Essays and Studies 2015

Series Editor: Elaine Treharne

The English Association

The objects of the English Association are to promote the knowledge and appreciation of the English language and its literatures, and to foster good practice in its teaching and learning at all levels.

The Association pursues these aims by creating opportunities of co-operation among all those interested in English; by furthering the recognition of English as essential in education; by discussing methods of English teaching; by holding lectures, conferences, and other meetings; by publishing journals, books, and leaflets; and by forming local branches.

Publications

The Year's Work in English Studies. An annual bibliography. Published by Blackwell.

The Year's Work in Critical and Cultural Theory. An annual bibliography. Published by Blackwell.

Essays and Studies. An annual volume of essays by various scholars assembled by the collector covering usually a wide range of subjects and authors from the medieval to the modern. Published by D.S. Brewer.

English. A journal of the Association, *English* is published four times a year by the Association.

English 4–11. A journal supporting literacy in the primary classroom, published three times a year

The Use of English. A journal of the Association, *The Use of English* is published three times a year by the Association.

Newsletter. A *Newsletter* is published three times a year giving information about forthcoming publications, conferences, and other matters of interest.

Benefits of Membership

Institutional Membership

Full members receive copies of *The Year's Work in English Studies*, *Essays and Studies*, *English* (4 issues) and three *Newsletters*.

Ordinary Membership covers *English* (4 issues) and three *Newsletters*.

Schools Membership includes copies of each issue of *English* and *The Use of English*, one copy of *Essays and Studies*, three *Newsletters*, and preferential booking and rates for various conferences held by the Association.

Individual Membership

Individuals take out Basic Membership, which entitles them to buy all regular publications of the English Association at a discounted price, and attend Association gatherings.

For further details write to the Membership Administrator, The English Association, The University of Leicester, University Road, Leicester, LE1 7RH.

Essays and Studies 2015

Writing Europe, 500–1450
Texts and Contexts

Edited by
Aidan Conti, Orietta Da Rold and Philip Shaw

for the English Association

D. S. BREWER

ESSAYS AND STUDIES 2015
IS VOLUME SIXTY-EIGHT IN THE NEW SERIES
OF ESSAYS AND STUDIES COLLECTED ON BEHALF OF
THE ENGLISH ASSOCIATION
ISSN 0071–1357

First published 2015
D. S. Brewer, Cambridge

D. S. Brewer is an imprint of Boydell & Brewer Ltd
PO Box 9, Woodbridge, Suffolk IP12 3DF, UK
and of Boydell & Brewer Inc.
668 Mt Hope Avenue, Rochester, NY 14620–2731, USA
website: www.boydellandbrewer.com

ISBN 978–1–84384–415–0

A CIP catalogue record for this title is available
from the British Library

The publisher has no responsibility for the continued existence or accuracy of
URLs for external or third-party internet websites referred to in this book,
and does not guarantee that any content on such websites is,
or will remain, accurate or appropriate

This publication is printed on acid-free paper

Printed and bound in Great Britain by
TJ International Ltd, Padstow, Cornwall

Contents

Illustrations

The editors, contributors and publishers are grateful to all the institutions and persons listed for permission to reproduce the materials in which they hold copyright. Every effort has been made to trace the copyright holders; apologies are offered for any omission, and the publishers will be pleased to add any necessary acknowledgement in subsequent editions.

Notes on Contributors

Rolf H. Bremmer Jr is Professor of English Philology and, by special appointment, Professor of Frisian Language and Literature at Leiden University on behalf of the Fryske Akademy. He has published widely in both fields, including more recently, with Kees Dekker, two volumes in the series Anglo-Saxon Manuscripts in Microfiche Facsimile. He is the author of *An Introduction to Old Frisian* and co-editor of *Directions for Old Frisian Philology*.

Stewart Brookes is a research associate based at the Department of Digital Humanities, King's College London. His publications include a co-edited volume of essays on digital palaeography (forthcoming); a study of variation in the handwriting of Aldred's gloss to the Lindisfarne Gospels; and articles on Ælfric's *Saints' Lives*. He is currently finishing a critical edition of Ælfric's adaptation of the biblical 'Book of Esther' and 'Book of Kings'.

Aidan Conti is an associate professor specialising in Medieval Latin at the University of Bergen. His work examines textual transmission, translations and other intersections between Latin and Northern vernacular literatures and languages. His current research focuses on identified copy-exemplar pairs as evidence for specific reading and writing events within general practices of medieval literacy.

Orietta Da Rold is University Lecturer in Literature and the Material Text: 1100 to 1500 at the University of Cambridge and a Fellow of St John's College. She has published on medieval manuscript culture and scribes, focusing chiefly on the period 1100–1500, and researches the codicology and palaeography of medieval manuscripts. She is the editor of *A Digital Facsimile of Cambridge, University Library, MS Dd.4.24 of Chaucer's Canterbury Tales*, and is currently working on a project on the significance of paper in late medieval books.

Helen Fulton is Professor of Medieval Literature at the University of Bristol. She has published widely on medieval English and Welsh literatures with a particular focus on political writing and cultural exchanges between Latin and vernaculars in medieval Britain. Her most recent book is the edited collection *Urban Culture in Medieval Wales*.

Marilena Maniaci is Professor of Palaeography at the Università degli studi di Cassino e del Lazio meridionale. She is the author of *Terminologia* *del libro manoscritto, Costruzione e gestione della pagina nel manoscritto bizantino, Archeologia del manoscritto*, and, more recently, *La syntaxe du codex. Essai de codicologie structural*, with Patrick Andrist and Paul Canart. She has also published articles on the materials (parchment and inks) and manufacturing techniques employed in Greek and Latin manuscripts, on the structure and description of complex codices, and on the codicology of the Latin Bible and of Greek and Latin liturgical rolls.

Débora Marques de Matos is in the final year of a PhD at the Departments of Digital Humanities and Theology and Religious Studies (Jewish Studies) at King's College London. Her research focuses on medieval Hebrew manuscripts from the Iberian Peninsula and the mobility and adaptability of Sephardic scribes. Her publications include articles about palaeography and decoration in late-medieval Sephardic manuscripts, Hebrew book illumination and the first full study of Parma MS 1959.

Annina Seiler is a research associate at the English Department of the University of Zurich. Her general research interests include English language history (especially graphemics and phonology), Old English language and literature, and the West Germanic languages. She is also interested in cultural aspects connected with literacy and orality in the Middle Ages, the functions of writing and the connections between Roman and runic writing. She has recently published a monograph on the scripting of the Germanic languages.

Philip Shaw is Senior Lecturer in English Language and Old English at the University of Leicester. His research covers various aspects of early medieval language and literature, focusing particularly on early Germanic dialects and personal names.

Peter A. Stokes is Senior Lecturer in Digital Humanities at the Department of Digital Humanities, King's College London. With a background in both computer engineering and palaeography, he has led research projects on digital methods in palaeography, including a Leverhulme Fellowship and the ERC-funded DigiPal project. He is currently co-investigator on the AHRC-funded 'Conqueror's Commissioners' and 'Models of Authority' projects. Major publications include *English Vernacular Minuscule from Æthelred to Cnut, circa 990–circa 1035*.

Nadia Togni is a lecturer at the University of Geneva, and specialises in Latin codicology, palaeography and medieval manuscript transmission. She is currently working on the circulation of the Giant Bibles from the eleventh to the twelfth century, and on book production in the abbey of Saint Peter of Perugia. She has published several articles on the Giant Bibles, and has authored *Monasteri benedettini in Umbria* and edited *Les Bibles atlantiques. Le manuscrit biblique à l'époque de la réforme de l'Église du XIe siècle*.

Svetlana Tsonkova is currently completing her PhD dissertation in the Department of Medieval Studies at the Central European University, Budapest. Her doctoral research is on medieval and early modern Bulgarian verbal magic and its role in everyday life. She is also a researcher in a research project on popular religion in Central and Eastern Europe, organised by the University of Pécs (Hungary). Her scholarly interests are in the fields of verbal charms, popular beliefs, popular demonology, crisis rites and daily-life applications of magic.

Matilda Watson is a research student within the DigiPal Project in the Department of Digital Humanities at King's College London. She is currently working on her PhD thesis, 'Manuscript Fragments, Christianisation and Digitisation: Contacts between England, Norway and Sweden in the Eleventh Century'. The thesis investigates fragments of eleventh-century liturgical manuscripts preserved in Scandinavian archives in order to study the influence of English manuscript culture in Norway and Sweden *c*. 1000–1100. As part of her PhD, Matilda has used the DigiPal framework to develop ScandiPal, a database of letterforms found in the manuscript fragments surviving in Scandinavia.

George Younge is Postdoctoral Research Fellow at the Centre for Medieval Literature (CML), an international centre of excellence based jointly at the Universities of York and Southern Denmark (Odense). Younge's published work focuses on vernacular literary culture in England during the high medieval period (*c*. 1000–1300), with a special concentration on the afterlife of Old English in the century after the Norman Conquest. His research interests include the European contexts for insular literature, interaction between English and French writers, and the use of vernacular sources by medieval artists. He is currently working on a monograph entitled *The Place of English in the Twelfth-Century Renaissance*.

Preface

ORIETTA DA ROLD, AIDAN CONTI
AND PHILIP SHAW

A SOPHISTICATED MARKET for the production and circulation of written texts, a concern with the establishment of national vernaculars as well as a forum for the exchange of religious, philosophical and literary ideas characterised medieval Europe. Explorations of this textual culture can fruitfully elucidate the prolonged and varied processes through which Europe and its constituent localities entered into modern reading, writing and communicative practices. Europe here is intended as an ideological concept which, despite present concerns and worries, does persist; indeed, the worries attest to the persistence of Europe's existence. To debate and consider the coherence of medieval Europe is important. It matters because it shows the tension between the unity and the diversity which still define Europe. The summer of 2015 will see the publication of a major literary history under the general editorship of David Wallace; this project is

[An] opportunity to consider how Europeans and their near neighbours defined and regenerated themselves following the greatest single catastrophe in their history [...] This is the first literary history of medieval Europe to be attempted in English. Eschewing conventional, anachronistic organization by "national blocks" – English literature, French literature, etc. – it considers literary activity in transnational sequences of interconnected places. Its vision of Europe, and of movement within Europe is, we believe, of acute contemporary relevance.[1]

As *Europe: A Literary History, 1348–1418* takes its reader on journeys through the literary encounters of Europe, *Writing Europe 500–1450: Texts and Contexts* brings together papers on a range of topics in medieval

---

[1] For an overview of the project and a very interesting visual journey of the literary exchange, see David Wallace, 'About this Project' in 'Europe: A Literary History, 1348–1418' <http://www.english.upenn.edu/~dwallace/europe/about. html> [accessed 2 January 2015]. The project is to appear in *Europe: A Literary History, 1348–1418*, ed. by David Wallace, 2 vols (Oxford: Oxford University Press, 2015 forthcoming).

manuscript studies and textual criticism, seeking to explore these issues from a pan-European perspective.

The focus on writing, which implicitly considers readers, is roughly chronologically defined between the fall of the Western Roman Empire and the introduction of printing in Europe. These two events had profound influences in defining pre-modern Europe and its global cultural, social and political influences – of which writing is a constituent paradigm. Thus this volume draws on a range of approaches and perspectives to manuscript studies, material culture, multilingualism in texts and books, book history, readers, audience and scribes across the medieval period in Europe.

The essays in the volume employ a variety of methodologies, some looking broadly across European traditions, while others present case studies within individual national and local milieux. Marilena Maniaci and Orietta Da Rold's survey of contemporary manuscript studies in Europe highlights the need for international collaboration and training in an active and developing field. Dialogues between traditional and new methods, national and linguistic practices, and, indeed, platforms and systems are all necessary to realise the promise of contemporary manuscript studies. Stewart Brookes and his colleagues focus on 'DigiPal', a successful project which has made a significant contribution in bringing together technology and human knowledge to answer palaeographical questions in a new way. The issue at stake here is methodological, and by applying this methodology to two other projects, 'ScandiPal' and 'SephardiPal', the authors demonstrate that digital palaeography works, but the exercise of human judgement is essential. Nadia Togni explores another important topic in medieval book production. Her discussion of the production and dissemination of Italian Giant Bibles reveals the ways in which they reflect the political and religious influence of the papacy during a key period of eleventh-century reform.

Rolf Bremmer's contribution considers a neglected chapter in the history of literacy in Frisia through the *arengas* and colophons written by early scribes. Detailing the use of common phrases and formulas, Bremmer argues that early Frisian scribal practices demonstrate that copyists actively participated in international diplomatic exchanges and scribal customs. And again, questions of literacy and language are considered by Aidan Conti, Helen Fulton and Annina Seiler. Conti's piece provides an invaluable survey of the Latin composition of medieval Norway, elucidating the problems and lacunae in our evidence as well as demonstrating the ways in which careful consideration of the surviving texts can help us to understand the nature and scale of Latin textual production during this period, and the ways in which it was in dialogue with broader trends in Latin literature in the European Middle Ages. Fulton discusses the importance and prestige of Welsh medieval literary culture, exploring, in particular, the European influences on this vernacular. Fulton shows how the manuscript transmission and the literary influence are both defined by European contacts but also define cultural and political choices. Seiler's examination of writing in early Germanic languages deals with the creation of vernacular spelling systems using the Latin alphabet. While Irish influences have often been cited for the development of digraphs to accommodate Germanic phonology, Seiler convincingly shows that Merovingian orthography provides a model for early English use of <th>, <ch> and <uu>.

With the essays by George Younge and Svetlana Tsonkova we move into additional cultural European contradictions. George Younge's article looks at the development and use of 'heathen' to refer to Jews in English texts of the twelfth century, thereby tracing the rise and development of antipathy towards the Jews of England within the work of scribes and translators of this period. Svetlana Tsonkova examines medieval Bulgarian charms, frequently preserved in *требници* or books of occasional prayers, but also in miscellanies, psalters, and books of hours. These practically oriented texts often have little to do with the Christian traditions, but have the formal and stylistic features of a Christian prayer and are organically incorporated among canonical content in books.

Some of these essays came into being as part of a larger exchange which took place in Bergen in 2012,[2] others were the outcome of subsequent discussions which this topic raised. The value of a journey is judged by what one has learnt on the way. The picture that this issue offers is no doubt incomplete, but it is a beginning. Indeed, it is the aim of this volume to encourage and develop additional conversations, international collaborations and transnational interactions on medieval Europe and its textual culture.

---

[2] 'Writing Europe Before 1470: A Colloquium' was held at the University of Bergen, 3–5 June 2012, more details can be found at <http://www2.le.ac.uk/ departments/english/news/conferences/writing-europe> [accessed 16 February 2015].

Acknowledgments

The editors would like to thank the Centre for Medieval Studies at the University of Bergen and the School of English at the University of Leicester for the generous contribution towards the organisation of the 'Writing Europe' Conference which inspired the preparation of this volume. The editors also wish to thank the contributors for their exemplary scholarship and professionalism in bringing this volume to completion. Our gratitude also goes to the many librarians who assisted with the access to books and material in their care. Orietta Da Rold is very grateful to Inan, Elif and Eren for their patience over the Christmas holidays. Final thanks go to the English Association for supporting this volume, and especially to Helen Lucas and Elaine Treharne.

Abbreviations

CDDM A. G. Watson, *Catalogue of Dated and Datable Manuscripts c.700–1600 in the Department of Manuscripts, the British Library*, 2 vols (London: British Library, 1979) and *Catalogue of Dated and Datable Manuscripts c.435–1600 in Oxford Libraries*, 2 vols (Oxford: Oxford University Press, 1984); P. R. Robinson, *Catalogue of Dated and Datable Manuscripts in Cambridge Libraries c.737–1600*, 2 vols (Cambridge: Brewer, 1998) and *Catalogue of Dated and Datable Manuscripts c.888–1600 in London Libraries*, 2 vols (London: British Library, 2004)

Colophons Bénédictines de Bouveret, *Colophons de manuscrits occidentaux des origines au XVIe siècle*, 6 vols (Fribourg: Éditions Universitaires Fribourg Suisse, 1965–82)

EETS Early English Text Society

    o.s.   original series

    s.s.   supplementary series

IMEP *The Index of Middle English Prose: Handlists* (21 vols to date; Cambridge: Brewer, 1996–)

MED *Middle English Dictionary*, ed. by Hans Kurath and others (Ann Arbor: University of Michigan Press and London: Oxford University Press, 1956–2001)

NIMEV Julia Boffey and A. S. G. Edwards, *A New Index of Middle English Verse* (London: British Library, 2005)

PL *Patrologia Latina*, ed. J.-P. Migne, 221 vols. (Paris, 1844–1903)

PMLA *Publications of the Modern Language Association of America*

Medieval Manuscript Studies: A European Perspective*

ORIETTA DA ROLD and MARILENA MANIACI

WHEN JEAN MALLON wrote his seminal treaty on Roman palaeography, he pointed out that the field is so large that scholars cannot be expected to explore it in detail. All one can do, he argued, is wander; however, after getting lost in a minefield of information, a scholar will always come back with something tangible.[1] It is equally difficult to define what contemporary medieval manuscript studies represent in Europe. The literature on the subject is obviously vast, and it is impossible to offer a thorough survey of the wide field it covers. It is, however, equally true that confronting ideas and practices across international and national borders may lead to profitable new research initiatives.

The ways in which scholars think about medieval manuscripts are as multifaceted as the taxonomies used to define the discipline, and scholarly practices vary across international and national borders. In the anglophone world, 'manuscript studies' is understood as an interdisciplinary endeavour, which started with the great effort of cataloguing manuscripts in British collections, and now intersects with a wide range of other disciplines from literary studies to textual transmission and editing, art history, history, cultural studies and sociology.[2] Other concerns in the field include detailed considerations on the dissemination, circulation and reception of

---

* This essay is the result of a close collaboration and engaging conversations between the authors. Each of us has brought to the argument her own experiences and research competencies, and we are aware that we cannot here cover the field in its entirety. Our aim is not to offer a comprehensive overview, systematically dealing with all areas and periods of the Western Latin and medieval vernacular manuscript tradition, but rather a series of thoughts on some aspects and issues of manuscript studies which seem to us worthy of further development, with particular reference to our specific areas of expertise. The essays in this volume offer additional contribution to our discussion.

[1] Jean Mallon, *Paléographie romaine* (Madrid: Instituto Antonio de Nebrija de Filologia, 1952).

[2] See, for instance, Raymond Clemens and Timothy Graham, *Introduction to Manuscript Studies* (Ithaca NY: Cornell University Press, 2007). For an historical overview, see Christopher De Hamel, 'Medieval Manuscript Studies', in *The Book Encompassed: Studies in Twentieth-Century Bibliography*, ed. Peter Hobley Davison

books, the development of medieval libraries, the growth of manuscript collections and the history of reading. In Europe, the terms palaeography and codicology are often called upon to denote and define the study of the medieval manuscript. Codicology is sometimes understood as an ancillary component of palaeography, when its independence is not categorically denied. In other contexts, the word codicology is used instead to indicate the study of the manuscript book as a whole, including, for example, matters relating to the history of handwriting.[3] More specific terms such as archaeology of the book, material codicology or – more recently – structural codicology have been introduced to emphasise the focus on the study of materials and to describe the physical structure of the medieval book.[4] These different labels will be used conventionally in the following pages as a common thread to navigate the most relevant and promising research trends, starting with a short overview on manuscript studies.

Manuscript studies

The field of manuscript studies can be broadly defined, especially in anglo-phone countries, as an interdisciplinary platform. This field is enjoying a popularity it has never seen before. Research on individual manuscripts, type of texts, *scriptoria* and writing environments, copyists, artists, decorative techniques, bindings, ownership, provenance, circulation and reception of books and texts is well documented in monographs, journal articles and essays as well as electronic publications, blogs, newsletters and web portals.[5] International congresses, workshops, seminars and conferences are also regularly organised to discuss manuscript culture and the

(Cambridge: Cambridge University Press, 1998), pp. 37–45. See also a variety of recent collective works, some of which are quoted in the following footnotes.

3   J. Peter Gumbert, 'Fifty Years of Codicology', *Archiv für Diplomatik*, 50 (2004), 505–526.

4   Marilena Maniaci, *Archeologia del manoscritto. Metodi, problemi, bibliografia recente* (Rome: Viella, 2002).

5   A good picture is offered by some of the key journals in the field, including the *Journal of the Early Book Society, Studies in the Age of Chaucer, Medium Aevum, Speculum*, the *History Reviews, The Review of English Studies* and *English Manuscripts Studies: 1100–1700* (although this last journal has apparently ceased publication). Main international publishers have also embraced the material turn in their monograph series and collection of essays, see, for example, Boydell and Brewer, Brepols, Cambridge University Press, Oxford University Press, The University of Chicago Press, Cornell University Press, the British Library, Ashgate, Brill, Viella, Carocci, Armand Colin and also smaller university publishers, such as

history of the book in the disciplines' own rights or in an interdisciplinary setting.[6]

The picture is certainly very lively, albeit difficult to capture and somehow marked by an evident caesura between anglophone tradition, which is often focused on local themes and materials, and Continental conventions. Here, the need of a deeper and more systematic communication between the north, south, west and east of Europe clearly emerges from the bibliography which is quoted by scholars, often restricted to their own national research environments. One of the key limitations is the increasing difficulty in reading publications in different languages by English-speaking scholars, and the slow acceptance of English as the *lingua franca* of manuscript studies outside the English-speaking world.

The field in Britain was defined by great scholars such as Humfrey Wanley, Henry Bradshaw, M. R. James, Neil Ker, Richard Hunt, Roger Mynors, Julian Brown, Malcolm Parkes, Ian Doyle and others, who were influenced by and worked closely with other scholars, for example, Elias A. Lowe, Bernhard Bischoff, Jean Destrez and Léon Marie Joseph Delaissé.[7] The impact that their work has had on our understanding of medieval manuscripts is immeasurable. These scholars pushed disciplinary boundaries in history, social, cultural, textual and literary studies to consider manuscripts worthy of close scrutiny and study in their own right. Their foundational rationale on how scholars should catalogue manuscripts still stands as one of the essential references. Their work shows that a cataloguer should go beyond his or her ability to describe the content of a manuscript, and prompted some of the first remarkable steps which then led to other new approaches and forged manuscript studies as an inter-

Leiden University Press. The web presence is too wide-ranging to be summarised here.

6 Key meetings include the biennial conference of the Comité international de paléographie latine (CIPL), the York Manuscript Conference, the Early Book Society conference, and the Writing Britain series. See also the programme of the 2014 New Chaucer Society Congress held in Reykjavík <http://newchaucersociety. org/pages/entry/2014-congress> [accessed 23 December 2014].

7 On Bradshaw, see Paul Needham, *The Bradshaw Method: Henry Bradshaw's Contribution to Bibliography*, Hanes Lecture (Chapel Hill: University of North Carolina at Chapel Hill, 1988). On the British tradition, De Hamel, 'Medieval Manuscript Studies', pp. 37–45, and also the writings by Julian Brown, in particular, 'Latin Palaeography since Traube', in *A Palaeographer's View: The Selected Writings of Julian Brown*, ed. by Janet Bately, Jane Roberts and Michelle Brown (London: Harvey Miller, 1993), pp. 17–37.

disciplinary field of enquiry.[8] In 1984, Derek Pearsall followed in these footsteps when he argued, 'There is a need to be conscious, always, of how behind every text presented in a modern edition, with all the reassuring apparatus of titles and text divisions, capital letters and full stops, paragraphs and line numbers, there lies the spoil heap of the manuscripts from which it has been drawn.'[9] This newly-gained awareness has ever since attracted literary and textual scholars to think more carefully about the material evidence of their editorial projects.[10] Seminal publications then appeared that greatly influenced the training of literary scholars both in the early and later medieval period.[11]

Again in 2000, Pearsall stressed that

The study of manuscripts is one of the most active areas of current research in medieval studies: manuscripts are basic primary material evidence for literary scholars, historians and art-historians alike, and there has been an explosion of interest over the past twenty or twenty-

---

[8]   Obvious reference works are E. A. Lowe, *Codices Latini Antiquiores: A Palaeographical Guide to Latin Manuscripts Prior to the Ninth Century*, 11 vols. and suppl. (Oxford: Clarendon Press, 1934–71; 2nd ed. of vol. 2, 1972) and N. R. Ker, *Catalogue of Manuscripts Containing Anglo-Saxon* (Oxford: Clarendon Press, 1957; repr. 1990).

[9]   D. Pearsall, 'Texts, Textual Criticism, and Fifteenth-Century Manuscript Production', in *Fifteenth-Century Studies: Recent Essays*, ed. by R. F. Yeager (Hamden, CT: Archon Books, 1984), pp. 121–36 (p. 121).

[10]   One must not forget the important and pivotal work done by the Early English Text Society to promote and make accessible medieval texts in the English vernacular. For a discussion, see the recent EETS volume, *Probable Truth: Editing Medieval Texts from Britain in the Twenty-First Century*, ed. by Vincent Gillespie and Anne Hudson (Turnhout: Brepols, 2013).

[11]   *Book Production and Publishing in Britain 1375–1475*, ed. by Jeremy Griffiths and Derek Pearsall (Cambridge: Cambridge University Press, 1989), but also all the publications derived from the York Medieval Manuscript Conference Series whose first proceedings were published in *Manuscripts and Readers in Fifteenth-Century England: The Literary Implications of Manuscript Study. Essays from the 1981 Conference at the University of York*, ed. by Derek Pearsall (Cambridge: D. S. Brewer, 1983). For the earlier medieval period, see, for example, *Anglo-Saxon Manuscripts: Basic Readings*, Garland Reference Library of the Humanities, ed. by Mary P. Richards (New York: Garland, 1994); *Words, Texts, and Manuscripts: Studies in Anglo-Saxon Culture Presented to Helmut Gneuss on the Occasion of His Sixty-Fifth Birthday*, ed. by Michael Korhammer (Cambridge: D. S. Brewer, 1992); *Anglo-Saxon Manuscripts and Their Heritage*, ed. by Phillip Pulsiano and Elaine Treharne (Aldershot: Ashgate, 1998); *Textual and Material Culture in Anglo-Saxon England, Manchester Centre for Anglo Saxon Studies*, ed. by D. G. Scragg (Cambridge: D. S. Brewer, 2003).

five years. Manuscript study has developed enormously: codices are no longer treated as inert witnesses to a culture whose character has already been determined by modern scholar, but are active participants in a process of exploration and discovery.[12]

This observation maintains its relevance fourteen years later. A number of thoughtful reviews have also recently appeared with the aim of reflecting on how the field has evolved, and how it could move forward.[13] In 2000, Ian Doyle showed a specific concern for terminological as well as codicological developments in manuscript studies.[14] More recently, A. S. G. Edwards argued that English manuscripts produced in the period c. 1200–1350 need further examination, and particular areas of interest are the origin and provenance of manuscripts, their production and the transmission of texts, with a special emphasis on regional production.[15] There is also a general consensus that the history of the book and material culture theories have deeply influenced much of what literary scholars do as a way of interpreting and accessing the past.[16]

[12] D. Pearsall, 'Introduction', in *New Directions in Later Medieval Manuscript Studies. Essays from the 1998 Harvard Conference*, ed. by D. Pearsall (York: The University of York-Centre for Medieval Studies, 2000), p. xi, but see also D. Pearsall, 'The Value/s of Manuscript Study: A Personal Retrospect', *Journal of the Early Book Society*, 3 (2000), 167–81.

[13] See, for instance, R. Hanna, 'Middle English Books and Middle English Literary History', *Modern Philology*, 102 (2004), 157–78; Orietta Da Rold, 'Re-sourcing the Production and Use of English Manuscripts 1060 to 1220', *Literature Compass*, 3.4 (2006), 750–66; Alexandra Gillespie, 'Analytical Survey: The History of the Book', *New Medieval Literatures*, 9 (2007), 245–86; Jessica Brantley, 'The Pre-History of the Book', *PMLA* 124.2 (2009), 1–15; T. Webber, 'English Manuscripts in the Century after the Norman Conquest: Continuity and Change in the Paleography of Books and Book Collections', in *Writing in Context, Insular Manuscript Culture 500–1200*, ed. by E. Kwakkel (Leiden: Leiden University Press, 2013), pp. 141–76.

[14] A. I. Doyle, 'Recent Directions in Medieval Manuscript Study', in *New Directions in Later Medieval Manuscript Studies*, pp. 1–4.

[15] A. S. G. Edwards, 'Directions in the Study of English Manuscripts, c. 1200–c. 1350', *English Manuscript Studies 1100–1700*, 17 (2012), pp. 280–8.

[16] See *The Cambridge History of the Book in Britain*, ed. by Nigel J. Morgan, and Rodney M. Thomson (Cambridge: Cambridge University Press, 2008); *The Cambridge History of the Book in Britain: Volume 3, 1400–1557*, ed. by Lotte Hellinga and J. B. Trapp (Cambridge: Cambridge University Press, 1999); *The Cambridge History of the Book in Britain: Volume 1. C.400–1100*, ed. by Richard Gameson (Cambridge: Cambridge University Press, 2011); *The Production of Books in England 1350–1500*, ed. by Alexandra Gillespie and Daniel Wakelin (Cambridge: Cambridge University Press, 2011).

The availability of online material has suddenly opened unexpected doors, giving access to a huge amount of data which facilitate new avenues for first-hand research.[17] It is particularly important that the training needed to guide students across this sea of information is not neglected,[18] and within this context it must not be forgotten that, as Doyle notes, 'we cannot do very well to study English texts and manuscripts in isolation from those in other languages and from other countries'.[19] The following sections look at how a summative and comparative approach to disciplines such as codicology and palaeography within a broad European context may offer ideas for future research themes and trends of development.

[17] This includes large digitisation projects or studies of individual manuscripts available either online or on DVD. For a recent example, see *A Facsimile Edition of the Vernon Manuscript: Oxford, Bodleian Library, MS. Eng. Poet. A. 1*, ed. by Wendy Scase (Oxford: Bodleian Library, 2011) and see also the accompanying volume, *The Making of the Vernon Manuscript: The Production and Contexts of Oxford, Bodleian Library, MS Eng. Poet. A .1*, ed. by Wendy Scase (Turnhout: Brepols, 2013).

[18] It is essential to teach MA, MPhil and PhD students what working with manuscripts means. This training is now offered in a variety of ways and is undertaken by universities and other professional bodies. See, for example, the 'London International Palaeography Summer School' <http://www.ies.sas.ac.uk/london-palaeography-summer-school> [accessed 23 December 2014]; the 'New Chaucer Society Graduate Student Workshop' and the 'ISAS Graduate Student Workshop'; the 'Quadrivium Project' <http://quadriviumproject.com/> and the 'Digging Deeper Project' <http://www.stanfordtexttechnologies.com/>. Most of the online sites, however, focus on palaeographical matters (mostly reading exercises) and offer very little by way of codicological instruction. See, for example, 'Scriptorium' <http://scriptorium.english.cam.ac.uk/>; 'Medieval Writing: History, Heritage and Data Source', <http://www.medievalwriting.50megs.com/>; 'Medieval Palaeography' <http://paleo.anglo-norman.org/medfram.html>; 'Paläographisches Lesetraining' <http://www.phil.uni-passau.de/histhw/palaeographie/index.html>; 'Palaeography: Reading Old Handwriting 1500–1800. A practical online tutorial' <http://www.nationalarchives.gov.uk/palaeography/>; 'Scottish Handwriting, 1500–1700' <http://www.scottishhandwriting.com/>. An exception is 'InScribe' at the University of London, which also offers training in codicology <http://www.history.ac.uk/research-training/courses/online-palaeography> [all accessed 23 December 2014].

[19] A. I. Doyle, 'Introductory Address', in *Late Medieval Religious Texts and Their Transmission: Essays in Honour of A. I. Doyle*, ed. by A. J. Minnis (Cambridge: D. S. Brewer, 1994), pp. 1–8 (p. 3).

Codicology

Material codicology is a particularly buoyant area, which witnessed great advances during the last decade of the twentieth century and the first two decades of the twenty-first century. This period saw the development of ambitious general and specific cataloguing initiatives, which opened up the possibility of systematic analysis of the material details of medieval codices. The sudden eruption of computing in the humanities, the rapid progress of laboratory techniques, the development of methodological practices of restoration and the promotion of a comparative approach to the history of the Oriental and Western manuscripts have pushed forward codicological research in different ways.[20] The most important, and debated, methodological innovation has been the proposal of the so-called quantitative codicology and the sociology of the medieval book. Between the 1980s and the end of the twentieth century, quantitative codicology aimed to compile a history of the book through the use of statistical analysis of large samples of data.[21] In terms of the archaeological analysis of materials and manufacturing techniques of the manuscript book, new studies have appeared on writing media (especially parchment and paper), inks and colours, the composition of quires, the *mise en page* and binding techniques.[22] Updated manuals offer more details on thematic strands which are emerging from the current codicological research on

[20] See Denis Muzerelle, 'Evolution et tendances actuelles de la recherche codicologique', *Historia, instituciones, documentos*, 18 (1991), pp. 347–74, and his 'Le progrès en codicologie', in *Rationalisierung der Buchherstellung im Mittelalter und in der frühen Neuzeit*, ed. by Peter Rück and Martin Boghardt (Marburg an der Lahn: Philipps-Universität, Institut für Historische Hilfswissenschaften, 1994), pp. 33–40; Gumbert, 'Fifty Years'.

[21] Ezio Ornato, 'L'histoire du livre et les méthodes quantitatives: bilan de vingt ans de recherches', in *La face cachée du livre mèdiéval. L'histoire du livre vue par Ezio Ornato, ses amis et ses collègues* (Rome: Viella, 1997), pp. 607–79.

[22] See, for example, *Ancient and Medieval Book Materials and Techniques*, ed. by Marilena Maniaci and Paola F. Munafò (Vatican City: Biblioteca Apostolica Vaticana, 1993); *Pergament. Geschichte, Struktur, Restaurierung, Herstellung*, ed. by Peter Rück (Sigmaringen: J. Thorbecke, 1991); Robert Fuchs, Christiane Meinert and Johannes Schrempf, *Pergament* (Munich: Siegl, 2001); Ezio Ornato, P. Busonero, P. F. Munafò and M. S. Storace, *La carta occidentale nel tardo medioevo* (Rome: Istituto centrale per la patologia del libro, 2001) and Monique Zerdoun Bat-Yehouda, *Les encres noires au moyen age* (Paris: CNRS, 1983, 2003). For a recent overview, see Orietta Da Rold, 'Materials', in *The Production of Books*, ed. by Gillespie and Wakelin, pp. 12–33.

the threshold of the new millennium.[23] It is, however, a shame that the most recent and complete handbooks are only available in Italian and thus remain poorly known in northern Europe.[24]

Without embracing the apodictic pessimism exhibited by Carlo Federici in decreeing the 'failure of the archaeology of the book',[25] it is undeniable that in recent times, the study of the materiality of the manuscript seems to have slowed its development, without exhausting its original creative impulse. This situation is, partly, a consequence of curtailing spaces reserved to humanistic knowledge – especially those of a more technical nature – and the lack of job opportunities within and outside academia. Furthermore quantitative codicology, which necessitates the analysis of data collected through long and patient survey and encoding, requires the mastery of basic statistical concepts virtually absent from the humanities curricula. The statistical approach, however, still continues to prove its great potential,[26] even though it does not seem to be able to open up beyond a small group of enthusiasts, or to diversify its methods and tools or to give rise to its own school. With few exceptions, scientific analyses, often hampered by difficulties related to cost, complexity of interdisciplinary dialogue and the growing restrictions on access to the originals, are developed within a few specific laboratories and groups of researchers, and their results, mostly based on restricted samples, cannot be safely extrapolated.[27] Finally, the contribution from the world of conservation to historical knowledge, although supported by a growing awareness and

[23] Maniaci, *Archeologia* and M. Luisa Agati, *Il libro manoscritto da Oriente a Occidente: per una codicologia comparata* (Rome: L'Erma di Bretschneider, 2009), both with full bibliography.

[24] Hanna notes how important it is for students to familiarise themselves with other European languages, but his bibliography mainly focuses of works in English with the exception of one Dutch title. See Ralph Hanna, 'Introduction', in *Introducing English Medieval Book History. Manuscripts, Their Producers and Their Readers* (Liverpool: Liverpool University Press, 2013), pp. xiii–xx.

[25] Carlo Federici, 'Sul fallimento dell'archeologia del libro', *Gazette du livre médiéval*, 45 (2004), 50–55.

[26] A volume which includes an overview on the main recent methods and results on quantative codicology is currently in preparation by Marilena Maniaci for Gruyter.

[27] Examples and references in *The Technological Study of Books and Manuscripts as Artefacts: Research Questions and Analytical Solutions*, ed. by Sarah Neate and others (Oxford: Archaeopress, 2011).

willingness to develop a theoretical framework, has increasingly focused on the analysis of materials and the structure of binding.[28]

Codicological research, however, has continued to advance on the historical study of materials and manufacturing techniques of books. It is impossible to provide an overview of the results in these few pages; suffice it here to say that some of the most prominent achievements, relate to the study of materials, in particular paper, the composition of quires, systems and types of ruling, the *mise en page* and *mise en texte* (especially in manuscripts with a challenging layout, for instance, those glossed), and the study of a specific mode of production such as the *pecia*. Maria Luisa Agati reviews these key issues in the second edition of her recent manual, and describes the state of the discipline with plenty of details, although a more critical overview or an outline on a future, additional perspective remains a *desideratum*.[29] Recent work on the recognition of the structural complexity of medieval manuscripts, which intensified in the last decade, appears as one of the most promising trends, especially for its impact on cataloguing practices, the study of manuscript traditions and the editing of texts. In particular, scholars have focused on the evolutionary nature of the medieval book as an artefact: the fact that it is subject to physical changes of various kinds over time, and that these changes, corresponding in turn to more or less evident shifts in its functions, can alter more or less visibly its original state. The importance of this approach was clearly highlighted by Gumbert in a speech in 2004, where he argued that 'The principal fact that the codicological eye may find is that the manuscript

---

[28] Apart from the numerous references collected in Maniaci, *Archeologia*, and, for the following decade, in Agati, *Il libro manoscritto*, see, for instance, the bibliography in progress on the web portal of the research centre 'Ligatus' <http://www.ligatus.org.uk/node/716> [accessed 23 December 2014].

[29] Here one ought to note the absence of recent state of the fields and bibliographies. M. Luisa Agati, 'Kodikologhia. Rolos, kathefthynseis kai nea synora', *Byzantina Symmeikta*, 21 (2011), pp. 195–216 <http://byzsym.org/index.php/bz/article/view/1059/969> [accessed 23 December 2014]) is written in Greek and rather elementary. In addition to the journals mentioned above, see *Bulletin*, *Gazette*, *Scrineum*, *Scripta* and *Manuscripta*. Essential bibliographical readings are the *Bulletin codicologique* of *Scriptorium*, and for the monographs the *Bibliographie* of the *Gazette*. A good idea of the vitality of the field can be gathered from the *Chronique*, up to number 30 of the same journal, which published key events relating to manuscript studies – conferences, seminars, courses, exhibitions and workshops (a similar service is now offered by the mailing list of the association APICES <http://www.palaeographia.org/apices/apices.htm> [accessed 23 December 2014]).

is not homogeneous but composite, or at least articulated in blocks'.[30] Unlike other themes, the study of what is improperly labelled as miscellany is transversely spread across distant traditions, which are often still, unfortunately, mutually impermeable.[31] The focus on the complexity of the medieval codex is also stimulating new reflection on the protocols of descriptions, which are increasingly challenged by the establishing of digital technologies, albeit in a still uncertain and heterogeneous form.[32]

The framework summarily traced here mainly concerns the study of the Latin and Greek manuscript tradition, certainly more evolved in terms of method and results; but one of the most important perspectives in codicological research goes under the name of comparative codicology, whose objectives were clearly anticipated about twenty years ago by Malachi Beit Arié, who notes,

> Only comparative study of similar and even disparate codicological features, styles of book scripts and their changes in different, similar, opposing or self-contained cultures will offer us satisfactory explanations and understanding. Similar practices in different circumstances will prove that they were not conditioned by social, economic, or cultural context, but were universally inherent in the making of a codex. Similar practices in similar circumstances would prove that they were conditioned by those circumstances, as in the case of the introduction of plummet. Different practices may be the consequence of factors other than technologiacal [sic], such as aesthetic conventions, economic or scholarly needs.[33]

---

[30] Gumbert, 'Fifty Years', p. 509.

[31] For a comprehensive overview, and bibliographical references, see Patrick Andrist, Paul Canart and Marilena Maniaci, *La syntaxe du codex. Essai de codicologie structurale* (Turnhout: Brepols, 2013). See also *Manuscript Miscellanies, c. 1450–1700*, an issue of *English Manuscript Studies 1100–1700*, 16 (2011), in particular, Alexandra Gillespie, 'Medieval Books, Their Booklets, and Booklet Theory', pp. 1–29, and Orietta Da Rold, 'Making the Book: Cambridge, University Library Ii.1.33', *New Medieval Literatures*, 13 (2012 for 2011), pp. 273–88.

[32] For a recent overview of current projects and key research questions, see *La descrizione dei manoscritti: esperienze a confronto*, ed. by Edoardo Crisci, Marilena Maniaci and Pasquale Orsini (Cassino: Dipartimento di Filologia e Storia, 2010).

[33] Malachi Beit Arié, 'Why Comparative Codicology?', *Gazette du livre médiéval*, 23 (1993), pp. 1–5 (p. 2). See, more recently, J. P. Gumbert, 'Our Common Codicology', *Comparative Oriental Manuscript Studies Newsletter*, 8 (2014), pp. 23–27. Comparative approaches mostly juxtapose the results of different contexts and cultures rather than directly studying sources with a common methodology. See, for example, *Recherches de codicologie comparée. La composition du codex au Moyen Âge, en Orient et en Occident. Communications présentées à la table ronde*

Comparing practices and phenomena belonging to different book cultures brings out similarities and differences and enables scholars to hypothesise and define, wherever possible, the reasons for book production. Comparative projects have put together scholars from different backgrounds and training and have focused, in particular, on the study of Eastern manuscript traditions. These projects have an emphasis on obvious connections with the Greek and Latin traditions,[34] and focus on the Mediterranean ones, but have also expanded the research context by looking at (geographically and culturally) more distant manuscript cultures, where the codex is not the main book form, or is completely unknown.[35] In the absence of adequate modern catalogues, scholars of different book cultures have begun to feel, with increasing urgency, the need for studies based on systematically collected and strictly encoded data.

Detailed quantitative work, based on the systematic collection and exploitation of material evidence, is still very much needed in the study of medieval book production, even more so in Britain. Some recent publications consider the vexed question of the application of a quantitative approach to the study of books of English origin,[36] but even a simple, complete count of the extant ones is still not available, which is surprising considering the fervent cataloguing work in recent years, and the diffusion

---

tenue à l'École Normale Supérieure les 5 et 6 Décembre 1990, ed. by Philippe Hoffmann (Paris: Presses de l'École Normale Supérieure, 1998); *Lire le manuscrit médiéval. Observer et décrire*, ed. by Paul Géhin (Paris: Colin, 2005) and Agati, *Il libro manoscritto*.

[34] Relevant here is the ESF Research Networking Programme COMST (Comparative Oriental Manuscript Studies) which has just published an introduction to a comparative study of Eastern manuscripts available at <http://www1.uni-hamburg.de/COMST/handbookonline.html> [accessed 17 April 2015].

[35] The varieties of manuscript cultures in Asia, Africa and Europe are currently being studied at the Centre for the Study of Manuscript Cultures of the University of Hamburg in an ambitious comparative project entitled 'Manuskriptkulturen in Asien, Afrika und Europa' <http://www.manuscript-cultures.uni-hamburg.de/> [accessed 23 December 2014]. One of the outcomes of this project is the planned publication of an *Encyclopedia of Manuscript Cultures in Asia and Africa* <http://www.manuscript-cultures.uni-hamburg.de/Enzy.html> [accessed 23 December 2014].

[36] See, for some methodological considerations, Orietta Da Rold, 'Fingerprinting Paper in West Midlands Medieval Manuscripts', in *Essays in Manuscript Geography: Vernacular Manuscripts of the English West Midlands from the Conquest to the Sixteenth Century*, ed. by Wendy Scase (Turnhout: Brepols, 2007), pp. 257–71, and more recently on palaeographical debates, see Peter A. Stokes, *English Vernacular Minuscule from Æthelred to Cnut, c. 990–c. 1035* (Cambridge: D.S. Brewer, 2014).

of digital technologies and electronic resources.[37] The quantification of the number of surviving British manuscripts is not a trivial mathematical exercise, but it is essential to discuss the unique multilingual and diverse position that Britain had in the medieval European book market. Even more important is the need to carry on the detailed and meticulous research that Neil Ker describes to Richard Hunt in a letter dated 16 January 1944, where he writes:

> I'm spending what spare time I have in Magdalene for the most part, and have nearly finished the palaeographical descriptions of the manuscripts. It has taught me a lot and I shall have to go back to my first descriptions and improve them. I've learnt that all manuscripts need looking at in the way that Lowe has looked at the oldest manuscripts, with due attention to the pricking, ruling, etc., and that a small book needs to be written about the subject.[38]

Doyle has published Ker's observations on the arrangements of hair and flesh in British manuscripts as well as his notes on ruling and pricking practices, and some observations on the preparation of the quires and the dating of some techniques are also provided, but more work is needed in this area.

---

[37] It is always difficult to quantify data, because this exercise depends on how the field is defined and relies on available catalogues. However, sources which could be usefully mined, apart from the immediate library catalogues, include the numerous projects now accessible via 'Manuscripts Online' <http://www.manuscriptsonline. org/> [accessed 23 December 2014], and cataloguing ventures such as Ruth J. Dean, *Anglo-Norman Literature: A Guide to Texts and Manuscripts* (London: Anglo-Norman Text Society, 1999), the more recent Maria Careri, Christine Ruby and Ian Short, *Livres et écritures en français et en occitan au XIIe siècle: catalogue illustré* (Rome: Viella, 2011). Also Helmut Gneuss, *Handlist of Anglo-Saxon Manuscripts: A List of Manuscripts and Manuscript Fragments Written or Owned in England up to 1100* (Tempe: Arizona Center for Medieval and Renaissance Studies, 2001) and Helmut Gneuss and Michael Lapidge, *Anglo-Saxon Manuscripts: A Bibliographical Handlist of Manuscripts Written or Owned in England up to 1100* (Toronto: University of Toronto Press, 2014); Ker, *Catalogue of Manuscripts*, and his *Medieval Manuscripts in British Libraries*, 4 vols (Oxford: Clarendon Press, 1969, 1977, 1983, 1992). The *CDDM* also offers additional information. For English texts, the work of the editors of the *NIMEV* and the *IMEP* is invaluable. On this issue, see also Wendy Scase, 'Afterword: The Book in Culture', in *The Production of Books*, ed. by Gillespie and Wakelin, pp. 292–98.
[38] A. I. Doyle, 'Introduction to Neil Ker's Elements of Medieval English Codicology', *English Manuscript Studies 1100–1700*, 14 (2008), 244–45.

An approach to manuscript cataloguing which properly takes into account material and structural issues can be equally rewarding. Ralph Hanna has meticulously addressed some of these issues, among which the division in booklets, in his catalogue of the manuscripts of Richard Rolle, and more work using this methodology ought to be encouraged.[39] Moving from these most important signs of progresses and new perspectives, other questions naturally arise, concerning the evolution of book manufacturing and writing techniques, the organisation of the scribal work and the possible dating and localisation of the outlined practices. Some aspects have been explored in Continental literature – though not always with definitive results – but no discussion has yet been published about British scribes.[40]

British book production is often anonymous: little information has survived about book makers, scribes, readers etc., but detailed work on accounts, books and medieval libraries has already made important connections indispensable to push knowledge further.[41] The work on detailed scribal practices and book production can lead to interesting observations which may contribute to date and localise books, but also to understand general trends.[42] For British medieval manuscripts, this is a challenge which ought to be embraced.

[39] Ralph Hanna, *The English Manuscripts of Richard Rolle: A Descriptive Catalogue* (Exeter: University of Exeter, 2010), but see also his methodological observations in Ralph Hanna, 'The Booklet in Medieval Manuscript Cataloguing', *Nottingham Medieval Studies*, 55 (2011), 231–48. On the (stimulating but not unambiguous) notion of 'booklet', see Andrist, Canart and Maniaci, *La syntaxe du codex*, I. *État de la recherché*, pp. 11–44.

[40] See the bibliography in Maniaci, *Archeologia*.

[41] On libraries, see, for example, Michael Lapidge, *The Anglo-Saxon Library* (Oxford: Oxford University Press, 2006) and *The Cambridge History of Libraries in Great Britain and Ireland: Volume I: to 1640*, ed. by T. Webber and E. S. Leedham-Green (Cambridge: Cambridge University Press, 2006), but also 'The Corpus of British Medieval Library Catalogues Project' <http://www. history.ox.ac.uk/research/project/medieval-libraries-of-great-britain-mlgb3.html> [accessed 23 December 2014] and 'The British Medieval Library Catalogues' <http://www.history.ox.ac.uk/research/project/british-medieval-library-catalogues. html> [accessed 23 December 2014].

[42] See a recent discussion in Orietta Da Rold, 'Codicology, Localization and Oxford, Bodleian Library, MS. Laud. Misc. 108', in *The Makers and Users of Medieval Books: Essays in Honour of A. S. G. Edwards*, ed. by Carol Meale and Derek Pearsall (Cambridge: D. S. Brewer, 2014), pp. 48–59.

Palaeography

In recent decades, the research on the materiality of the codex has shaped into some sort of coherent evolution; the same consistency is difficult to find in assessing the progress and the current directions of palaeography, understood as an historical discipline rather than a set of reading and deciphering techniques. Palaeography is affected to a greater extent than codicology by the constraints which are linked to the peculiarities of the national linguistic and graphic realities, the weight of local traditions,[43] and the persistent diversity in terminological uses.[44] Not surprisingly, research in palaeography has long remained substantially faithful to methodologies of ancient and deep-rooted tradition, and poorly permeable to the application of new techniques of investigation. In particular, the comparative approach to the history of writing has had a very limited success and has not recorded the same level of achievements as codicology.[45]

The most recent Italian handbook on the history of Latin writing, published in 2010 by Paolo Cherubini and Alessandro Pratesi,[46] is a useful contribution to the discipline for the abundance of information provided, and the consistency of bibliographical notes that are included at

---

[43] For a thematic bibliography, see 'Theleme. techniques pour l'historien en ligne: études, manuels, exercices, bibliographies' <http://theleme.enc.sorbonne.fr/bibliographies/paleographie/objets_methodes_problemes> [accessed 23 December 2014], and the rich *Bibliographie de paléographie latine* (over 1500 titles, updated November 2011) collected by M. H. Smith, 'Paléographie' at <http://www.academia.edu/1744242/Bibliographie_de_pal%C3%A9ographie_latine> [accessed 23 December 2014]. For an overview and a state of the field from the 1950s, see note 57 below.

[44] On the scientific status and functions of palaeography, see, recently, Daniele Bianconi, 'Paleografia: riflessioni su concetto e ruolo', in *Storia della scrittura e altre storie*, ed. by Daniele Bianconi (Rome: Accademia Nazionale dei Lincei, 2013), pp. 7–29, with updated bibliography.

[45] The state of the field is still not far from that described by Armando Petrucci, 'Paleografia greca e paleografia latina: significati e limiti di un confronto', in *Paleografia e codicologia greca. Atti del II colloquio internazionale (Berlino-Wolfenbüttel, 1983)*, ed. by Dieter Harlfinger and Giancarlo Prato, in collaboration with Marco D'Agostino and Alberto Doda (Alessandria: Edizioni dell'Orso, 1991), I, pp. 463–84, and Alessandro Pratesi, 'Paleografia greca e paleografia latina o paleografia greco-latina?', in *Studi storici in onore di Gabriele Pepe*, ed. by Mario Sansone (Bari, 1969), pp. 161–72 (repr. in Alessandro Pratesi, *Frustula palaeographica* (Florence: Olschki, 1992), pp. 129–41).

[46] Paolo Cherubini and Alessandro Pratesi, *Paleografia latina. L'avventura grafica del mondo occidentale* (Vatican City: Scuola Vaticana di paleografia, diplomatica e archivistica, 2010).

the bottom of each chapter, but it is also highly (if not exceedingly) representative of a single historical tradition. Latin palaeography is presented as a 'history of the continuous development of the signs of the Latin alphabet and those which supplement it. [...] It is investigated with its own methodology in the intrinsic mechanisms and external causes that contribute from time to time to modify the structure and appearance [of the signs].'[47] In the introduction, the possibility of joining the study of writing and reading to the history of society and culture is mentioned, as well as an acknowledgment of the study of writing as a system of signs in motion, but this structuralist approach, which was theorised in the work of Emanuele Casamassima (the author of the most lucid work on the mechanism of graphic change after Jean Mallon) is briefly dismissed as hardly persuasive to the objectives of the discipline. The authors state a similar, or even stronger, scepticism towards the application of quantitative methods to palaeography or laboratory techniques.[48]

And yet, the Italian palaeographic (or palaeographic-codicological) tradition has shown trends and tendencies that go beyond the rather crystallised vision proposed by Cherubini and Pratesi. An important contribution to the knowledge of late-medieval graphics tendencies has resulted in the systematic cataloguing of dated and datable manuscripts located in Italian libraries. For the past twenty years, these catalogues have been collecting exceptional documentation in both its quantitative richness and typological variety:[49] an incredibly varied landscape of scribes and hand-

---

[47] Cherubini and Pratesi, p. 9. 'storia del continuo divenire dei segni dell'alfabeto latino e di quelli che lo integrano [...] indagata con una propria metodologia nei meccanismi intrinseci e nelle cause esterne che concorrono di volta in volta a modificarne struttura ed aspetto'.

[48] See, for example, Cherubini and Pratesi's particularly ungenerous judgement of the work by Albert Derolez on the palaeography of Gothic scripts. Cherubini and Pratesi, pp. 479–80.

[49] For a discussion on the 'Manoscritti datati d'Italia' Project, see <http://www.manoscrittidatati.it> [accessed 23 December 2014]. The website also lists all the published and forthcoming volumes. See also Teresa De Robertis, 'La catalogazione dei manoscritti datati d'Italia', in *Conoscere il manoscritto: esperienze, progetti, problemi. Dieci anni dal progetto Codex in Toscana*, ed. by Michaelangiola Marchiaro and Stefano Zamponi (Firenze: SISMEL – Edizioni del Galluzzo, 2007), pp. 125–43. On methodological considerations on cataloguing medieval manuscripts, see Stefano Zamponi, 'Obiettivi, modelli e limiti della catalogazione: alcuni problemi aperti', in *Zenit e Nadir II. I manoscritti dell'area del Mediterraneo: la catalogazione come base della ricerca. Atti del seminario internazionale (Montepulciano, 6–8 luglio 2007)*, ed. by Benedetta Cenni and others (Montepulciano: Thesan & Turan, 2007), pp. 21–33.

writings, mainly belonging to the Late Middle Ages, and still largely unexplored, whose full understanding also requires an awareness of the close interactions between book hands and the documentary hands of notaries and merchants, who are often active as copyists of books.[50] The attention paid to cataloguing, which is increasingly, if not generally, understood as research activity in its own right, encourages the perception of the medieval manuscript as an inseparable unity of materiality, content and script. The contributions to our understanding of book production that this awareness has produced in recent years are remarkable.[51] Advances have been shown in specific contexts of book production: for example, individual persons and categories of copyists have been identified, their work within specific contexts has been investigated and the codicological sensitivity of some more well known than others has been studied, as reflected in the physiognomy of their own book collections or the attention paid to the aspect and layout of the books containing their own work.[52] A particularly lively strand of investigation is dedicated to the

---

[50] See Teresa De Robertis, 'Aspetti dell'esperienza grafica del Quattrocento italiano attraverso i Manoscritti datati d'Italia', *Aevum. Rassegna di scienze storiche, linguistiche e filologiche*, 82, 2 (2008), pp. 505–22, and Nicoletta Giovè, 'I copisti dei manoscritti datati', *Aevum. Rassegna di scienze storiche, linguistiche e filologiche*, 82, 2 (2008), pp. 523–41.

[51] For example, the Franciscan book production, studied by Nicoletta Giovè, 'Il codice francescano. L'invenzione di un'identità', in *Libri, biblioteche e letture dei frati Mendicanti (secoli XIII–XIV). Atti del XXXII Convegno internazionale (Assisi, 7–9 Ottobre 2004)* (Spoleto: Fondazione Centro Italiano di Studi sull'Alto Medioevo, 2005), pp. 375–418; Nicolettà Giovè and Stefano Zamponi, 'Manoscritti in volgare nei conventi dei frati Minori: Testi, tipologie librarie, scritture (secoli XIII–XIV)', in *Francescanesimo in volgare (secoli XIII–XIV), Atti del XXIV Convegno internazionale (Assisi, 17–19 Ottobre 1996)* (Spoleto: Centro Italiano di Studi sull'Alto Medioevo, 1997), pp. 301–36; on the books and handwriting of merchants, see Marco Cursi, 'Il libro del mercante: tipicità ed eccezioni', in *La produzione scritta tecnica e scientifica nel Medioevo: libro e documento tra scuole e professioni*, ed. by Giuseppe De Gregorio and Maria Galante (Spoleto: Cisam, 2012), pp. 147–93; on merchants and their hands, see, for example, Irene Ceccherini, 'Merchants and Notaries: Stylistic Movements in Italian Cursive Scripts', *Manuscripta*, 53 (2009), pp. 239–83 (with full bibliography).

[52] Amongst the most representative works on Dante's manuscripts: Sandro Bertelli, *La tradizione della 'Commedia'. Dai manoscritti al testo*, I. *I codici trecenteschi (entro l'antica Vulgata) conservati a Firenze* (Florence: Olschki, 2011) and *I manoscritti della letteratura italiana delle Origini. Firenze, Biblioteca Medicea Laurenziana* (Florence: Sismel – Edizioni del Galluzzo, 2011); Marisa Boschi Rotiroti, *Codicologia trecentesca della Commedia. Entro e oltre l'antica Vulgata* (Rome: Viella,

theme of authorship, a subject also discussed at a recent meeting of the Comité international de paléographie latine.[53]

Compared with the last decades of the twentieth century, the methodological discussions on issues such as the palaeographic method, the techniques and description of scripts and hands,[54] the criteria for dating and localisation have been overall less lively.[55] It is not a coincidence that Albert Derolez, in the introduction to his significant monograph on the palaeography of Gothic manuscripts, explicitly explores the 'crisis of

2004); on Boccaccio: Marco Cursi, *Il Decameron: scritture, scriventi, lettori. Storia di un testo* (Rome: Viella, 2007) and *La scrittura e i libri di Giovanni Boccaccio* (Rome: Viella, 2013); on Petrarch, Stefano Zamponi, 'Il libro del Canzoniere: modelli, strutture, funzioni', in *'Rerum vulgarium fragmenta'. Codice Vat. lat. 3195. Commentario all'edizione in fac-simile*, ed. by Gino Belloni and others (Rome and Padua: Editrice Antenore, 2004), pp. 13–72, and Maddalena Signorini, 'Sul codice delle *Tusculanae* appartenuto a Francesco Petrarca (Roma, *BNC*, Vittorio Emanuele, 1632)', *Studi romanzi*, 1 (2005), pp. 107–39; 'S. Gregorio al Celio e un codice della biblioteca di Francesco Petrarca', *Culture del testo e del documento*, 18 (2005), pp. 5–23; 'La scrittura libraria di Francesco Petrarca: terminologia, fortuna', *Studi medievali*, 48 (2007), pp. 839–62; on Coluccio Salutati, *Coluccio Salutati e l'invenzione dell'Umanesimo. Catalogo della mostra (Florence, Biblioteca Medicea Laurenziana, 2 novembre 2008–30 gennaio 2009)*, ed. by Teresa De Robertis and others (Florence: Mandragora, 2008).

[53] *Medieval Autograph Manuscripts. Proceedings of the XVIIth Colloquium of the Comité International de Paléographie Latine, held in Ljubljana, 7–10 September 2010*, ed. by Nataša Golob (Turnhout: Brepols, 2013), in particular, Teresa De Robertis, 'Una mano tante scritture. Problemi di metodo nell'identificazione degli autografi', pp. 18–38; see also *'Di mano propria'. Gli autografi dei letterati italiani. Forlì, 24–27 novembre 2008*, ed. by G. Baldassari and others (Rome: Salerno Editrice, 2010). For an interest in autographs of Italian authors, see *Autografi dei letterati italiani. Le origini e il Trecento*, I, ed. by Giuseppina Brunetti, Marco Fiorilla and Marco Petoletti (Rome: Salerno Editrice, 2013); *Il Quattrocento*, I, ed. by Francesco Bausi and others (Rome: Salerno Editrice, 2014); two other volumes of the same series are devoted to autographs of sixteenth-century authors. For autographs in the Occitan language, see Giuseppina Brunetti, *Autografi medievali francesi* (Rome: Salerno Editrice, 2014).

[54] See *Methoden der Schriftbeschreibung*, ed. by Peter Rück (Marburg: J. Thorbecke, 1999).

[55] Among the (positive) exceptions, see the remarks on dating (and localising) criteria, by Denis Muzerelle, 'Dating Manuscripts: What is at Stake in the Steps Usually (but Infrequently) Taken / Dater les manuscrits: les enjeux d'une démarche (trop peu) usuelle', *Journal of the Early Book Society*, 11 (2008), pp. 167–80, and the reflection on theoretical, technical and historical aspects of cursive writing, developed in the periodical meeting of the 'Seminario permanente sulla corsività / Séminaire permanent 'Écritures cursives' / Workshop on cursive handwriting', comprising an international group of scholars.

paleography',[56] drawing attention to the problematic nature of the scientific status of the discipline and the weakness and fragmentation of its methodological assumptions. This 'crisis' is contrasted with a stimulating, if not universally agreed, effort of objectivity in the classification and nomenclature of Gothic scripts, grounded on the collection of a large amount of data and the definition of types, based on the systematic analysis of the morphology of letter forms, ligatures and abbreviations.

This is not the place to give an account of the individual studies which have been dedicated to different palaeographical topics.[57] It will be enough to remember that in Northern European research, methodological contributions and specific palaeographical analysis are often contextualised in a broader and more generic framework in which the search for a historical, literary-historical, prosopographical and sociological background on centres and contexts of production, copyists, practices of teaching and learning how to write tend to prevail.[58] An interest oriented towards more specific palaeographic issues is not completely absent: examples may be seen in the advancement in the study of documentary scripts in the work of Marc Smith;[59] in the application of advanced statistical techniques to the study of the dynamics of medieval handwriting and its material and physiological limitations in the reflections of Denis Muzerelle;[60] or in the independent application of quantitative palaeography in the current work

---

[56] Albert Derolez, *The Palaeography of Gothic Manuscript Books from the Twelfth to the Early Sixteenth Century* (Cambridge, Cambridge University Press, 2003), p. 7.

[57] For a *status questionis* on the main periods and typologies of graphs, see *Actes du XIVe colloque du Comité international de paléographie latine, Enghien-les-Bains, 2003*, published in *Archiv für Diplomatik*, 50 (2004). A good bibliography up to 2010 is available, by Marc H. Smith, *Paléographie. Bibliographie d'histoire de l'écriture manuscrite en caractères latins de l'Antiquité à l'époque moderne*, https://www.academia.edu/1744242/Bibliographie_de_pal%C3%A9ographie_latine [accessed 23 December 2014].

[58] See, for a confirmation, the papers presented at the congresses of the Comité international de paléographie latine (CIPL), listed on the website <http://www.palaeographia.org/cipl/colloq.htm> [accessed 23 December 2014].

[59] Marc H. Smith, 'Les "gothiques documentaires": un carrefour dans l'histoire de l'écriture latine', *Archiv für Diplomatik*, 50 (2004), 417–65.

[60] Denis Muzerelle, 'Le geste et son ombre: essai sur le "rapport modulaire" des écritures', *Gazette du livre médiéval*, 35 (1999), pp. 32–45 and 'Jeux d'angles et jeu de plume. Première partie: retour sur l'hypothèse du biseautage de la plume', *Gazette du livre médiéval*, 60 (2013), 1–27.

of Maria Gurrado (for the study of French cursive book hand) or Erik Kwakkel (for the definition of criteria in the transition from Caroline to Gothic script).[61]

Methodology and terminology are often associated concerns in the writings of palaeographers on the British side of the Channel. Malcolm Parkes, in particular, tried to rationalise the nomenclature of scripts in the late medieval period, and in his last book contextualised the activity of medieval British scribes within social and regional environments.[62] The recent effort made by Peter Stokes to define English Vernacular minuscule between 990 and 1035 as a national graphic achievement based on the joint contribution of Continental and Insular practices also deserves mention here, although the methodology applied fits more appropriately within the recent framework of digital palaeography.[63] More work on later scripts may also help to discuss further local scribal practices and the coexistence of set and cursive scripts in English manuscript production, as well as the ways in which they intersect with French and Latin manuscripts.[64]

A salient development of British palaeography is the current fervent work on scribal identifications. British book production is mostly anonymous, a marked difference with other European realities. In late medieval Bologna, writing contracts were registered with the city authority, and this type of evidence has provided precious information on the social identity of the scribes, their training, the type of work they were copying, their identity and their clientele and, of course, the time spent transcribing books.[65] Scribes active in fifteenth-century Rome have been studied, and of course much is known about Paris, through the work of Richard and

---

[61] Maria Gurrado, 'Les écritures cursives livresques en France (1250–1420). Essai de paléographie quantitative d'après le catalogue des manuscrits datés' (unpublished thesis, École nationale des chartes, Paris, 2011) <http://theses.enc. sorbonne.fr/2011/gurrado> [accessed 23 December 2014].

[62] Essential here are the seminal works by M. B. Parkes, *English Cursive Book Hands, 1250–1500* (Oxford: Clarendon Press, 1969) and *Their Hands before Our Eyes: A Closer Look at Scribes* (Aldershot: Ashgate, 2008). For a response on terminology, see Elaine Treharne, 'Medieval Manuscripts: The Good, the Bad, the Ugly', in *The Genesis of Texts: Essays in Honour of A. N. Doane*, ed. by Matt Hussey and Jack Niles (Turnhout: Brepols, 2012), pp. 265–87.

[63] See, for a discussion, the essay by Brookes and others in this volume, pp. 25.

[64] Daniel Wakelin, 'Writing the Words', in *The Production of Books*, ed. by Gillespie and Wakelin, pp. 34–58.

[65] Giovanna Murano, *Copisti a Bologna: 1265–1270* (Turnhout: Brepols, 2006).

Mary Rouse among others.[66] Scholars over the years have contributed to the field with articles, books and essays.[67] Precentors' accounts – or accounts in general – can offer some information about the operating mechanisms of the medieval book market within specific environments, and this is an area which would be worth expanding.[68] A recent book by Linne Mooney and Estelle Stubbs has uncovered a wealth of information on scribes working in the City of London:[69] an important starting point which again demonstrates how the mode of writing and copying books may show significant resemblances across national boundaries.

New trends (digital palaeography, neuropalaeography)

Over recent decades, the development of new digital technologies has created the conditions for a new digital shockwave in a scientific community, characterised by a substantial continuity of objectives and research practices, despite the variety of approaches. As a result, digital palaeography has emerged as a new trend in a position of sharp discontinuity with traditional approaches.

Digital palaeography is indeed a diverse array of methods, techniques and research practices very dissimilar in assumptions and purposes. The general assumption underlying them is that the evolution of digital technologies – as applied to the study of books, but especially of ancient and medieval scripts – profoundly changes not only our research practices,

---

66 Elisabetta Caldelli, *Copisti a Roma nel quattrocento* (Rome: Viella, 2006); H. Rouse Richard and A. Rouse Mary, *Manuscripts and Their Makers: Commercial Book Producers in Medieval Paris, 1200–1500* (London: Harvey Miller, 2000).

67 See, for example, D. G. Scragg, *A Conspectus of Scribal Hands Writing English, 960–1100* (Cambridge: D. S. Brewer, 2012), M. B. Parkes, *Their Hands before Our Eyes*; Simon Horobin, 'Manuscripts and Scribes', in *Chaucer: Contemporary Approaches*, ed. by Susanna Fein and David Raybin (University Park, PA: Pennsylvania State University Press, 2010), pp. 67–82; Graham Pollard, 'The University and the Book Trade in Medieval Oxford', *Beiträge zum Berufsbewusstsein des mittelalterlichen Menschen, Miscellanea Mediaevalia*, 3 (1968), 336–44; and 'The Medieval Town Clerk of Oxford', *Oxoniensia*, 31 (1966), 44–76.

68 M. Gullick, *The Precentor's Accounts of Ely Cathedral Priory* (Hitchin: Red Gull Press, 1989), N. R. Ker, 'Medieval Manuscripts from Norwich Cathedral Priory', *Transactions of the Cambridge Bibliographical Society*, 1 (1949–53), 1–28.

69 L. R. Mooney and Estelle Stubbs, *Scribes and the City: London Guildhall Clerks and the Dissemination of Middle English Literature, 1375–1425* (York: York Medieval Press, 2013), and see also the 'Late Medieval English Scribes' Project <http://www.medievalscribes.com> [accessed 23 December 2014].

but also the very nature of the historical knowledge that we have of them. The complete digitisation of the existing manuscript heritage has gone in a few years from a utopian perspective to a realistic horizon,[70] and the development and dissemination of reproduction technologies as well as the possibilities of image manipulation have certainly changed, if not necessarily determined, the way in which we look at medieval books. This situation is not dissimilar to what happened at the beginning of the last century with the spread of facsimiles, which opened up the long and neglected field of books and scripts. However, the variety of accomplishments, projects and experiments which can be traced back to the field of digital palaeography (and less clearly to digital codicology) still suffers from confusion between instrumental uses of the digital technologies and processes and the elaboration of new methodological paradigms. This confusion can be seen, for example, by scrolling the table of contents of two recent collections of essays devoted to digital palaeography and codicology which juxtapose, with a generic confidence in the heuristic potentials of technology, contributions dedicated to digital photography, cataloguing, scientific examination of the material characteristics of the book, reading practices, classification and analysis of handwriting, and encoding of texts and codicological details.[71]

Regarding the presentation, communication and circulation of materials and scientific results (images, text and descriptions both in open or closed forms, but also information and research hypotheses published by social communities), it is undeniable that technology and the Internet offer wide-ranging possibilities. However, the scientific and cultural implications related to the need to manage and exploit in a correct and proper form the abundance of information in circulation, or easily acquired in

---

[70] Ezio Ornato, '*Bibliotheca manuscripta universalis*. Digitalizzazione e catalografia: un viaggio nel regno di Utopia?', *Gazette du livre médiéval*, 48 (2006), 1–13 and 'La numérisation du patrimoine livresque médiéval: avancée décisive ou miroir aux alouettes?', in *Kodikologie und Paläographie im digitalen Zeitalter, Kodikologie und Paläographie im digitalen Zeitalter*, ed. by Franz Fischer, Christiane Fritze and Georg Vogeler (Nordested: Books on Demand, 2010), pp. 85–115 <kups.ub.uni-koeln.de/4345/1/07_ornato.pdf> [accessed on 23 December 2014]).

[71] *Kodikologie und Paläographie im digitalen Zeitalter – Palaeography and Codicology in the Digital Age*, ed. by Malte Rehbein, Patrick Sahle and Torsten Schaßan (Norderstedt: Books on Demand, 2009) <http://kups.ub.uni-koeln. de/2939/> [accessed 23 December 2014] and *Kodikologie und Paläographie im digitalen Zeitalter*, ed. by Fischer, Fritze and Vogeler <http://kups.ub.uni-koeln. de/4337/> [accessed 23 December 2014].

digital format, ought not to be underestimated, nor reduced to a sum of purely technical problems. This is particularly true with regard to electronic cataloguing. For electronic catalogues to function seamlessly, they require the achievement of adequate interoperability standards which necessarily involve a coherent and significant investment in the selection of languages, encoding and presentation protocols, but, more importantly, a relative homogeneity in the description and encoding of codicological, palaeographical and art-historical details. This is a commitment so far underestimated, in the name of a misguided defence of the uniqueness of the manuscript and the resulting variety of descriptive practices. In the same vein, the development of a shared multilingual terminology remains a *desideratum*. A digital dictionary has been started but left unfinished for codicology (with the notably patchy presence of English) and is still substantially unfulfilled for palaeography.[72]

The most prominent potential and pitfalls are those related to the application of methods of automatic processing of the image to medieval handwriting. Leaving aside the purely instrumental purposes (such as automatic transcription of texts), the experiments in progress are marked by differences in orientation and perspectives that are too often underestimated. On the one hand, initiatives such as the DigiPal project (in which context the aforementioned volume by Peter Stokes is included),[73] or the above-mentioned research conducted by Erik Kwakkel,[74] have combined the newfound interest in objectivity, reproducibility and multiplication of comparability, which electronic models particularly privilege, with tried-and-tested traditional palaeographical methods which trust the selection and the interpretation of the graphical features to the subjectivity of the researcher. On the other hand, methodologies have been proposed which tend more or less consciously to transfer the responsibility for processing the data, and the judgement that follows, from the scholar to the computer. In this case, the computer is not used as an aid in the creation of historically-based classifications, but as a source for patterns and classifications produced automatically, whose results are only assessed

[72] Apart from the valuable but still incomplete attempt by Peter Gumbert, *Words for codices* [2010] <www.cei.lmu.de/extern/VocCod/WOR10–1.pdf>; <www.cei.lmu.de/extern/VocCod/WOR10–2.pdf>; <www.cei.lmu.de/extern/VocCod/WOR10–3.pdf> [all accessed on 24 December 2014].

[73] See, in this volume, Stewart Brookes and others. A bibliography on Digital Palaeography up to 2010 is also available on the DigiPal website <http://www.digipal.eu/general-bibliography/> [accessed 23 December 2014].

[74] See p. 19.

at a later stage.[75] Overall, a need is felt for a more solid exchange and connection between the complexity of historical knowledge, which has been accrued from a long tradition of scientific research, and the development of new approaches. A constructive dialogue between traditional and digital methodologies ought to be built on a consolidation or revision of the results already achieved, and ought to assist in the formulation of those new questions and research hypotheses which cannot be achieved with traditional methods.

Apart from digital palaeography, another innovative trend is represented by the proposal to conjoin palaeographical approaches to research developed in cognitive sciences (neuropalaeography), with the aim of recognising the role of hand movements in the morphologic transformation of the characters,[76] in order to achieve a 'comprehensive understanding of the movement of the hand when writing'.[77] However, beyond the explanation of the advantages of the contribution of the cognitive approach to the analysis of medieval handwriting and the definition of its limits, the concrete practical application and interpretative effectiveness of neuropalaeography still remain to be fully explored.

A number of key issues and research perspectives relating to the study of medieval manuscripts have been highlighted, without aspiring to

---

[75] For an overview, see Denis Muzerelle, 'À la recherche d'algorithmes experts en écritures médiévales', *Gazette du livre médiéval*, 56–57 (2011), pp. 5–20 (= *Analyse d'image et paléographie systématique: travaux du programme Graphem*, ed. by Denis Muzerelle and Maria Gurrado); see also the other essays in that volume and the summary of the round table entitled 'Applications actuelles de l'informatique à la paléographie: quelles méthodes pour quelles finalités?', pp. 119–30.

[76] Maria Gurrado, 'Capire la scrittura: l'approccio delle scienze cognitive', *Gazette du livre médiéval*, 58 (2012), pp. 18–50 (with full bibliography); Marc Smith, 'Les formes de l'alphabet latin, entre écriture et lecture', *La vie des formes*, Paris, 14 Octobre 2011 <http://www.college-de-france.fr/site/colloque-2011/symposium-2011-10-14-10h45.htm> [accessed 23 December 2014]: 'Les formes et structures de l'écriture latine ont sans cesse évolué depuis plus de deux mille ans, qu'il s'agisse de l'aspect individuel des lettres ou des configurations toujours plus complexes dans lesquelles elles sont mises en œuvre pour former un texte, une page, un document ou un livre. Les formes infiniment diverses et subtilement articulées que nous employons aujourd'hui, répondant à autant de paramètres conventionnels – fonctionnels, cognitifs, techniques, socioéconomiques ou esthétiques –, sont ainsi le résultat d'une complexe sédimentation historique. Il importe d'autant plus de resserrer le dialogue entre les sciences qui étudient l'écriture dans son fonctionnement présent et celles qui rendent compte de sa formation au fil des siècles.'

[77] Gurrado, p. 48.

completeness, in the preceding pages. They contribute to define a vivid picture of recent achievements, work in progress and future perspectives, whose future evolution is unpredictable, in a context in which the speed (exciting or confusing, according to the points of view) of digital progress is associated with the growing uncertainty that weighs on the spaces and resources allocated to humanities research. It is, of course, impossible to predict the future and some further developments will increasingly have to deal with a number of general instances, which may be worth emphasising at the end of this short survey on manuscript studies in Europe. They include: the importance of working comparatively on British and Continental (northern and southern European) manuscript production; the need to strengthen the interaction between the different scholarly traditions and, finally, the opportunity to develop common training programmes in manuscript studies at an international level.

The DigiPal Project for European Scripts and Decorations

STEWART BROOKES, PETER A. STOKES, MATILDA WATSON AND DÉBORA MARQUES DE MATOS*

Introduction

PALAEOGRAPHY HAS OFTEN been considered, both by its practitioners and its critics, as something of an art, relying on the expertise of a small number of experienced scholars whose decision-making processes may be difficult or impossible to explain. As David Ganz notes, the consequence of this is that palaeographers are 'all too often regarded as repositories of authoritative dogma'.[1] Any such system for the transfer of knowledge depends, of course, on a combination of respect and trust, and should either of these waver, there is the potential for the relationship to be resented or to break down. Albert Derolez calls attention to this, observing that the discipline is in crisis due to a lack of transparency:

> when an extremely experienced palaeographer declares that a given manuscript was written in Northern France in the first half of the thirteenth century, but fails to indicate the criteria on which this statement is based, he may be a perfect connoisseur, but he is not being an effective teacher. What is more, he unconsciously contributes to the present-day crisis of palaeography as a discipline.[2]

* The authors wish to thank the other members of the DigiPal team, particularly Geoffroy Noël and Giancarlo Buomprisco, without whose contribution to the project this article would not have been possible. We also gratefully acknowledge the financial support of the European Research Council: the research leading to these results received funding from the European Union Seventh Framework Programme (FP7) under grant agreement no. 263751.

1 David Ganz, '"Editorial Palaeography": One Teacher's Suggestions', *Gazette du livre médiéval*, 16 (1990), 17–20 <http://www.palaeographia.org/glm/glm. htm?art=ganz> [accessed 24 December 2014]. For ease of reference all of the URLs and images in this article may be found at: http://www.digipal.en/blog/writing-europe.

2 Albert Derolez, *The Palaeography of Gothic Manuscript Books: From the Twelfth to the Early Sixteenth Century* (Cambridge: Cambridge University Press, 2003), p. 9.

One response to the perception of dependence on a few highly-skilled practitioners has been the development of computer-based methods of palaeography. However, the attendant problem with many such approaches is that they exchange the authority of the palaeographer for the authority of the computer, or so-called 'black box'.[3] In the hypothetical extreme, operators feed vast quantities of data into a computer and receive 'answers' but with little understanding of how these results were achieved, how to interpret them, or whether it is possible to refine the output. Although the reality is more nuanced than this, palaeographers grounded in traditional methodologies have sometimes been reluctant to accept findings from computer-based research even when the advantages of quantitative and statistical approaches seem clear.[4]

With these issues in mind, the project team of the *Digital Resource and Database for Palaeography, Manuscripts and Diplomatic* (DigiPal) set out to offer a visible and replicable methodology to allow people to explore palaeographical data and to communicate their evidence and accompanying argument to a wider audience.[5] Addressing the needs of both expert palaeographers and those with less specialised teaching and research interests in manuscript studies, DigiPal provides a web-based framework for annotating digital images, interrogating the data, and ordering and presenting the results. The intention is to move palaeography away from the exclusive knowledge-base which has led to accusations of 'vagueness and subjectivity'[6] and toward an evidence-based approach in which

---

[3] Lior Wolf and others, 'Computerized Paleography: Tools for Historical Manuscripts', *IEEE International Conference on Image Processing* (ICIP), 2011 <http://www.cs.tau.ac.il/~wolf/papers/lettercharts.pdf> [accessed 24 December 2014]; Lambert Schomaker, 'Writer Identification and Verification', in *Advances in Biometrics: Sensors, Systems and Algorithms*, ed. by Nalini K. Ratha and Venu Govindaraju (London: Springer Verlag, 2008), pp. 247–64 (p. 260).

[4] For an argument setting out the potential benefits of quantitative palaeography, see Derolez, pp. 7–9; for concerns about 'cross-examining' the computer's results, see Tom Davis, 'The Practice of Handwriting Identification', *The Library*, 8 (2007), 251–76 (p. 266 n. 27).

[5] 'Digital Resource and Database for Palaeography' (DigiPal) was a four-year project (2011–2014) based at the Department of Digital Humanities, King's College London <http://www.digipal.eu> [accessed 24 December 2014]. The website includes both the database and supporting documentation and resources.

[6] Peter A. Stokes, 'Computer-Aided Palaeography, Present and Future', in *Kodikologie und Paläographie im digitalen Zeitalter – Palaeography and Codicology in the Digital Age*, ed. by Malte Rehbein, Patrick Sahle and Torsten Schaßan (Norderstedt: Books on Demand, 2009), pp. 309–38 (p. 312).

findings can be readily reproduced, shared and tested. In this paper, we describe the basic functionality of the DigiPal framework and then present applications of that framework to different corpora, namely English Vernacular minuscule of the eleventh century which is the central test-case for DigiPal; a group of Latin manuscript fragments which survive in Scandinavian archives dated from the tenth to eleventh centuries (ScandiPal); and medieval Hebrew manuscripts copied and decorated in the Iberian Peninsula during the second half of the fifteenth century (SephardiPal). The methodology is designed to be applicable to a wide range of script and even decoration, and therefore cuts across many of the issues that underlie the study of writing in Europe during the medieval period and beyond.

The DigiPal Project (by Stewart Brookes)

As researchers with strong interests in both palaeography and digital humanities, it was our intention to bring the benefits of a computer-based approach to the study of medieval handwriting. Therefore, we set out to create new methodologies for analysing, classifying, presenting and curating palaeographic content. As this paper shows, a further objective was to build a framework of palaeographic tools suitable for extension to corpora beyond the DigiPal test-case of English Vernacular minuscule.

We began by reviewing the online resources for studying manuscripts from the medieval period and found that they were either based on textual descriptions or were designed to offer digital surrogates for manuscripts in the form of individual images or a 'turn the pages' style of presentation. At the time of DigiPal's inception, the most significant research projects that covered material in our specific timeframe were 'The Production and Use of English Manuscripts 1060 to 1220' (hereafter EM 1060 to 1220) and the 'MANCASS C11 Database: An Inventory of Script and Spellings in Eleventh-Century English' (hereafter C11 Database).[7] Led by Orietta Da Rold, Takako Kato, Mary Swan and Elaine Treharne, EM 1060 to

---

[7] *The Production and Use of English Manuscripts 1060 to 1220*, ed. by Orietta Da Rold and others (University of Leicester, 2010; last update 2013), <http://www.le.ac.uk/ee/em1060to1220> [accessed 23 January 2015]. Donald Scragg and others, *ManCASS C11 Database Project* (Manchester: Manchester Centre for Anglo-Saxon Studies, 2005). Regrettably, the website for the C11 Database <http://www.arts.manchester.ac.uk/mancass/C11database> has, at the time of writing, not been functional for over a year and communication with the maintainers suggests that there is no intention to provide access. Some of its content is available from the 'Wayback Machine' hosted at the Internet Archive: <http://web.archive.org/

1220 set out to identify and describe all those manuscripts containing English which were written in England between 1060 and 1220. The website is comprised of textual descriptions of the manuscripts and their content, often with detailed information about the letter-forms of individual scribes (the aspect most of interest to our project). The project website was conceived as an electronic book rather than a database and not designed to support the sort of palaeographic queries of interest to the DigiPal team, such as whether there were any patterns in the treatment of ascenders by the scribes in this period; how often ascenders are wedged or split; and whether they are short or tall. Many of the descriptions in EM 1060 to 1220 contained the information in which we were interested, and the provision of a Google-powered search engine took us tantalisingly close to being able to locate it, especially as one can use the standard Google search operators such as quotation marks to return more precise results and the Boolean operators 'OR' and 'AND' to combine searches (for example: "split ascender" OR "split descenders"). The problem with searching for specific phrases in this way is that the descriptions of the letter-forms were written by a number of different researchers and, as one might expect, their vocabulary varies. Thus, a precise search for "split ascenders" would miss 'ascenders are tall and split', 'split-topped ascenders' and 'long ascenders, split, with elaborate flags'. This last issue touches on a wider matter: the details in the descriptions vary and do not all, for example, draw the distinction between the different types of **g** and this means that it is not possible to distinguish between Caroline and Insular in a search for 'closed tail of **g**'. In the end, the only way to not miss information is to use generalised search terms without quotation marks and accept that the results will include material that is not relevant. It would not, of course, be fair to EM 1060 to 1220 to see this as a shortcoming as we were looking to search in detail for specific features of script and this was not something for which the project website was intended. Having said that, our experience of trying to search for data in EM 1060 to 1220 helped to formulate our intentions when designing DigiPal, especially when considering facilities for structured searching and also when devising a way to ensure descriptions of letter-forms were constrained to a standard template. A final point to note in the context of Digital Humanities is that while the current website is an important resource for studying the manuscripts described, the researchers involved in EM 1060

web/20060619193332/http://www.arts.manchester.ac.uk/mancass/C11database/>
(<http://goo.gl/OvHZGj>) [accessed 21 November 2014].

to 1220 have secured the long-term future of their work by marking up their descriptions in Text Encoding Initiative (TEI) format – a considerable effort – and generously allowing other projects (including DigiPal) to make free use of their 'raw' TEI data in their online resources.[8]

The second project we examined, the C11 Database, had a scope similar to that envisaged for DigiPal, covering the whole corpus of writing that has survived in Old English from *c.* 980 to 1099.[9] The C11 Database took as its focus a subset of the alphabet, examining minuscule **a**, **æ**, **c**, **d**, **e**, **g**, **h**, **s**, **þ**, **ð**, **y** and majuscule **A**, **Æ**, **D**, **E**, **G**, **H**, **M**, **N**, **T**, **Ð**, the tironian abbreviation **7**, and five forms of ascenders which were classified as 'straight', 'wedged', 'clubbed', 'notched' and 'looped'.[10] The project website presented letters in visual form, but rather than using digitised images of manuscripts, the team created their own 'idealised' (the term used by Alexander Rumble, co-director of the project) abstractions of letter-forms from scans (see Fig. 1). Each 'idealised' letter was assigned a reference number, the first three numbers of which indicate a script type; for example, '5_2_3' refers to 'Anglo-Saxon minuscule *c.* 850–1100'. Additional numbers were used to indicate particular features of the letter-form, so 'd_5_2_3_2_1' refers to '**d** with short and rounded ascender' and 'd_5_2_3_2_2' to '**d** with long and straight ascender'.[11] Obviously, these numbers are only of use to others if the system is explained and unfortunately the C11 Database team did not document how their system of numbers maps to palaeographic features beyond these two examples. Consequently, there is no way of decoding the numeric sequences 's_5_2_3_1_1_1' or 'y_5_2_3_2_1_1' in Fig. 1, nor is it possible to determine which script form is indicated by the '3_2_2' of **Ash** and '2_2_2' of **A** in place of the more frequent '5_2_3'. Another issue is that the 'idealised' letter-forms often bear little resemblance to the actual writing of the scribes under discussion. For the purposes of comparison, I have combined the letter-forms displayed by the C11 Database with those of

---

[8] An example of the way we have reused data from EM 1060 to 1220 in the DigiPal database and added illustrative images can be seen in one of the hand descriptions for Cambridge, Corpus Christi College, MS 111: <http://www.digipal. eu/digipal/hands/299/descriptions/> [accessed 28 May 2015].

[9] A. Rumble, 'The Palaeographical Material in the C11 Database', in *C11 Database* <http://web.archive.org/web/20060621190544/http://www.art.man.ac.uk/ english/mancass/data/PalaeogIntro.pdf> (<http://goo.gl/8vHTGb>) [accessed 20 November 2014].

[10] Rumble, p. 2.

[11] Rumble.

Manchester Centre for Anglo-Saxon Studies

SEARCH FOR LETTER COMBINATIONS

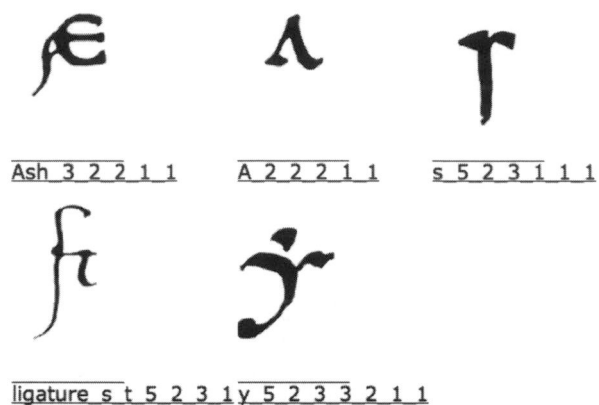

Figure 1: Searching for letter-forms in the *CII Database*.

a digital image of the corresponding manuscript (see Fig. 2). Note the 'idealised' **æ** has a 'high eye' not seen in the scribe's hand; the tail of the **g** is closed in the 'idealised' version, but open in the manuscript; and the ascender of the **þ** has a flag not present in the manuscript. Directly above the 'idealised' letters, the CII Database includes Ker's comment that this is a forward-sloping hand, drawing attention to a further problem which is that the database's 'idealised' letters are upright and do not reflect the characteristic slope of the handwriting which can be seen in the detail from the manuscript image included in Fig. 2. The problem here is not the 'idealisation' as such, but rather that the images in the CII Database do not communicate to the user which palaeographical features the project team considered significant and therefore what it is that distinguishes one 'idealised' form from another. [12]

The overview of EM 1060 to 1220 and the CII Database in the preceding paragraphs is, of course, very much from the perspective of the

[12] For further discussion of this, see also Peter A. Stokes, 'Palaeography and the "Virtual Library" of Manuscripts', in *Digitizing Medieval and Early Modern Material Culture*, ed. by Brent Nelson and Melissa Terras, Medieval and Renaissance Texts and Studies, 426 (Tempe, AZ: Arizona Center for Medieval and Renaissance Studies, 2012), pp. 137–69 (pp. 151–55).

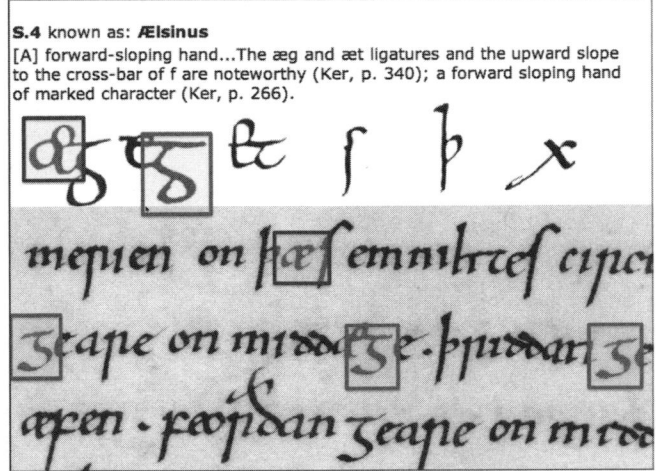

S.4 known as: **Ælsinus**
[A] forward-sloping hand...The æg and æt ligatures and the upward slope to the cross-bar of f are noteworthy (Ker, p. 340); a forward sloping hand of marked character (Ker, p. 266).

Figure 2: *The C11 Database* and superimposed beneath it an annotated image from London, British Library, MS Cotton Titus D XXVII, fol. 42v. (© The British Library Board)

research interests of the DigiPal team, and not a reflection of the successes those two projects achieved within their respective remits. Rather, our intention here is to highlight the importance of our research questions to the way that we approached the design of the DigiPal framework and the wider issue of creating a platform for a more transparent communication of palaeographic argument. In regard to transparency, it was of formative influence to note that neither of the earlier projects used their computer-based medium to move away from the idea of the palaeographer as a repository of authoritative knowledge. Indeed, EM 1060 to 1220 was never designed to do this, and the C11 Database makes for further obscurity with its numeric descriptions, the details of which are known only to the researchers on the project. Two essential aspects for an evidence-based approach are, of course, to display the data and explain the terminology used. With this in mind, we divided the DigiPal project into four main components. The first is a web-based framework (essentially, a database and a set of tools linked through a web interface) designed for computer-assisted palaeography and curation of data. The second is the creation of a fine-grained terminology to describe letter-forms (or allographs, as they are referred to in DigiPal, with an allograph being a variant form of a character; for example, Insular **d** and Caroline **d**). The third component applies that framework to our main test-case, the entire corpus of surviving

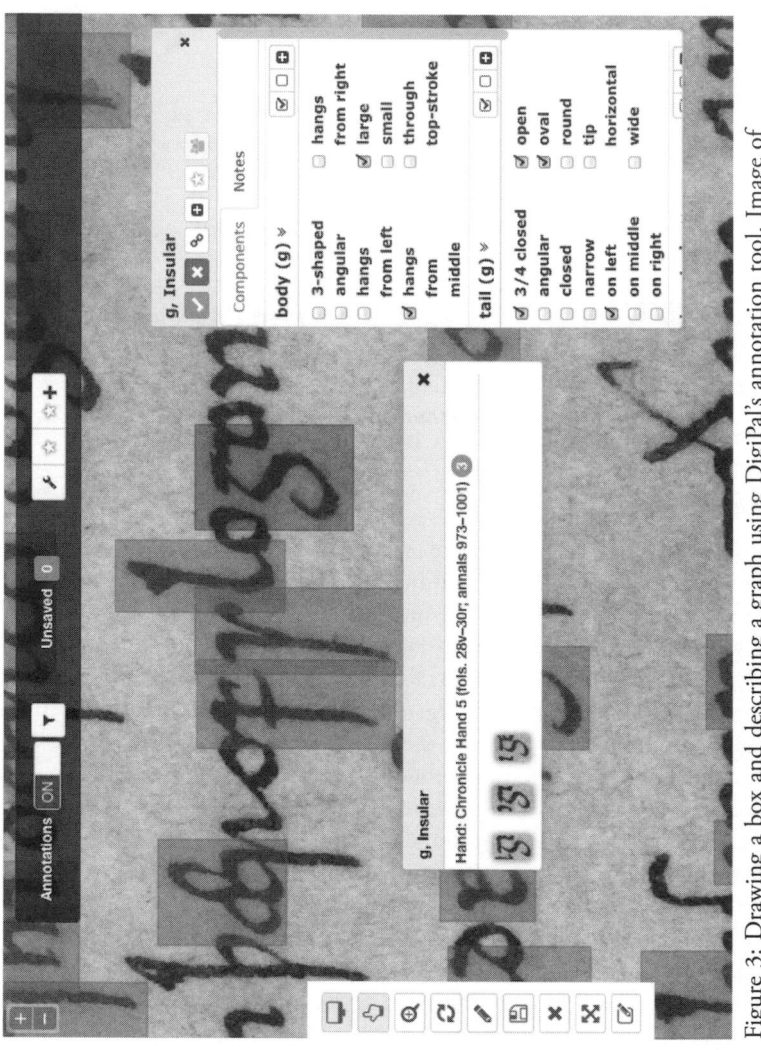

Figure 3: Drawing a box and describing a graph using DigiPal's annotation tool. Image of Cambridge, Corpus Christi College, MS 173, fol. 29v.

English Vernacular minuscule from the eleventh century.[13] Finally, the fourth component is the publication of research based on results derived from the analysis of the data through the framework and the writing of blog posts which detail the underlying principles of DigiPal.

In the initial stages of the project we examined the manuscripts within our corpus and selected examples of each scribal hand for inclusion in our database of eleventh-century English Vernacular minuscule, requesting new digital photography in those cases where digital images were not already available.[14] A pragmatic consideration was that the cost of purchasing images restricted the number of examples of each scribal stint we could include in the DigiPal database. (The framework itself is not limited in this way and could be used across a complete manuscript or many manuscripts.) As noted earlier, our intention was to combine the textual description of letter-forms traditionally used by palaeographers with images of those letter-forms. In order to do this, we created an annotation tool to draw boxes around samples of a scribe's allographs. Just how many instances of each allograph are annotated relies upon the judgement of individual researchers and will vary according to their research questions and the nature of the material they are studying. In theory, every instance of each allograph could have an annotation box drawn around it, but having hundreds of often near-identical letter-forms would seem unlikely to add to our understanding of the features of a particular scribal hand. In the case of the DigiPal case-study, English Vernacular minuscule, it was thought to be sufficient to capture four or five examples of each variant of an allograph, with scope for further inclusion as necessary.

As boxes are drawn, a dropdown menu is used to associate the annotation with an allograph and a tick-box system is used to describe the letters (or graphs, as individual instances of an allograph are referred to within DigiPal). While the decision-making processes during the selection and description stages are reliant on the judgement of the researchers working on DigiPal, the benefit of a tick-box system is that it fosters consistency

---

[13] We are grateful to Donald Scragg, who generously shared material from *A Conspectus of Scribal Hands Writing English, 960–1100* (Cambridge: D. S. Brewer, 2012) prior to its publication. The corpus of eleventh-century vernacular scribal hands used in DigiPal is based on that established by Scragg in the *Conspectus*, although we have extended the list where that seemed appropriate in the course of examining the manuscript evidence.

[14] We acknowledge the support of the Parker Library and Stanford Digital Library in providing us with images from their digitised collections at an early stage, and particularly the kind assistance of Suzanne Paul (then sub-librarian at the Parker Library) and Ben Albritton of Stanford.

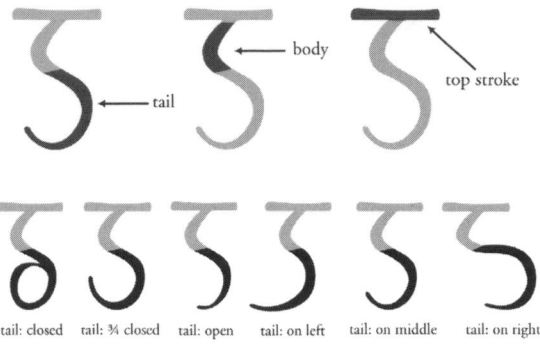

tail: closed   tail: ¾ closed   tail: open   tail: on left   tail: on middle   tail: on right

Figure 4: Descriptive labels for component parts of **g** and features of the tail of **g**.

and avoids the problems associated with scholars using variant or variable language (see Fig. 3).[15]

When devising the terminology for use within DigiPal, we divided each allograph into component parts. For example, an Insular **g** is made up of the component parts 'top-stroke', 'body' and 'tail' (see Fig. 3 for an image of Insular **g** being annotated and Fig. 4 for a key to the component parts of the **g**). Each component may have one or more features associated with it. In Fig. 3, the body of the Insular **g** 'hangs from the middle', is 'large' and the tail of the g is 'three-quarters closed', 'open' and has an 'oval' shape. As can be seen in Fig. 4, the potential options for describing the tail of **g** include 'closed', 'three-quarters closed' or 'open', and the tail might 'extend to the left' of the body, 'hang from the middle' or 'extend to the right'. As explained, the methodology used for DigiPal is to select several representative examples of each allograph from each page rather than draw a box around every occurrence. If, for example, the same scribe wrote Insular **g** with both a closed tail and an open tail, we select a few examples of each form, including variations as relevant. As each box is drawn, an optional viewer window can be used to display the graphs in order to allow comparison. (The allograph viewer can be seen in Fig. 3 displaying the three instances of Insular **g** that have been annotated.) The

[15] Only members of the DigiPal project team can draw the boxes which are included in the database. There is, however, a tool for creating annotations (not saved as part of the database) which visitors to the site can use to draw boxes around any part of an image and add explanatory text and even images which may then be shared with others. For an example, see <http://goo.gl/CxJAAv> [accessed 24 December 2014].

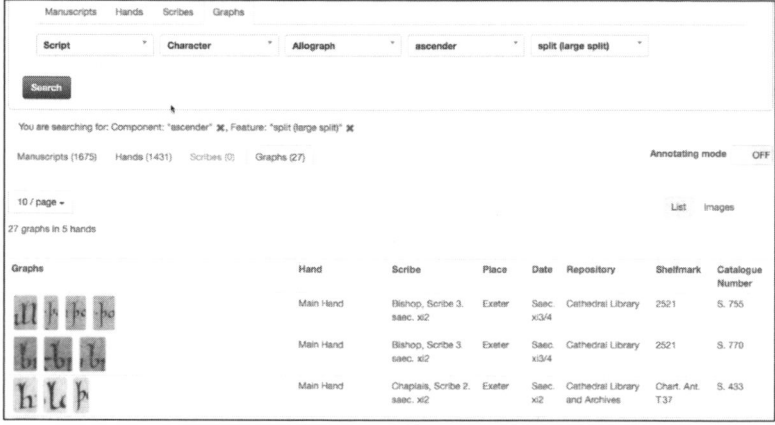

Figure 5: A subset of the search results for ascenders which are split.

allograph viewer thus serves as a visual reference guide to the graphs that have been chosen, acting as another aid to consistency because it reduces the need to rely on memory. If one clicks on a graph within the allograph viewer, the page moves to that graph (a facility that is also available for public users visiting the site).

The DigiPal framework offers a number of opportunities for searching the images and text-based descriptions within the database. To get a feel for the corpus, you can move from the general to the particular, browsing complete manuscript images; filtering according to repository to narrow the results; restricting the search to a range of dates; or choosing a particular named scribe, such as Ælfric or Wulfstan. In the same way, one may conduct a very general search for all those graphs which we have described as examples of **g** (which would show Insular and Caroline forms); or opt for criteria which limit the results to a specific script and features, such as 'Insular **g** with a tail that is open'. Clicking on any of the displayed cut-out graphs takes you to the manuscript viewer which displays those graphs within the word in which they are written and in the wider context of the complete folio. Palaeographers are of course interested in more than complete allographs, noting how scribes repeat similar strokes (or components) across different letters. With this in mind, we may return to our earlier research question and use DigiPal to search for all graphs with ascenders, or more specifically for those with ascenders which are split (see Fig. 5). As we shall see in the study of the DigiPal corpus which follows, the ability to determine the treatment of, for instance, ascenders and minims can be of central importance to palaeographic discussion. As we hope to make clear, the fundamental difference that the DigiPal framework makes is that assertions can be tested and easily retested against the evidence while providing a means to share results.

DigiPal and English Vernacular minuscule (by Peter Stokes)

As noted above, the DigiPal project comprises four key components: an online framework for the study of script; the creation of a detailed and consistent system of terminology to describe allographs within the framework and beyond; the application of the framework to particular case-studies; and the study and analysis of the results within their broader context in order to gain new understanding of the scripts and their history. The third of these is the topic of this section, and specifically the principal case study of the DigiPal project, namely English Vernacular minuscule. This script emerged in Anglo-Saxon England at the end of the tenth century and was practised throughout the eleventh.[16] It was used for writing in the vernacular, as opposed to Anglo-Caroline minuscule which was used for writing in Latin.[17] Vernacular minuscule was used in the production of a large number of manuscripts from the Anglo-Saxon period, and indeed the only surviving copies of many of the most important texts in Old English come down to us in books written in this script, including Beowulf, much of the Anglo-Saxon Chronicle, most of the surviving homilies, and boundary clauses from a number of royal and episcopal diplomas (as well as writs). Furthermore, the script presents some challenges of its own. As noted, it was written alongside Anglo-Caroline, and at least some scribes wrote both scripts together; the two therefore interacted with each other, to the degree that Neil Ker described English Vernacular minuscule of the second half of the eleventh century as 'thoroughly Caroline' despite the consistent differences in letter-form

---

[16] For a full discussion of this script, see Peter A. Stokes, *English Vernacular Minuscule from Æthelred to Cnut, circa 990–circa 1035* (Cambridge: D. S. Brewer, 2014).

[17] The principal studies of Anglo-Caroline minuscule are T. A. M. Bishop, *English Caroline Minuscule* (Oxford: Oxford University Press, 1971); David N. Dumville, *English Caroline Script and Monastic History: Studies in Benedictinism, A.D. 950–1030* (Woodbridge: Boydell, 1993); and Rebecca Rushforth, 'English Caroline Minuscule', in *Cambridge History of the Book in Britain, Volume 1: c. 400–1100*, ed. by Richard Gameson (Cambridge: Cambridge University Press, 2011), pp. 197–224.

(or allographic variation, to use more precise terminology).[18] However, the Vernacular minuscule of the early eleventh century underwent significant changes and variation, apparently even between contemporary scribes at a single *scriptorium*.[19] This is presumably in part due to the political turmoil of the period, with Danish incursions and ultimately conquest through the 990s and 1010s. However, palaeographers have tended at least to imply, if not to state, that the Anglo-Caroline of this period was more stable and less varied, and this in turn could suggest that standards and perhaps even education or training for the Caroline script was somehow more rigorous than that for the Vernacular.[20] This in turn raises questions about who was writing in eleventh-century England. Were scribes exclusively monastic, as one might assume? Presumably not, given that the canons at Exeter during Leofric's episcopate (1046–1072) undoubtedly produced books, but the question remains who else was doing so.[21] Indeed, recent work has indicated that approximately 1200 distinct scribal hands can be identified from the 'long' eleventh century for writing in English alone, and many more again once Latin is added.[22]

These research questions lie behind the DigiPal project and its application to eleventh-century writing in the vernacular. Not all of them can be addressed by use of the DigiPal framework, of course, but many key

---

[18] N. R. Ker, *Books, Collectors and Libraries: Studies in the Medieval Heritage*, ed. by Andrew G. Watson (London: Hambledon, 1985), p. 34; N. R. Ker, *Catalogue of Manuscripts Containing Anglo-Saxon* (Oxford: Clarendon Press, 1957), p. xxxii.

[19] For one example among many, see discussion and illustration of London, British Library, MS Cotton Vitellius A XV (fols 94–209), the manuscript containing the only surviving copy of Beowulf (among other texts); these hands have been discussed at length by many including Kevin Kiernan, *Beowulf and the Beowulf Manuscript*, 2nd edn (Ann Arbor, MI, 1996) and David N. Dumville, 'Beowulf Come Lately: Some Notes on the Palaeography of the Nowell Codex', *Archiv für das Studium der neueren Sprachen und Literaturen*, 225 (1998), 49–63.

[20] Contrast the discussions by Ker and Stokes in notes 15 and 17 above with the relatively straightforward sequence of styles presented by those cited in note 16, above.

[21] The most recent full-length study of book production at Leofric's Exeter is by Erika Corradini, 'Leofric of Exeter and his Lotharingian Connections: A Bishop's Books, c. 1050–72' (unpublished doctoral thesis, University of Leicester, 2008) <http://hdl.handle.net/2381/7639> [accessed 21 March 2010].

[22] Scragg, *Conspectus*, and David N. Dumville, 'English Libraries before 1066: Use and Abuse of the Manuscript Evidence', in *Anglo-Saxon Manuscripts: Basic Readings*, ed. by Mary P. Richards (New York: Routledge, 1994), pp. 169–219. I am not aware of any estimates to date of the number of surviving scribal hands writing Latin from the eleventh century in England.

insights can be gained nevertheless. In order to do this, an application of the DigiPal framework has been populated with approximately 1500 scribal hands in about 1600 manuscripts and charters and (at the time of writing) about 750 images of manuscripts and charters, marked up with annotations of about 55,000 individual letters for analysis. This allows researchers (and, indeed, anyone else) to explore the corpus in numerous ways.

An example of DigiPal's application to Vernacular minuscule is the question of scribal variation. Neil Ker wrote of Anglo-Saxon script that it showed 'no single characteristic type of writing and no obvious course of development' from about the 990s until the 1040s or so.[23] Although Ker did not clearly distinguish between writing in Old English and in Latin, scholars since have tended to infer that writing in the vernacular varied more than that used for Latin. Similarly, although Ker was here referring to variation across different hands, and indeed probably different scriptoria, elsewhere he and others have pointed to the variation within hands: that is, the degree to which scribes, again when writing Old English, would vary their script. This is a question which can be tested very easily using the DigiPal framework.

One hand that demonstrates very little internal variation is that of the adjurations on pages 303–9 of Cambridge, Corpus Christi, MS 146, a manuscript written at Winchester Cathedral, or perhaps Canterbury Cathedral. Despite being written in Old English, and despite being dated to early in the eleventh century, nevertheless the graphs are very consistent in their production and also show almost no allographic variation: in other words, the scribe wrote very consistently, using the same form of letter throughout and writing that same form very consistently.[24] Indeed, the only allographic variation is found in **s**, where the scribe used the low Insular form, the round majuscule form and the long form somewhat like the Caroline but with a descender. Even here there are patterns, however: the long form is found consistently before **d** or **t**, where the stem of the former or top-stroke of the latter could interfere with the hook of low **s**; the round form is most often in initial position; and the low form was used elsewhere (including sometimes initially). Slight variation is also evident in **e**, where both horned and round forms are used,

---

[23] Ker, *Books*, p. 34.
[24] The full results can be seen (and explored) at http://digipal.eu/digipal/hands/306/graphs/. Unless otherwise specified, for all the following references the *DigiPal* database was accessed on 14 April 2014.

but complex letters which typically caused difficulty for scribes, such as æ, **g** and **ð**, show remarkable consistency. Significantly, the same is evident when looking at the scribe's Caroline script, where a very similar level of consistency is evident. Indeed, when comparing graphs of letters which have the same form in both Caroline and Vernacular script, such as **m**, **n**, **b**, **l** and so on, the similarity across the two hands is striking. Ascenders show the typical wedge in a Vernacular context and are tapering in Anglo-Caroline, but other than this the letters are utterly indistinguishable.

In stark contrast to this consistency is a manuscript such as London, British Library, MS Cotton Tiberius A XIII (fols 1–118). This is a cartulary compiled by the community of Worcester Cathedral during the first quarter of the eleventh century. It was written by at least five scribes, with others adding notes and other texts at around the same time. The level of allographic variation within hands is again relatively small. However, the variation in execution of graphs is much larger than that of Cambridge, Corpus, MS 146, and the variation between scribes in the same manuscript is also very large indeed. This can be seen most evidently by comparing images of graphs of all letters comprised of minims in the manuscript,[25] and perhaps even more evident when comparing ascenders.[26]

The results so far are undoubtedly superficial, coming as they do from only one manuscript each. However, similar tendencies can be observed more generally from the *scriptoria* in question. Only eighteen scribal hands writing Old English can be attributed to Winchester Cathedral,[27] and there is undoubted variation between them, but nevertheless similarities can be observed. For example, the letter **g** typically has an open tail and something of a forward lean in the first half of the century, after

---

[25] For this, see DigiPal > Search: 'G. 366', Graph Component='minim': <http://digipal.eu/digipal/search/?terms=%22G.+366%22&component=minim&s=1&basic_search_type=graphs&result_type=graphs&view=list> (<http://goo.gl/oUuXWg>)

[26] DigiPal > Search: 'G. 366', Graph Component='ascender': <http://digipal.eu/digipal/search/?terms=%22G.+366%22&ordering=&years=&result_type=graphs&view=list&pgs=&from_link=true&basic_search_type=graphs&script=&character=&allograph=&component=ascender&feature=&s=1> (<http://goo.gl/tdQYSS>).

[27] Scragg, *Conspectus*, lists seven as certainly from Winchester Old Minster, namely numbers 182, 586, 662, 663, 735, 1006 and 1042. For the list of eighteen, see *DigiPal* > Search: Hand Place = 'WiOM': <http://www.digipal.eu/digipal/search/? result_type=hands&hand_place=WiOM> (<http://goo.gl/5YtKTi>).

which it is much more upright and rounded.[28] A pointed top is often found in a early in the century, and a rounded form from the mid-century onwards.[29] Perhaps more significant is the ascenders, which have a long, thin form with prominent wedge early in the century, and from the mid-eleventh century are shorter and thicker.[30] Similar tendencies are also evident in hands attributed to the New Minster at Winchester, and to Winchester generally.[31] Very different, however, are the hands attributed to Worcester. The rounded form of a which was evident at Winchester is typical of Anglo-Saxon script of the middle and second half of the eleventh century; indeed, not for nothing is this sometimes called Anglo-Saxon Round minuscule. However, this form seems to be less prevalent in hands attributed to Worcester, even for those dated to the second half of the eleventh century.[32] Round forms are found, for example in Hand 2 of London, British Library, MS Cotton Otho C I, vol. ii, a copy of Werferth's translation of Gregory's Dialogues dated to the mid-eleventh century and tentatively attributed to Worcester,[33] or the main hand of Cambridge, Corpus Christi College, MS 557, a binding-fragment again of the mid-eleventh century and again tentatively attributed to Worcester.[34] Perhaps clearer cases are Oxford, Bodleian Library, MS Junius 121, MS Hatton 113 and MS Hatton 114, all of which have been attributed to Worcester during Wulfstan's episcopate (1064–83) and clearly show the rounded forms.[35] However, other late hands still show a vertical back with pointed top which shows much greater continuity throughout the

[28] DigiPal > Search: Hand Place = 'WiOM', Graph Character: 'g'. <http://digipal. eu/digipal/search/?terms=WiOM& result_type=graphs&view=list &basic_search_ type=graphs&character=g> (<http://goo.gl/U3ng7j>).

[29] DigiPal > Search: Hand Place = 'WiOM', Graph Character: 'a'. <http:// digipal.eu/digipal/search/?terms=WiOM&result_type=graphs&view=list &character=a> (<http://goo.gl/KoWrNK>).

[30] DigiPal > Search: Hand Place = 'WiOM', Graph Component: 'ascender'. <http:// digipal.eu/digipal/search/?terms=WiOM&result_type=graphs&view=list&basic_ search_type=graphs&character=a> (<http://goo.gl/7HxspT>).

[31] DigiPal > Search: Hand Place = 'WiNM', Graph Component: 'ascender' (etc.).

[32] DigiPal > Search: Hand Place= 'Worcester', Graph Character: 'a': <http://www.digipal.eu/digipal/search/?result_type=graphs&hand_ place=Worcester&character=a> (<http://goo.gl/uA6w54>).

[33] DigiPal > Search: 'Hand 2 (62–139v5): <http://digipal.eu/digipal/hands/674/ graphs>.

[34] DigiPal > Search: 'Corpus 557': <http://digipal.eu/digipal/hands/438/graphs>.

[35] At the time of writing these are not yet in the *DigiPal* database: see, however, the detailed descriptions in EM 1060 to 1220.

century than is evident at Worcester, a point which seems to support the suggestion that scribes at the latter institution were not keeping up with developments elsewhere.[36] For example, Coleman is a scribe who can be securely attributed to Worcester at the very end of the eleventh century; although his writing is primarily marginal comments and glosses, nevertheless his **a** shows an upright back and pointed top. The same also goes for Hand 3 in 'Hemming's Cartulary' (MS Cotton Tiberius A XIII, fols 119–200), and the main hand in the 'Nero Middleton Cartulary' (London, British Library, MS Additional 46204), although not for the hand of the 'Hemming' scribe himself.[37] Indeed, at the time of writing, forty hands attributed to Worcester have been catalogued, of which all but eight show point-topped **a**. This percentage stands in sharp contrast to that of Winchester, discussed above, particularly considering that all but two of these eight have been dated to the first half or middle of the eleventh century.[38] Perhaps even greater variation is evident in ascenders attributed to Worcester scribes, with very little obvious correlation between length and date at least until the heavily Norman-influenced script which appears at the very end of the century, apart perhaps from a possible tendency to sometimes write Anglo-Caroline with shorter ascenders than those of the Vernacular.[39]

The discussion presented here is necessarily brief and inconclusive. A small sample of scribal hands is insufficient for drawing general conclusions about practices across the country, particularly given the impossibility of knowing what proportion of manuscripts survive, and the degree to which this represents what was originally produced. However, we argue that DigiPal's approach constitutes an advance compared with what came earlier. First, the framework as applied here presents all known surviving writing in English datable to the eleventh century. This is very different

---

[36] For this lack of 'keeping up developments', see Stokes, *English Vernacular Minuscule*, 203–24.

[37] <http://digipal.eu/digipal/hands/1276/graphs>; <http://digipal.eu/digipal/hands/2/graphs>; <http://digipal.eu/digipal/hands/160/> (and see further DigiPal > Scribes Name: 'Hemming' http://digipal.eu/digipal/scribes/3/).

[38] For the full list, see DigiPal > Search: Hand Place='WiOM', Hand Allograph='a, Insular': <http://www.digipal.eu/digipal/search/?result_type=graphs&hand_place =Worcester&character=a&allograph=Insular> (<http://goo.gl/enJJ5h>).

[39] For all ascenders, see <http://digipal.eu/digipal/search/?place=Worcester&result_ type=graphs&pgs=100&basic_search_type=graphs&component=ascender> (<http://goo.gl/eR15XB>). For 'Norman-influenced' hands, see, for example, Hand 1 of MS Cotton Tiberius A XIII (fols 119–200): <http://digipal.eu/digipal/hands/1275/graphs>.

from the normal tendency to study a small group of manuscripts or scribes, perhaps from a single *scriptorium* or representing a particular genre of text. The examination of small groups of manuscripts or of particular scribes is still valuable – such focused studies are necessary and produce important results – but it is also born to some extent of necessity, due to the diffi-culties of accessing material scattered across tens of repositories in poten-tially two or three continents (if not more).[40] By addressing the whole corpus of over one thousand scribal hands, with around seven hundred of these represented in digital images, regardless of genre and drawing from multiple repositories, a very different perspective can be gained.[41]

DigiPal to ScandiPal (by Matilda Watson)

While the initial case study for the DigiPal framework was English Vernac-ular minuscule of the eleventh century, the tools that the framework offers for computer-assisted palaeography were designed to be productive for other corpora. This flexibility meant that I was able to apply the frame-work to my own research area, the group of manuscript fragments which survive in Scandinavian archives and which date to approximately before the year 1100; the resulting database and website is called ScandiPal.[42]

As noted above, one of the strengths of the DigiPal framework is that the researcher can decide what is annotated and described, recognising that different corpora have their own specific requirements and research questions. My rationale with ScandiPal is to study the different scribal hands that appear in the fragments and to investigate where the scribes

---

[40] For locations of manuscripts and charters containing Old English from *c.* 990–*c.* 1035, see Stokes, *English Vernacular Minuscule*, pp. 30–4.

[41] For further discussion of this, including some further conclusions that can be gained by such an approach, see especially Stokes, *English Vernacular Minuscule*.

[42] The ScandiPal database is not currently publicly available because of the need to obtain image permissions and pay for reproduction rights. However, it may be possible to make all or parts of the database more widely accessible in the future. The images used in this article are of the manuscript fragment, Oslo, NRA, MS Lat. Fragmenter 202, 1–2. The fragment is owned by The National Archives of Norway (NRA) in Oslo. The images of the fragment used in this article were taken by and are reproduced with the permission of Dr Åslaug Ommundsen (University of Bergen). Note that in order to gain as much detail as possible in the images reproduced of the fragment reproduced in this article, it has not always been possible to reproduce the ScandiPal annotations, although these have been used where possible.

may have come from and the circumstances of production for each manuscript. The aim of ScandiPal is to illuminate the beginnings of manuscript production and scribal culture in Scandinavia, and particularly the role of the English Church, in the first centuries of Christianisation. Because of the fragmentary and disconnected nature of my corpus, it was desirable to gain as much detail as possible about each item and each hand. In order to do so, I annotated what I judged as a representative number of instances of every letter-form and character, including those found in interlinear additions and corrections. The nature of the corpus also necessitated including a wider variety of forms than those within DigiPal's remit (primarily minuscule letter-forms, punctuation and abbreviation marks), and so I have annotated initials, rubrics and erasures.

The fragments in ScandiPal's database date from the tenth to the eleventh century and are the remnants of manuscripts produced for use by the Church. The fragments contain liturgical texts in Latin. Many of the fragments come from outside of Scandinavia, particularly from countries such as England, France and Germany.[43] ScandiPal's focus is on material argued to be English or which may have been influenced by English manuscript culture but produced in Scandinavia.[44] The latter group provides evidence for the presence of local *scriptoria* in Scandinavia in the eleventh century. Time and practical considerations mean that ScandiPal is currently limited to fragments extant in Norway and Sweden, primarily in the national archives of both countries, although there are other relevant collections elsewhere.[45]

---

[43] I am indebted to Michael Gullick's lists of the fragments in Norwegian and Swedish archives: Michael Gullick, 'Preliminary Observations on Romanesque Manuscript Fragments of English, Norman and Swedish Origin in the Riksarkivet (Stockholm)', in *Medieval Book Fragments in Sweden. An International Seminar in Stockholm, 13–16 November 2003*, ed. by Jan Brunius (Stockholm: Kungl. Vitterhets Historie och Antikvitets Akademien, 2005), pp. 31–82; Michael Gullick, 'A Preliminary List of Manuscripts, Manuscript Fragments and Documents of English Origin or the Work of English Scribes in Norway Datable to before 1225', in *Latin Manuscripts of Medieval Norway: Studies in Memory of Lilli Gjerløw*, ed. by Espen Karlsen (Oslo: Novus Press, 2013), pp. 123–98.

[44] For discussion of how to identify the origin of a fragment, see Michael Gullick, 'A Preliminary Account of the English Element in Book Acquisition and Production in Norway before 1225', in *Latin Manuscripts*, ed. Karlsen, pp. 103–22; Jan Brunius, *From Manuscripts to Wrappers: Medieval Book Fragments in the Swedish National Archives*, Skrifter utgivna av Riksarkivet 35 (Stockholm: Riksarkivet, 2013), pp. 57–64.

[45] As well as smaller collections in Norway and Sweden, which have not been comprehensively included in ScandiPal, there are also extensive national collections

The majority of the medieval manuscripts of Norway and Sweden became fragments during the sixteenth and seventeenth centuries. The ruling administrations in Sweden and Norway (the latter was at that time ruled from Denmark) ordered parchment manuscripts to be collected by officials for re-use as binding materials for new tax account books which were being drawn up on paper.[46] Leaves of parchment were either wrapped around the tax books as covers or cut into small pieces to strengthen the sewn bindings.[47] As a result, the fragments in ScandiPal's corpus vary in size from scraps of only a few centimetres to complete bifolia.[48] There are about five to six thousand manuscript fragments in Norwegian archives and around 23,000 in Sweden. The number of fragments argued to be English or which show English influence is subject to much debate; for my research with ScandiPal, I have established a corpus of one hundred fragments from Norwegian archives and thirty-five from Sweden.[49] In

in Denmark, Finland and Iceland, introduced in *The Beginnings of Nordic Scribal Culture, ca 1050–1300: Report from a Workshop on Parchment Fragments, Bergen 28–30 October 2005,* ed. by Åslaug Ommundsen (Bergen: Centre for Medieval Studies, University of Bergen, 2006), pp. 1–61 (pp. 15–36) <https://bora.uib.no/bitstream/handle/1956/2403/Ommundsen_Report_2006.pdf> (<http://goo.gl/qV3Lm3>) [accessed 17 November 2014].

[46] Åslaug Ommundsen, 'From Books to Bindings – and Back: Medieval Manuscript Fragments in Norway', *Gazette du livre médiéval,* 52 (2008), pp. 34–44. <http://www.palaeographia.org/glm/glm.htm?art=ommundsen> (<http://goo.gl/88vkyI>); Gunnar Pettersen, 'Katalogisering av latinske membranfragmenter som forskningsprosjekt: Del 1', in *Arkivverkets forskningsseminar gardermoen 2003,* Rapporter og retningslinjer 16 (Oslo: Riksarkivaren, 2003), pp. 43–58; Brunius, *From Manuscripts to Wrappers,* pp. 13–33.

[47] I use parchment as a general term to mean calfskin, goatskin or sheepskin, as defined in the *Oxford English Dictionary* as 'a piece of animal skin, esp. from a sheep or goat, dressed and prepared as a surface for writing'. From 'parchment, n.', in *Oxford English Dictionary Online,* Oxford University Press <http://www.oed.com/view/Entry/137746?redirectedFrom=parchment> (<http://goo.gl/qQGA9u>) [accessed 18 November 2014]. Bernhard Bischoff also uses parchment as an umbrella term for different animal skins in his introduction to his book: Bernhard Bischoff, *Latin Palaeography: Antiquity and the Middle Ages,* trans. by Daíbhí Ó Cróinín and David Ganz (Cambridge: Cambridge University Press, 1990), pp. 9–11.

[48] The Norwegian fragments tend to be smaller than those from Sweden because most of the earliest tax account books in Norway (i.e. those from the sixteenth century) were destroyed after they were archived. This is discussed in more detail by Åslaug Ommundsen in 'From Books to Bindings' (paragraph 3).

[49] The numbers cited here are not exhaustive and are based on my own assessment of which fragments are English or English-influenced. Note also that I have counted individual fragments separately, rather than counting fragments from a

many cases, the fragments come from the same volume and so the number of manuscripts represented is far fewer than the numbers imply.

One of ScandiPal's main objectives is to see whether the database can shed light on the early products of Norwegian or Swedish *scriptoria*. There is extensive debate on how to identify the output of early local *scriptoria* which I summarise briefly here:[50] for example, local spellings, handwriting which might suggest someone learning a script, awkwardness in the script suggesting the difficult conditions of working in a nascent *scriptorium*,[51] contents of the liturgy,[52] presence of local saints and notation,[53] among others. My study focuses on script and consequently I will discuss a fragment that exemplifies some of the features that may point toward a local *scriptorium*. The aim of this case study is to show how ScandiPal has underlined and extended the observations of others to shed light on the issue of identifying early Scandinavian *scriptoria*.

The manuscript now known as Missal 3 (Mi 3) survives in two complete leaves: Oslo, NRA, MS Lat. Fragmenter 202, 1 and 2. As with the Old English material discussed above, a question that has often arisen in relation to Mi 3 is the degree of idiosyncrasy or variation in the scribal hands in this fragment. Lilli Gjerløw first pointed out the peculiarities of the forms of **a**, **e** and **g** in the context of a more extensive discussion on the content and (often incorrect) spelling of Mi 3 and concluded that 'skriften er høyst eiendommelig. Man skulle tro boken var skrevet i Norge

---

single identified book together as one, which explains some of the differences between the numbers here and those of the articles cited in Gullick, 'A Preliminary List of Manuscripts', pp. 123–98.

[50] For discussion, see Gullick, 'A Preliminary Account', pp. 103–22; Espen Karlsen, 'Katalogisering av latinske membranfragmenter som forskningsprosjekt: Del 2', in *Arkivverkets forskningsseminar gardermoen 2003*, Rapporter og retningslinjer 16 (Oslo: Riksarkivaren, 2003), pp. 58–88; Jan Brunius, *From Manuscripts to Wrappers*, pp. 73–80; Åslaug Ommundsen, 'The First Norwegian Scribes and their Teachers', in *Teaching Writing, Learning to Write, Proceedings of the XVIth Colloquium of the Comité International de Paléographie Latine*, ed. by P. R. Robinson, Kings College London Medieval Studies, 22 (King's College London: Centre for Late Antique and Medieval Studies, 2010), pp. 131–45.

[51] Erik Niblaeus, 'German Influence on Religious Practice in Scandinavia, c. 1050–1150' (unpublished doctoral thesis, King's College London, 2010), pp. 71–5.

[52] See discussions by Lilli Gjerløw, such as, 'Missaler brukt i Bjørgvin bispedømme fra misjontiden til Nidarosordinariet', in *Bjørgvin bispestol: Byen og bispedømmet*, ed. by P. Jukvam (Bergen: Universitetsforlaget, 1970), pp. 73–127.

[53] John Toy, *English Saints in the Medieval Liturgies of Scandinavian Churches*, Henry Bradshaw Society Subsidia, 6 (Woodbridge: Boydell Press, 2009).

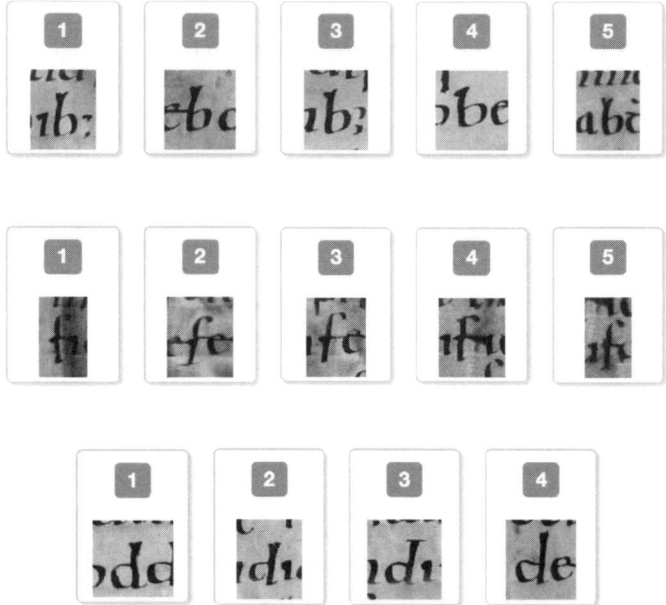

Figures 6–8: Variation in graphs of the allograph 'b, Caroline', 'f, Caroline' and 'd, Caroline' for Mi 3 in ScandiPal.

engang i 1100–tallet.'[54] Espen Karlsen highlighted some of the unusual features of the script, such as the unusually small **a** and narrow breaks between words, concluding the fragment is from 'et lokalt *scriptorium* etter engelsk model'.[55] Michael Gullick has also commented on the 'imitative' nature of the script and suggested the origin is uncertain and probably not English.[56] Likewise, K. D. Hartzell described the writing as 'malformed, waywardly written' and characterised by the forms of **a**, **f**, **s** and the use

---

[54] 'The script is very quaint. One should believe that the book was written in Norway at some point in the eleventh century.' Lilli Gjerløw, 'Missaler brukt i Oslo bispedømme fra misjontiden til Nidarosordinariet', in *Oslo bispedømme 900 år: Historiske studier*, ed. by Fridtjov Birkeli, Arne Odd Johansen and Einar Molland (Oslo: Universitetsforlaget, 1974), pp. 131–58 (p. 79). Unless otherwise specified, all translations are my own.

[55] 'A local scriptorium following an English [script] model.' Espen Karlsen, 'Katalogisering av latinske', p. 66.

[56] In both, Gullick, 'A Preliminary List', p. 149 and an unpublished draft-list of the fragments in the National Archives in Oslo (2008), kindly made available to me by Gullick in personal communication.

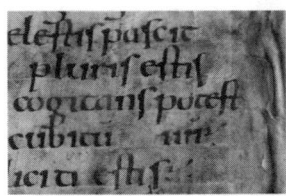
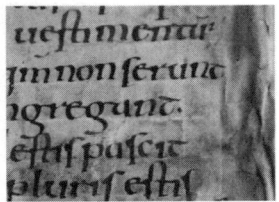

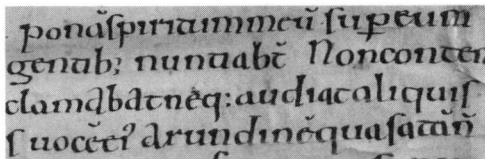
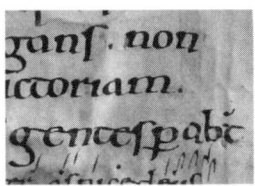

Figures 9a–d: Variation in spacing and line-ends in the main hand of Mi 3.

of **&** and **st** ligatures.[57] Hartzell also notes the poor word division and inaccurate spelling leading to the tentative conclusion that it was 'written in England (?)'.[58] All of these scholars make important points about the hand of the main text scribe of Mi 3, yet their descriptions, while valid, do not necessarily meet Derolez's criteria of being 'clear and convincing'.[59]

Annotating examples of each letter in ScandiPal gives an overview of the extent of inconsistency between many characters, an aspect not normally highlighted by palaeographers, and provides a more comprehensive perspective on Mi 3 and the question of origin. Examples of some of the inconsistencies between characters are illustrated in Fig. 6 through Fig. 8, where it is immediately apparent that the scribe is erratic in his treatment of, for instance, the bowl of **d,** the wedges on the ascenders of **b** and **d**, and the foot serifs on **f**.

In addition to this variation in the execution of allographs, it is also clear that the scribe did not plan his writing well. The lengths of lines vary greatly (Figs 9a–c); letters sometimes become increasingly cramped as the scribe reaches the end of the line (especially in Fig. 9d); the base line is inconsistent (for instance, the fluctuation in the base-line of Fig. 9c); and the size of the letters varies considerably, both between occurrences of the

[57] K. D. Hartzell, *Catalogue of Manuscripts Written or Owned in England up to 1200 Containing Music* (Woodbridge: Boydell in association with the Plainsong and Medieval Music Society, 2006), no. 230.

[58] Hartzell, no. 230.

[59] Derolez, p. 7.

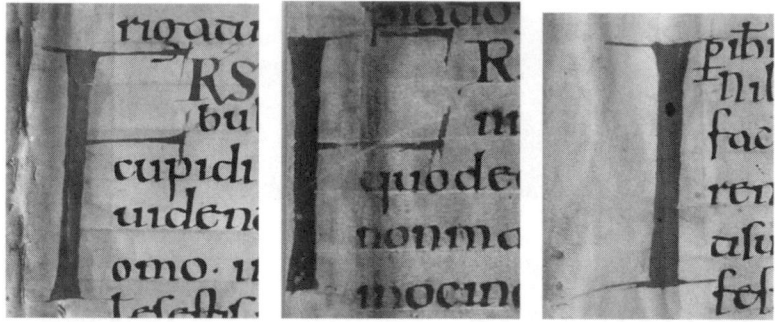

Figures 10a–c: Variation and lack of planning in execution of initials in Mi 3.

Figure 11: Corrections of scribal dittography in Mi 3.

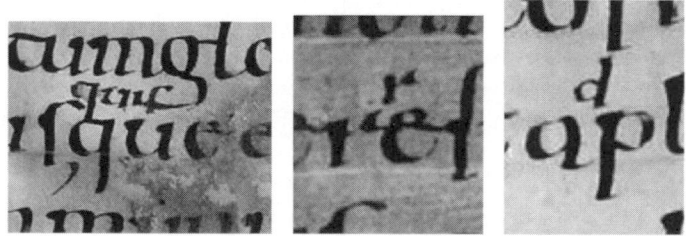

Figures 12a–c: Insertions by the main scribe (?) in Mi 3.

same letter and also between adjacent letters (especially letter **a** in Fig. 9d); spacing between words is also erratic (Fig. 9d), indicating that the scribe either did not understand the text or was copying from an exemplar written in *scriptio continua*.

The scribe of the main text did not plan well for spaces for the initials (for example, in the stroke of the bottom hair-line at the base of **f** in

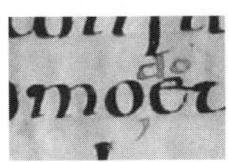  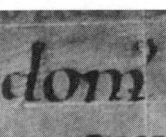

Figures 13a–c: Insertions by other scribes in Mi 3.

Fig. 10b). The initials themselves are also rather carelessly executed, for example, the hairline at the base of the minim of the majuscule **I** or the hairlines at the ends of the hook and tongue strokes of the majuscule **F** (Fig. 10a); the two initial **F**'s are different sizes (that of Fig. 10a occupies six of the ruled lines, while that of Fig. 10b is drawn within five).

In addition to the spelling mistakes highlighted by Gjerløw and Hartzell, there are also a number of examples of dittography by the main text scribe, and then he or another scribe crossed out the repetitions with different coloured ink (see Fig. 11).

The main scribe also inserted a number of interlinear corrections, for example on fol. 2r (Fig. 12a); that the insertions are by the same scribe is evident in the similar execution of **q** (compare with main hand in Fig. 12b): the line curves down slightly at the join between the bowl and the top of the ascender forming a slight point to the top of the ascender, while the **u** of the insertion (Fig. 12a) and in the main text below (Fig. 12b) has the same downward slope to the wedge on the first minim, followed by a less triangulated and thinner wedge on the second minim; furthermore the insertion has the same traits of a fluctuating base-line and poor lineation, as well as the same colour ink (as shown in Fig. 12).

There are also a number of insertions by different scribes. For example, the **d** of the insertion in Fig. 13a has a hairline at the top of the ascender, which protrudes significantly to the right, whereas the scribe of the main text drew a wedged ascender on **d** and never adds a hairline. The insertion in Fig. 13a is possibly the same hand as that of Fig. 13b. The hand of the insertion in Fig. 13b uses an Insular **a** and it should be noted that the abbreviation in *habem[us]* is executed quite differently from the same abbreviation by the main text scribe in *dom[us]* (f. 1r), as shown in Fig. 13c, and differences in the execution of **m** and *punctus elevatus* also point to a different hand from the main text scribe. The scribe of the insertions shown in Fig. 13a (and possibly Fig. 13b) may have been the one who corrected the main text scribe by crossing through mistaken repetitions because the ink seems to be the same colour, although this is by no means conclusive.

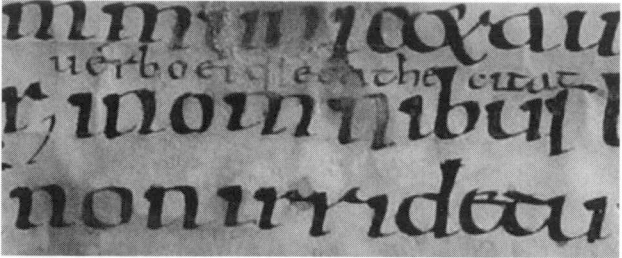

Figure 14: Insertions by a further scribe (?) in Mi 3.

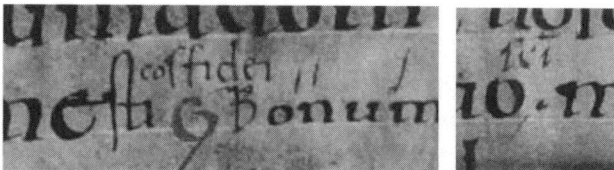

Figures 15a–b: Additional insertions in Mi 3.

The most extensive addition may be by yet another scribe (Fig. 14). The insertion is too short to attain any level of certainty, and there are some similarities with the main text hand: the form of the **r** with the forked, small spit hook, which joins the minim approximately three quarters of the way up from the baseline; the top stroke of the **t** slants down in *citat*; and the scribe has also used Insular **a**. The hand is either the same as that of the main text or very similar; if a different hand, then the scribe may have been working in the same *scriptorium* as the main text scribe. It should be noted that the insertion in Fig. 14 is in different ink from the main text and other insertions.

There are a number of additional insertions: that shown in Fig. 15a may be by the same scribe as the main text, while that of Fig. 15b looks like a later hand.

Although there is not space to do so in detail here, it is worth considering further who the scribes were who added the interlinear insertions because this may have implications for the circumstances of early manuscript production in Norway. The scribe of Fig. 13b (and possibly Fig. 13a) and the scribe of Fig. 14 (if different from the main text scribe) both use Insular **a** and their script may be approximately dated to the eleventh century, leading to the tentative suggestion that there may be the traces of several scribes working together in an early *scriptorium*. Even if the scribes were not working together or in the same place, the presence of several hands in Mi 3 indicates a number of relatively proficient scribes in Norway whose hands arguably exhibit the faint influence of English script models, at an early date. This cautious suggestion depends on the interpretation of the main text scribe's hand, as well as the other aspects of Mi 3 mentioned above, such as content and spelling. Unfortunately, there is not space to review these arguments in more detail here.

Annotating Mi 3 has provided a more comprehensive perspective on Mi 3, encompassing some of the hands that add to and correct the main text. The 'quaint' or 'wayward' aspect of the main text scribe's hand, noted by other scholars, has also been explored and extended through annotations of Mi 3 in ScandiPal to highlight the inconsistency and hesitancy in the scribe's execution of each letter-form, the fluctuation of the base-line, the varying line lengths and lack of planning in the scribe's execution, the mistakes and insertions, and the inexpertly drawn initials. When taken in conjunction with the spelling errors and Gjerløw's assertion that the content preserves a liturgical memory 'om den benediktinske misjonen i Norden',[60] ScandiPal has helped to underline the attribution of Mi 3 to an early Norwegian *scriptorium*. Dating the fragment is problematic and would require more space than is available, but the script points to the mid eleventh century. It will have to suffice to argue here that the foot serifs on the minims of many letters, the wedges, the combination of Insular and Caroline **a**, as well as the rotundity and spacing of the characters, might suggest that the script, or its model, belongs to *c*. 1050.

Now that the characters, scribal hands and features of the layout of Mi 3 have been annotated, these can be searched for and compared with other scribal hands and fragments in the ScandiPal database. These can be used to establish profiles for the scribes on the fragments and to explore where and when these scribes may have been active and to contribute to the scholarly debate over native *scriptoria* in Norway and Sweden before 1100.[61] ScandiPal provides a framework for discussing and studying the fragments in detail and a database enabling one to search for connections between scribal hands and fragments, and these links can then be extended and explored through wider investigation and discussion.

---

[60] 'Of the Benedictine mission in Scandinavia.' Gjerløw, 'Missaler brukt', p. 81.
[61] This work is currently underway as the topic of my PhD thesis. The list of fragments that I suggest may have been produced in *scriptoria* in Norway or Sweden in approximately the eleventh century is a work in progress.

SephardiPal (by Débora Marques de Matos)

The research discussed so far in this paper focuses on the study of texts written in Western scripts. From the outset, however, the DigiPal framework was designed with the intention that it be suitable for use with a wide range of languages and alphabets and also the decorative features of manuscripts (as I shall show below). The flexibility to move beyond the Latin-based alphabet has been well tested with my project which applies the DigiPal framework to a group of medieval Hebrew manuscripts copied and decorated in the Iberian Peninsula and other related regions (a geo-cultural area known in medieval Hebrew as 'Sepharad'). The resultant database and website, SephardiPal, has at its centre questions about the salient characteristics of scribes and artists who worked on Sephardic manuscripts produced during the second half of the fifteenth century.[62] The concept of 'salient characteristics' has been used successfully to ascertain authorship in works of art.[63] The same conceptual framework can be applied to manuscript studies, with handwriting and patterns of decoration being considered as salient characteristics. This study is performed from an 'integral' standpoint, that is, by providing a context for the salient characteristics which takes into account the historical and material aspects of the manuscripts. My final intention with SephardiPal is to demonstrate the significance of patterns of migration of Sephardic scribes and artists in the late fifteenth century, which in turn can help us establish the existence of commercial and family networks within the Sephardic world prior to the sixteenth and seventeenth centuries.

Throughout the Middle Ages Hebrew script was written in three modes: Square, Semi-cursive and Cursive;[64] while the latter two were more 'personal' modes of writing, Square script was employed in religious texts and it was (and still is) regulated by rabbinic instructions covering many aspects such as ductus, modulus, angle of writing, and contrast or

[62] The development of SephardiPal is part of PhD research undertaken at the Departments of Digital Humanities and Theology and Religious Studies at King's College London.
[63] Peter Bajcsy and Maryam Moslemi, 'Discovering Salient Characteristics of Authors of Art Works', IS&T/SPIE Electronic Imaging 7 (2010), 7531–10.
[64] It broadly corresponds to the threefold classification of Latin Gothic script: formata, media and currens, as named by Julian Brown and summarised by Michelle Brown, A Guide to Western Historical Scripts from Antiquity to 1600 (Toronto: University of Toronto Press, 1990).

the weight of letters.[65] Hebrew palaeographers must deal with an issue that has not arisen in the discussion so far, namely the highly stereotyped nature of script, particularly visible in Square script. This was due to the fact that professional scribes produced script that was highly standardised, being careful to avoid individualistic calligraphic flourish in a process of imitation of a script stereotype ideal, and with the wish to preserve geo-cultural traditions.[66] Thus, the high level of conformism to the script may be misleading, suggesting a smaller number of hands than was in fact involved.[67]

Despite this, there is scope for individual expression on the part of scribes, but if we are to find it we have to look beyond the level of script. As Malachi Beit-Arié points out, '[w]hile a scribe uses a common shape of letter, he selects from a large variety of the para-scriptural elements practised in his geo-cultural area'.[68] Beit-Arié identifies four main types of these para-scriptural elements: catchword decoration and its placement; devices for producing even left margins (either by dilating or compressing the final characters of the line); auxiliary signs (headings, pericope signs and so on); and several variants of the tetragrammaton (the writing of the name of God). Some practices are deliberate choices on the part of scribes, but they can also be subconscious. To this we should add that codico-logical practices and decorative elements can equally provide important evidence to establish the origin of manuscripts and contribute to ascertaining authorship.

Most proposed quantitative methods for the study of Hebrew script are based on the measurement of characters, outline, angles and space between letters; however, the very experts who have suggested these approaches have concluded that the difficulties presented by these methods are insuperable and do not seem to contribute significantly to the identification of hands.[69] A major impact of the stereotyped nature of Square script for the

[65] See, for example, Israel Meir and Yona Vogel, *Mishnas Sofrim: A Translation of the Mishna Berura Dealing with the Laws of Writing the Ashuris Script* (Monsey, NY: Jewish Learning Exchange / Tanenbaum College, 1984).

[66] Late medieval Hebrew script can be divided into five distinctive geo-cultural groups: Sepharad, Ashkenaz, Italy, Byzantium and Yemen.

[67] Malachi Beit-Arié, 'Stereotype and Individuality in the Handwriting of Medieval Scribes', in his *The Makings of the Medieval Hebrew Book: Studies in Palaeography and Codicology* (Jerusalem: Magnes Press, 1993), pp. 77–92.

[68] Beit-Arié, 'Stereotype and Individuality', p. 79.

[69] Colette Sirat and M. Dukan, *Écriture et civilisations* (Paris: Centre national de la recherche scientifique, 1976); Ada Yardeni, *The Book of Hebrew Script* (Jerusalem: Carta, 1997).

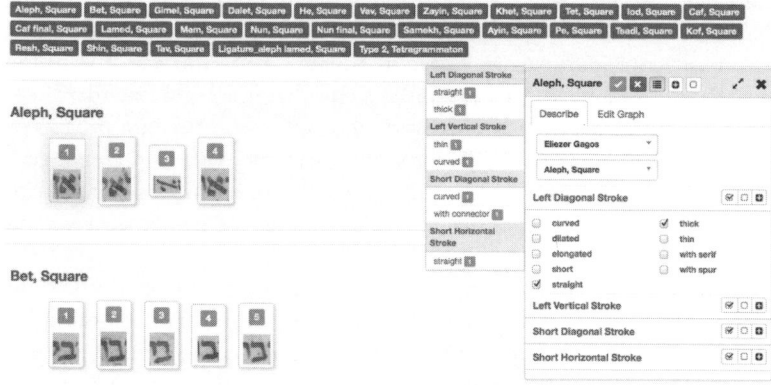

Figure 16: Describing forms of *aleph* in SephardiPal.

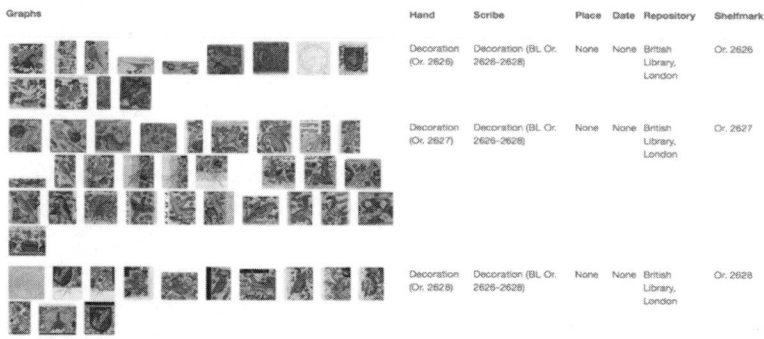

Figure 17: Searching for decorative elements in SephardiPal.

field of Hebrew palaeography is that most traditional studies end with the determination of the geo-cultural area of production and, when possible, a date of copy, but do not extend to any attempt at scribal identification. This means in turn that there is no defined ontology nor a coherent terminology for the description of script and para-scriptural elements. With this in mind, it seemed essential to create a system of morphological descriptors for letter-forms, components and para-scriptural elements. Equally important was the facility to link the terminology to images and it was these two requirements which made the approach taken by the DigiPal framework especially suited to my research questions. Examples of annotating, searching and describing letter-forms and decoration in SephardiPal are shown in Figs 16–18.

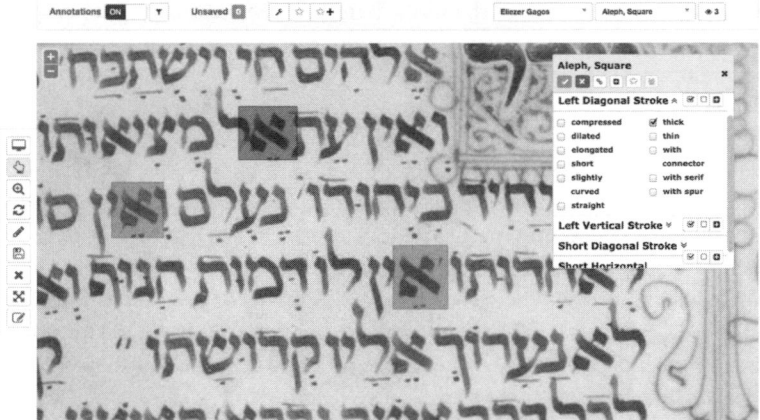

Figure 18: Annotations of graphs of *aleph* in SephardiPal. The image being annotated is Paris, Bibliothèque Nationale de France, MS hébr. 592, fol. 25v.

The first point to consider is that Hebrew uses an *abjad* writing system, meaning that only consonants are written out; vowels are marked using a system of dots and strokes and are added after the writing of the consonantal text. This vocalisation (and also cantillation) was often carried out by a scribe other than the copyist of the main text. For these reasons, and given the focus in my research on Square script, vowels are not considered in SephardiPal. Similarly to DigiPal and ScandiPal, my methodology focuses on complete letter-forms and letter strokes. Applying the framework in this way reveals that, contrary to expectation and despite the strict rules surrounding the copying of sacred texts, there are some strokes that do seem to be distinctive.

Another means of identification of authorship is through the analysis of manuscript decoration. Programmes of decoration have been an essential element to determine origin. For instance, despite the absence of colophons, the use of violet filigree with details in gold in some late fifteenth century manuscripts (for instance, London, British Library, MS Additional 27167 and MS Additional 15283) is consistent with other decorative programmes used in Portuguese manuscripts and therefore these manuscripts have been associated with Portugal. One of the innovative and distinctive aspects of SephardiPal is the annotation of samples of decoration. The way they are described and organised follows the same model used for letter-forms and characters in both DigiPal and ScandiPal.

Just as different notions of the term 'letter' can be expressed along a spectrum from abstract ideal (the allograph) through individual expression (the idiograph) to physical manifestation (the graph),[70] so can decorative elements: the relationship character – allograph – idiograph (and graph) can be transferred to decoration, and similarly, components and features are shared by different decorative 'characters' and 'allographs'. For instance, a carpet-page, that is a full-page decoration resembling a carpet (which is common in Sephardic manuscripts), can be divided into components such as 'frame', 'panel', 'rosette' and so on. In order to accomplish this, I created terminology to describe the main elements of decoration found in full-page decoration, *masora* and ways of marking passages in the text.[71] Some elements proved to be more complex and so were sub-divided into components and sub-components. The terminology is currently a work-in-progress, but it has allowed me to organise and curate a wide range of decorative elements in the SephardiPal database. On the basis of the corpus of images I have annotated, it is already possible to observe that common decorative structures (such as carpet pages or borders) are repeated using different elements, and that scribes adapted the visual aesthetic to meet regional tastes. We see this in Bibles, where the decorative structures, including initial word panels and borders, may be functionally similar, but are materialised in a range of artistic languages. For instance, in the second half of the fifteenth century, borders from Andalusia were created with delicate and intricate micrographic patterns, forming a myriad of knots and other ornaments, while those associated with Lisbon tend to be sumptuous, colourful and peppered with animals, hybrids and others fictitious elements.

In conclusion, as a framework and tool for the study of Hebrew manuscripts, SephardiPal has great potential. As with DigiPal, it brings new methods in Digital Humanities to the study of medieval handwriting and patterns of decoration from a contextualised point of view, allowing users to search, view, retrieve and curate data. Most of the existing databases for the study of Hebrew manuscripts have focused on the codicology of Hebrew manuscripts, providing detailed text descriptions with some

---

[70] For this terminology, see Davis, 'The Practice', pp. 254–55.

[71] Bibles and other religious texts usually included marginal notes known as masora. These are instructions for the vocalisation, accentuation, cantillation, verse counts, notation of single words, specific spellings, pronunciation and so on, along the margins of the manuscripts in minuscule script. They are written in the upper and lower margins (*masora magna*), in the inter-columnar spaces and outer margins (*masora parva*), and at the end of each book (*masora finalis*).

supporting images.[72] SephardiPal, in contrast, puts visual access to images and annotation at the forefront, combining this with detailed palaeographic and decorative information.[73] In the longer term, a database of script and decorative elements will enable comparison with other groups of manuscripts beyond my initial corpus of late fifteenth century Sephardic manuscripts. Finally, the development of SephardiPal will be essential to an understanding of how scribes and artists hitherto viewed as conservative can be seen to adapt to new markets. In turn, this will help us identify the origin of scribes and local artistic tendencies. As my research with SephardiPal suggests, immigrant scribes often continue to use distinctive elements throughout their professional writing lives;[74] on the other hand, decoration usually denotes adaptation to local tastes, although 'betraying' the technique and portfolio of the artists.

Conclusion

As we hope to have shown, the DigiPal framework allows scholars (and, indeed, anyone else) to explore palaeographical and decorative material and to communicate the results of that exploration along with the visual evidence to support their arguments. While the ability to test assertions and interrogate the evidence is a crucial step forward, it is worth reminding ourselves that the system is not truly objective. For example, the question of how to judge similarity or variation between different graphs is left very much up to those creating the annotations, as is the decision as to which, or how many, digital images to select for inclusion when compiling the respective databases. This seems like a desirable situation to us: although the framework would allow for the annotation of, for instance, every occurrence of the letter **a** in a corpus of over a thousand scribes, in practice such a profusion of detail is unlikely to be helpful to any palaeographer. Rather, it is the role of scholars to exercise judgement

---

[72] *SfarData: The Codicological Database of the Hebrew Palaeography Project* (Jerusalem: Israel Academy of Sciences and Humanities [n.d.]) <http://sfardata. nli.org.il/> [accessed 13 May 2014].

[73] There is already a thematic compilation of motifs that appear in Hebrew manuscripts, however it is not online and only available in some major libraries: see Bezalel Narkiss and Gabrielle Sed-Rajna, *Index of Jewish Art: Iconographical Index of Hebrew Illuminated Manuscripts* (Jerusalem: Israel Academy of Sciences and Humanities; Paris: Institut de recherche et d'histoire des textes, 1976).

[74] Beit-Arié, 'Stereotype and Individuality'.

in their area of expertise, a duty which is sometimes forgotten in a drive for the perceived benefits of an (impossible) objectivity.[75] Our goal with the DigiPal framework is allow for palaeographic argument to be communicated in a clear and unambiguous manner and, as far as possible, enable those outside the field to understand it and those within the field to verify it. It remains to be seen whether DigiPal's methodology will answer the challenge raised by Albert Derolez, namely 'how [...] to proceed in such a way that the description of a specimen of handwriting is as clear and convincing to its reader as it is to its author'.[76] In the meanwhile, if palaeographers are no longer seen as 'repositories of authoritative dogma' then the DigiPal project and its framework will have achieved one of its objectives, and our understanding of writing in Europe and beyond will be that much richer as a result.[77]

[75] Compare G. Thomas Tanselle's observations about textual criticism: 'The search for properly "scientific" method has been perhaps the dominant thread running through the history of textual criticism [...] Too often, however, rigor of method has been equated with the minimization of human judgment.' G. T. Tanselle, 'The Varieties of Scholarly Editing', in *Scholarly Editing: A Guide to Research*, ed. by D. C. Greetham (New York: The Modern Language Association of America, 1996), pp. 9–32 (pp. 18–19).

[76] Derolez, p. 7.

[77] In addition to the three projects discussed in this paper, a number of others that make use of the DigiPal framework are underway, including NumiPal (a project at the Bibliothèque nationale de France, studying the epigraphy of Merovingian coins); InsPal (examining Greek and Latin inscriptions from Thracia, based at King's College London); Models of Authority: Scottish Charters and the Emergence of Government 1100–1250 (Universities of Glasgow, Cambridge and King's College London); The Conqueror's Commissioners: Unlocking the Domesday Survey of South-Western England (with the University of Oxford and King's College London); and The Workshop of Matthew Paris at St Albans, AD 1230–1259 (King's College London).

Italian Giant Bibles: The Circulation and Use of the Book at the Time of the Ecclesiastical Reform in the Eleventh and Twelfth Centuries

NADIA TOGNI

Italian Giant Bibles

ITALIAN GIANT BIBLES – *Bibbie atlantiche* in Italian, *Bibles atlantiques* or *atlantes* in French, *Reisenbibeln* in German – constitute a distinctive group within the Latin Vulgate family, be it in terms of format, text or decoration. These large lectern Bibles contained both the Old and New Testaments in one manuscript that could be divided into two or more volumes.[1]

The Italian Giant Bibles were designed as a manifestation of the religious renewal and the new ecclesiastical unity promoted by the Roman Church in the eleventh and twelfth centuries.[2] This movement is commonly called the Gregorian Reform, from the name of Pope Gregory VII (1073–1085) who surrounded himself with a group of reformers within the papal court. He adopted measures to strengthen the moral integrity and independence of the clergy and theorised the principles of reform.

Roman reformers elaborated and produced various types of book, which were new both in terms of format and content, to restore the *auctoritas* of the Roman Church and guard against claims from the emperor and other ecclesiastical principalities. The monumental aspect and the textual

---

[1]   On Italian Giant Bibles, see *Le Bibbie atlantiche: il libro delle scritture tra monumentalità e rappresentazione*, ed. by Marilena Maniaci and Giulia Orofino (Milan: Centro Tibaldi, 2000) and *Les Bibles atlantiques: le manuscrit biblique à l'époque de la réforme de l'Église au XIe siècle*, ed. by Nadia Togni (Florence: Sismel, 2015).

[2]   Peter Brieger, 'Bible Illustration and Gregorian Reform', *Studies in Church History*, 2 (1965), 154–64; Ovidio Capitani, 'La riforma gregoriana', in *Le Bibbie atlantiche*, pp. 7–13; Guy Lobrichon, 'Riforma ecclesiastica e testo della bibbia', in *Le Bibbie atlantiche*, pp. 15–26 (French translation: 'La bible de la réforme ecclésiastique. Aspects textuels (XIe siècle)', in *La bible au Moyen Âge*, Les médiévistes français, 3 (Paris: Picard, 2003), pp. 94–108).

uniformity of the Giant Bibles became the emblem of ecclesiastical reform in the eleventh century.

Characteristics of Italian Giant Bibles

This type of biblical manuscript has monumental and very spectacular dimensions: it can be 600 millimetres high and 400 millimetres wide. Nevertheless, striking dimensions are not the only distinguishing features of Italian Giant Bibles. Their uniformity is due to several material and textual elements, namely:

- The division of the manuscript's material structure into blocks of quires that hold complete textual units, either a single biblical book (e.g. Job or Psalms) or a group of biblical books (e.g. Octateuch or Prophets);
- The use of a standardised Carolingian minuscule font;
- A two-column page layout;
- Each column of text being between 55 and 60 lines long;
- The use of large ornamental initials, placed at the beginning of each biblical book, to punctuate the text divisions of the Bible in an artistic way;
- Two monumental initials: F (*Frater*) at the beginning of Saint Jerome's Epistle, and I (*In*) at the beginning of Genesis, that take the whole page, to mark the beginning of the manuscript and of the whole biblical text;
- The Canon Tables are displayed on four pages, placed between the Old and the New Testaments;
- The introduction of biblical books by additional texts: prologues, prefaces, chapters and so on.

All these elements are manifest in the production of Giant Bibles from their very beginning in the middle of the eleventh century. They were systematically used in the making of most biblical manuscripts produced in the second half of the eleventh century and the beginning of the twelfth. The history of biblical manuscripts includes other examples of monumental manuscripts produced in the large and complex framework of a pastoral, cultural and ideological unification programme, such as the Carolingian Bibles of the ninth century. Nevertheless, Italian Giant Bibles were an exceptional and unprecedented editorial enterprise: they represent an intensive production of biblical manuscripts, whose production grew and reached a peak in just one century.

Much debate has surrounded the matter of localising the *scriptoria* in which these manuscripts were produced. Scholars have established that early Giant Bibles were made in various ateliers closely connected to the papal court. These *scriptoria* were very likely situated in the Umbrian-Roman region of Italy, in the south of Umbria and on the outskirts of Rome.[3] However, some recent studies speak clearly of an exclusively Roman production of early Giant Bibles.[4] Later, at the beginning of the twelfth century, when connections between Giant Bibles and the Gregorian Reform became weaker, manuscript production shifted to the region of Tuscany. This implied a certain remoteness from the original model, to the point where Tuscan Bibles form a blurred and scattered constellation whose material and textual characteristics are less uniform that those of the earliest Umbrian-Roman Bibles.[5]

The production of Umbrian-Roman and Tuscan Giant Bibles is characterised by the use of two different types of geometrical decorated initials, placed at the beginning of each biblical book: hollow shaft initials and full shaft initials.[6] In the hollow shaft initials, the body of the letter encloses rectangular compartments surrounded by a yellow band with a red fillet; each compartment is filled with foliated, floral or abstract elements and interlace that are more or less intricate; the extremities of the strokes may be decorated with interlaced knots and foliated clusters (Fig. 1). Full shaft initials have the body formed by a very bright ribbon of one colour

3   Paola Supino Martini, *Roma e l'area grafica romanesca (secoli X–XII)*, Biblioteca di scrittura e civiltà, 1 (Alessandria: Edizioni dell'Orso, 1987), pp. 31–33; Paola Supino Martini, 'La scrittura delle scritture (sec. XI–XII)', *Scrittura e Civiltà*, 12 (1988), 101–18 (pp. 106–08).

4   Lobrichon, 'Riforma ecclesiastica e testo della bibbia', pp. 18–19; Larry M. Ayres, 'Le Bibbie atlantiche: Dalla riforma alla diffusione in Europa', in *Le Bibbie atlantiche*, pp. 27–37 (pp. 33–34); Marilena Maniaci and Giulia Orofino, 'L'officina delle Bibbie atlantiche: Artigiani, scribi, miniatori: Problemi ancora aperti', in *Come nasce un manoscritto miniato*, ed. by Francesca Flores d'Arcais and Fabrizio Crivello (Modena: Panini, 2010), pp. 197–212.

5   Knut Berg, *Studies in Tuscan Twelfth-Century Illumination*, Scandinavian University Books (Oslo: Universitetsforlaget, 1968); Maria Grazia Ciardi Duprè, 'Le Bibbie atlantiche toscane', in *Le Bibbie atlantiche*, pp. 73–80; Laura Alidori Battaglia, 'Illustrazione e decorazione delle Bibbie atlantiche toscane', in *Les Bibles atlantiques*, pp. 153–70.

6   Edward B. Garrison, *Studies in the History of Medieval Italian Painting*, 4 vols (Florence: L'Impronta, 1953–1962), I, pp. 10–35, 37–68, 83–114, 159–76; II, pp. 47–68, 97–112, 151–58, 217–27; III, pp. 33–81, 119–69, 281–99; IV, pp. 277–367; Lucinia Speciale, 'Dalla lettera all'immagine: la decorazione delle Bibbie atlantiche', in *Le Bibbie atlantiche*, pp. 65–71 (pp. 65–69).

Figure 1: Hollow Shaft Initial, B (*Beatus*), Psalms, initial's dimensions 85 x 121 mm. Geneva, Bibliothèque de Genève, MS lat. 1, fol. 149r, col. B.

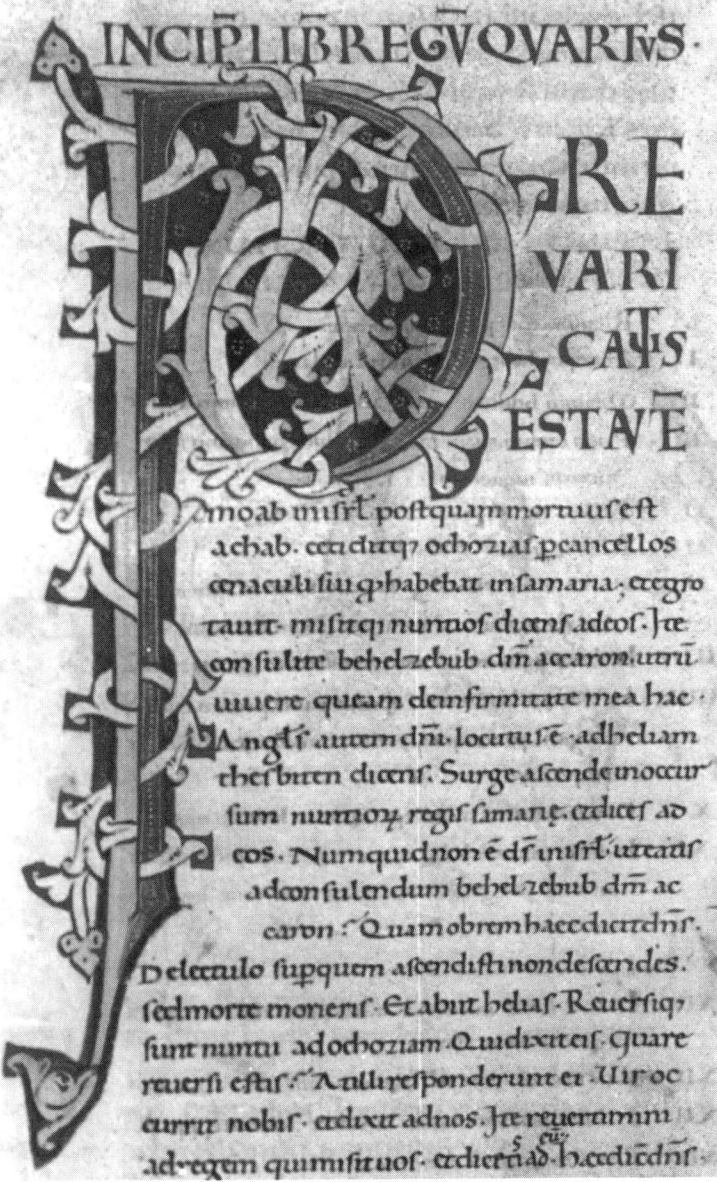

Figure 2: Full Shaft Initial, P (*Prevaricatus*), IV Kings, initial's dimensions 85 x 121 mm. Perugia, Biblioteca comunale Augusta, MS L 59, fol. 133v, col. A.

64 NADIA TOGNI

(yellow) or two colours (yellow and red); some interlaced white stems climb exuberantly over this ribbon (Fig. 2).

The inventory of Italian Giant Bibles

Based on modern bibliography, I have made an inventory of ninety-nine biblical manuscripts, whether in a single volume or several volumes. Furthermore, I have counted sixty-five fragments of nineteen other biblical manuscripts.[7] In total, I have now listed up to 118 Giant Bibles.[8] These 118 manuscripts are located and preserved in libraries worldwide, mostly in Italy, but also in Switzerland, Germany, Austria, France, Spain, England and Croatia. Several other manuscripts or fragments of Giant Bibles exist, that have crossed the Atlantic Ocean and are now preserved in libraries in New York, Stanford and Washington. All the biblical manuscripts and fragments with their places of conservation are displayed in a histogram, in which we have indicated the town where specimens are located, without specifying the particular libraries in which they are deposited (Fig. 3). Therefore one can see that twenty-two of the manuscripts are in Florence,[9] seventeen are preserved in the Vatican Library and twelve are in Rome.[10] In each of the other places of conservation there are just one, two or three such manuscripts.

As far as fragments are concerned, the situation is very different. In just two cases are an important number of identified biblical fragments preserved in the same place: Perugia, with sixteen fragments in the historical archives of Saint Peter's abbey and in the city library; and Venice,

---

[7] As part of a research project of the Department of Theology of the University of Geneva, I have identified and classified Italian Giant Bibles in a data processing system called BIBLION, which was developed for the analysis of this type of manuscript. About BIBLION, see Nadia Togni and Laurent Moccozet, 'BIBLION. A Data Processing System for Italian Giant Bibles', in *Proceeding of 5th International Technology, Education and Development Conference* (Valencia: IATED, 2011), pp. 4017–26; Nadia Togni, Laurent Moccozet, 'BIBLION. Système d'analyse informatisé des bibles et manuscrits atlantiques', in *Les Bibles atlantiques*, pp. 55–70.

[8] Nadia Togni, 'Inventario delle bibbie atlantiche', in *Les Bibles atlantiques*, pp. 509–18.

[9] Eighteen biblical manuscripts in the Medicea Laurenziana Library, two in the National Library of Florence, two in the Riccardiana Library.

[10] That is, three in the Angelica Library, three in the National Library of Rome, two in the Vallicelliana Library and two in the Casanatense Library, one in the Alessandrina Library and one in the San Giovanni in Laterano archives.

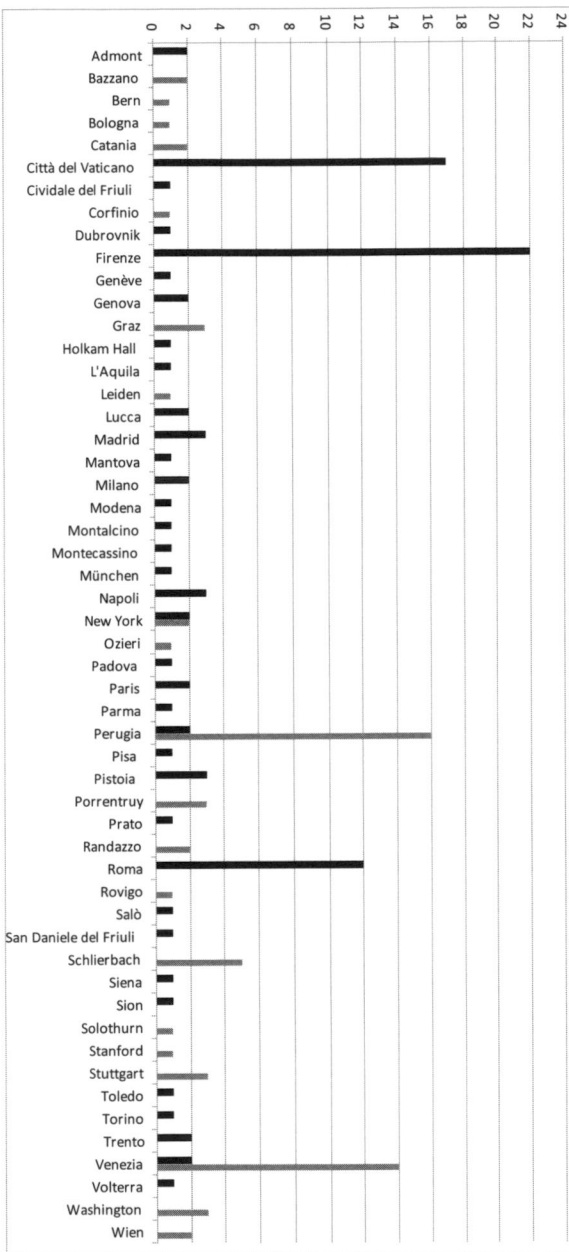

Figure 3: Places of conservation of Giant Bibles; biblical manuscripts in black, biblical fragments in grey.

with fourteen fragments in the state archives. Historical and palaeographic research shows that Perugia's fragments all belonged to the same biblical manuscript, which I refer to as 'Terza Bibbia di San Pietro',[11] while Venice's fragments all belonged to one biblical manuscript, that is, the San Marco di Vedana Bible.[12]

Italian giant liturgical manuscripts

In the second half of the eleventh century and at the beginning of the twelfth, when the production of Italian Giant Bibles still represented the expression of the most rigorous and strict policy of the first reformers, biblical manuscripts were rapidly sent from Rome and the Umbrian-Roman region to the ecclesiastical institutions for which they were destined. These institutions were either restructured or new monastic and canonical communities. They did not have their own collections of books with the necessary texts for use in choral liturgy and personal preaching and for the instruction of young monks and canons. Usually, Giant Bibles were commissioned along with several manuscripts of the same type and the same format: giant liturgical manuscripts, such as lectionaries, homiliaries, *Passiones Sanctorum*, works of the Church Fathers and other liturgical texts.

A complete and homogenous collection of giant liturgical manuscripts linked to a Giant Bible manuscript is the Troia collection, which Archbishop William gave to the chapter of the cathedral between 1108 and 1137.[13] In the Middle Ages, Troia was a very important diocese in the south-east of Italy; founded in 1019, it had from its very beginning the status of a diocese immediately subject to the pope. Archbishop William

---

[11] About this manuscript, see pp. 76–77.

[12] Lucilla Sandra Magoga, 'Sopravvivenze di codici nel fondo San Marco di Vedana dell'Archivio di Stato di Venezia', in *La Certosa di Vedana: storia, cultura e arte in un ambiente delle Prealpi bellunesi*, ed. by Lucilla Sandra Magoga and Francesco Marin (Florence: Olschki, 1998), pp. 137–58.

[13] The town of Troia is in the region of Apulia. On Troia's collection of giant manuscripts, see Gabriella Braga, Giulia Orofino and Marco Palma, 'I manoscritti di Guglielmo II, vescovo di Troia, alla Biblioteca Nazionale di Napoli: primi risultati di una ricerca', in *Libro, scrittura, documento della civiltà monastica e conventuale nel basso medioevo (secoli XIII–XV)*, ed. by Giuseppe Avarucci and others, Studi e Ricerche, 1 (Spoleto: Centro italiano di studi sull'Alto Medioevo, 1999), pp. 437–70; Gabriella Braga, 'I manoscritti del vescovo Guglielmo II: significato di una scoperta', in *Le Bibbie atlantiche*, pp. 87–90.

was a strong partisan of ecclesiastical reform, which he promoted in his diocese and in the chapter of his cathedral.

As this example shows, the purchasers of giant manuscript collections were high-ranking prelates of the Roman Church or princes committed to the moral and spiritual reform of the clergy. They had strong and continuous relationships with the papal court and they went more or less frequently to Rome, where they were informed of this big editorial enterprise of Giant Bibles and liturgical manuscripts. This led them to decide to equip their churches or monastic foundations with these monumental manuscripts as a sign of their loyalty to the Roman Church and to the pope.

Provenance of Italian Giant Bibles and liturgical manuscripts

In this paper, I specifically deal with the origin of the Giant Bibles and the liturgical manuscripts linked to them, focusing on the recipients of these manuscripts. This will allow us to connect the production of Giant Bibles with the promotion of the Gregorian Reform in the second half of the eleventh century. This way, it is possible to identify the pastoral and ideological strategy implied in the purchasing of such books for monastic and canonical communities. The analysis of the origins of Giant Bibles and liturgical manuscripts is very interesting and provides very rich and meaningful results regarding the circulation and use of this specific type of book.

Based on current research, I have produced a histogram that represents the number of biblical and liturgical manuscripts whose provenance can be identified (Fig. 4).

I have listed the towns of the monastic and canonical institutions to which thirty-one Giant Bibles and forty giant liturgical manuscripts were first destined and where they were used during the eleventh and twelfth centuries. This histogram represents the number of biblical manuscripts and liturgical manuscripts, including fragmentary specimens. The histogram shows that most of the ecclesiastical institutions in possession of Giant Bibles and liturgical manuscripts were in Italy. Several giant manuscripts were sent to ecclesiastical foundations in northern Italy. Among them is the Giant Bible of Mantua,[14] which was probably given to the

---

[14] About this manuscript, see Giuseppa Z. Zanichelli, '34. Mantova, Biblioteca Comunale, 131 (A V 1)', in *Le Bibbie atlantiche*, pp. 229–30.

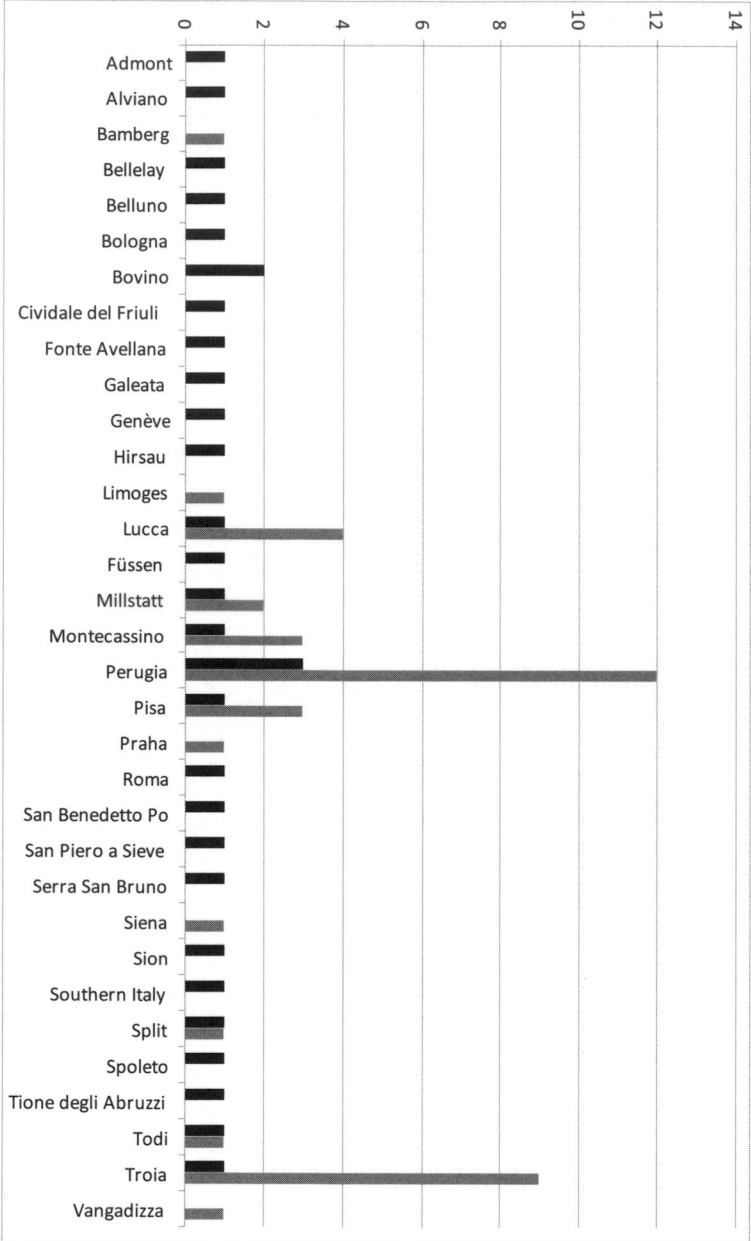

Figure 4: Provenance of Giant Bibles and liturgical manuscripts; Giant Bibles in black, giant liturgical manuscripts in grey.

abbey of San Benedetto of Po by Matilda of Tuscany (1046–1115), the main Italian supporter of Pope Gregory VII during the Investiture Controversy. On the other hand, in the centre of Italy there is a concentration of a relatively high number of giant manuscripts, in Perugia, Fonte Avellana, Todi, Spoleto, Saint Eutizio and Alviano. Finally, in southern Italy, the presence of Bibles from the beginning of the eleventh century is much more scarce, with the exception of the cathedrals of Troia and Bovino.[15]

According to Fig. 4, the highest number of Giant Bibles and giant liturgical manuscripts whose provenances we know are in Perugia and in Troia. In both cases we actually have a large and detailed bibliography regarding the complete collections of giant Italian manuscripts (Bibles and liturgical manuscripts) which were specially given to an ecclesiastical institution, respectively to Saint Peter's abbey in Perugia and the cathedral chapter in Troia. Besides, both in Perugia and Troia, the proportion between the number of Bibles and the number of liturgical manuscripts is absolutely correct, since one biblical manuscript usually came along with a set of liturgical books.

Four regions of provenance of Umbrian-Roman giant biblical and liturgical manuscripts

There are four regions where the circulation of Umbrian-Roman Giant Bibles and liturgical manuscripts seems to have been very significant, in order to express the support of the local Church to the reform movement. These regions are: the 'Pays Romands' region in the north-west corner of the Alps, the southern region of the Holy Roman Empire, the Umbria region in the centre of Italy and the Adriatic shores of the medieval kingdom of Croatia and Dalmatia. We have localised these four regions on the map below (Map 1).

The 'Pays Romands' region

The 'Pays Romands' region corresponds to Upper Burgundy (also called Transjurane Burgundy or Transjurania) in the Second Kingdom of Burgundy, which was incorporated into the Holy Roman Empire in

---

15 Two Giant Bibles, now in the Vatican Library, were used in Bovino cathedral until 1900, when the chapter gave them to Pope Leo III: Vatican City, Biblioteca Apostolica Vaticana (BAV), MS Vat. lat. 10510; BAV, MS Vat. lat. 10511.

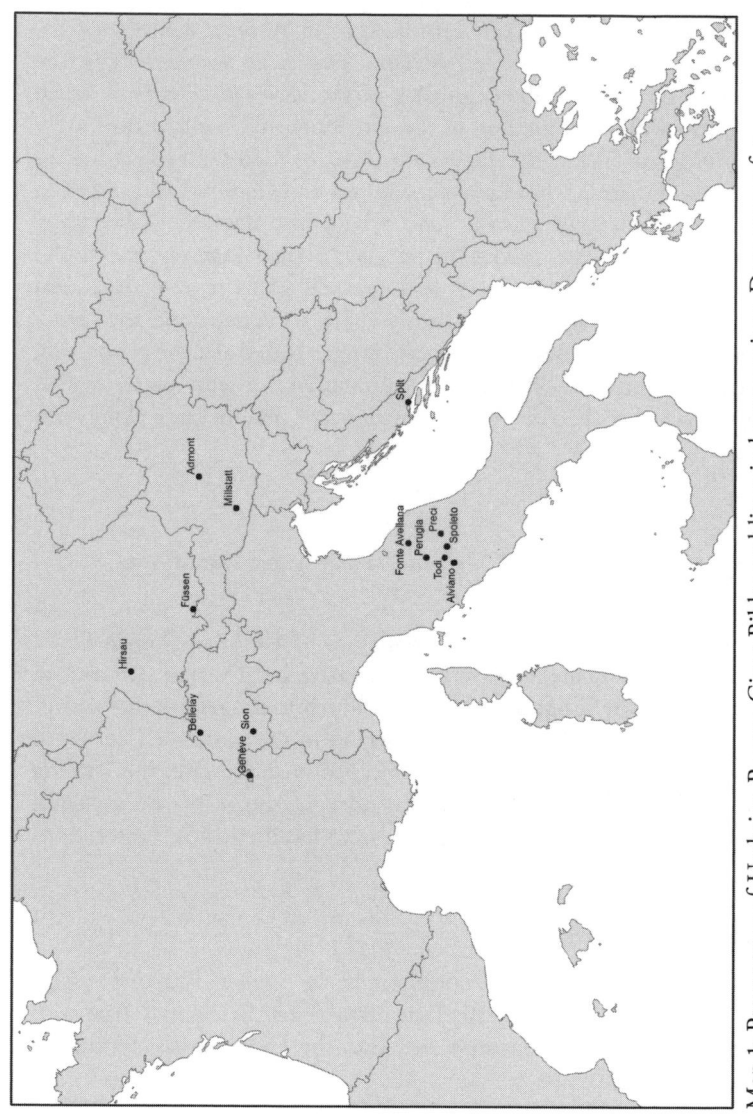

Map 1: Provenance of Umbrian-Roman Giant Bibles and liturgical manuscripts. Data source for administrative boundaries: GISCO – Eurostat (European Commission) © EuroGeographics for the administrative boundaries.

1032, after King Rudolph III died without any surviving heir.[16] In the 'Pays Romands' we have identified three ecclesiastical institutions that, between 1050 and 1142, received a Giant Bible, with some other giant liturgical manuscripts: Geneva cathedral chapter, Sion cathedral chapter and Bellelay abbey.

Giant Bible of Geneva cathedral chapter
Among the earliest Italian Giant Bibles is the Geneva Bible, the only one we can date more or less exactly.[17] Frederic, bishop of Geneva from 1032 to 1073, commissioned this manuscript in Rome, where he was in 1050 with other reformers of the Second Kingdom of Burgundy, such as Archbishop Hugues de Salins, *legatus* of Pope Nicholas II and prince of the German Empire. In the Roman pontifical court, Bishop Frederic would have been aware of the production of monumental biblical and liturgical manuscripts which were the spectacular expression of ecclesiastical reform. He therefore decided to purchase a Giant Bible with a complete collection of liturgical and patristic manuscripts and offered it to the canonical chapter of his cathedral in Geneva. The Giant Bible survives, but the collection of liturgical and patristic manuscripts has been lost, and we only have a list with titles and contents.[18] The donation of a Giant Bible with a collection of liturgical manuscripts to the Geneva cathedral chapter is evidence of Bishop Frederic's commitment to the promotion of the ecclesiastical reform in his diocese. Graphic and ornamental analogies show that several copyists and illuminators worked on the same group of biblical manuscripts which was formed by the Bible of the cathedral chapter of Sion, in the 'Pays Romands' region, and the Bibles of Admont abbey, Hirsau abbey and Füssen abbey, in the south of the Holy Roman Empire. Therefore, we can assume that these biblical manuscripts were

---

[16] Geographically speaking, the 'Pays Romands' area is the region extending from the Jura Mountains to the Rhone Valley, roughly corresponding to the present-day French-speaking districts of Switzerland. About the 'Pays Romands' region in the Middle Ages, see Agostino Paravicini Bagliani, 'Introduction', in *Les pays romands au Moyen Age* (Lausanne: Payot, 1997), pp. 5–8.

[17] Geneva, Bibliothèque de Genève, MS lat. 1. About this manuscript see Nadia Togni, 'La bible atlantique de Genève et la bible atlantique de Sion: un genre de manuscrit biblique à l'époque de la réforme ecclésiastique du XIᵉ siècle en Suisse' (unpublished doctoral thesis, University of Geneva, 2008), pp. 402–606.

[18] This booklist is edited in: Nadia Togni, 'La bible atlantique de la cathédrale de Sion (Archives du Chapitre de Sion, Ms. 15)', *Vallesia. Bulletin annuel de la Bibliothèque et des Archives cantonales du Valais, des Musées de Valère et de la Majorie*, 64 (2010), 153–92 (p. 157, n. 12).

produced in the same place and in the same *scriptorium*, and it is interesting to see that all these Bibles were first intended for religious institutions north of the Alps.

Giant Bible of Sion cathedral chapter
It is speculated that a few years after the bishop of Geneva commissioned the Giant Bible for the Geneva cathedral chapter, Ermenfroi, bishop of Sion from 1054 to 1087/1090, presented a Giant Bible to the chapter of his cathedral.[19] Like Frederic of Geneva, Bishop Ermenfroi restructured the rule of the canonical chapter and he was very close to the Roman curia and the ecclesiastical reform promoted by the pope, especially at the beginning of his episcopate, even if he supported the imperial policy of Henry IV, who appointed him chancellor of the empire.

Giant Bible of Bellelay abbey
In the diocese of Basel, we have another example of a Giant Bible donated by a high prelate of the Roman Church. Four fragments, now preserved in Berne, Porrentruy and Solothurn libraries, were part of a Giant Bible which was intended for the Premonstratensian abbey of Bellelay, in the Bernese Jura.[20] Ortlieb of Frohburg, the bishop of Basel (1136–1164) who played a leading role in the foundation of the abbey between 1140 and 1142, is credited with the donation of the manuscript to the Premonstratensian canons of Bellelay. The origins of this abbey can be traced to the search of canons coming from Lac du Joux for wild swamps they could turn into fertile and hospitable lands. However, the monastery's foundation also resulted from the influence of Bishop Ortlieb of Frohburg on the south-western border between the diocese of Basel and the territory of Moutier-Grandval abbey. Therefore, this donation of a Giant Bible became a symbolic act of laying new canonical foundations under his episcopal authority.

---

[19] Sion, Archives du Chapitre cathédral, MS 15. Description of the manuscript by Nadia Togni, 'La Bible Atlantique de la Cathédrale de Sion'. Digital reproduction: 'Sion/Sitten, Archives du Chapitre/Kapitelsarchiv, Ms. 15' in *E-Codices: Virtual Manuscripts Library of Switzerland* <http://www.e-codices.unifr.ch/fr/list/one/acs/0015> [accessed 23 January 2014].
[20] Bern, Burgerbibliotek, Cod. 749.7; Porrentruy, Archives de l'ancien evêché de Bâle, MS B 133/12, MS B 133/21, MS B 133/32; Solothurn, Zentralbibliothek, MS B_1496_09. About the Bellelay Bible, see Nadia Togni, 'Frammenti di una Bibbia atlantica provenienti dall'abbazia Premostratense di Bellelay', *Revue Suisse d'Histoire*, 58 (2008), 379–406; Ian Holt, *Handschriftenfragmente in der Zentralbibliothek Solothurn: Eine Auswahl* (Solothurn: Zentralbibliothek, 2012), pp. 24–25.

The Holy Roman Empire

During the second half of the eleventh century, a certain number of Giant Bibles and liturgical manuscripts were sent to abbeys founded in the south of the Holy Roman Empire, in the north-east region of the Alps, namely Admont, Millstatt, Hirsau and Füssen.

Giant Bible of Admont abbey

A Giant Bible, in two volumes, was presented to the Benedictine abbey of Admont, the *Monasterium ad Montes*, the oldest existing monastery in Styria. Based on a library inventory dated to 1370, we can identify the donor of the biblical manuscript as Archbishop Gebhard of Salzburg (1010–1088): 'Biblia tota in duobus maximis voluminibus quam dedit Gebehardus fundator'.[21] In 1074, Archbishop Gebhard of Salzburg established Admont abbey, thanks to an endorsement from Saint Hemma of Gurk, in the Carinthian March of Styria. He equipped the monastic library with everything necessary for monastic life, including books, as is related in the *Vita Gebehardi*.[22] The Giant Bible was found among the various manuscripts given by Gebhard, and is still preserved in the Admont monastic library.[23]

Giant Bible and liturgical manuscripts of Millstatt abbey

Archbishop Gebhard of Salzburg also seems to have been the donor of a Giant Bible to the Benedictine abbey of Millstatt. This abbey was founded as a proprietary monastery by Count Aribo (1024–1102) on his estates in Carinthia.[24] Though no charter is preserved, a later chronicle mentions a tithe agreement from about 1070 between Aribo and Archbishop Gebhard of Salzburg. It is presumed that the Benedictine abbey was founded before 1077, when Archbishop Gebhard of Salzburg was exiled. The monks may have come from Hirsau; moreover, the first known abbot of Millstatt around 1122 came from Admont. Just like Admont abbey, Archbishop Gebhard of Salzburg presented the Millstatt monastic community with a

---

21 Admont, Stiftsbibliothek, MS C–D.

22 'Vita Gebehardi episcopi Constantiensis', ed. by Wilhelm Wattenbach, in *Annales et chronica aevi Salici: vitae aevi Carolini et Saxonici*, Monumenta Germaniae Historica, Scriptores, 10 (Hannover: Hahn, 1852), pp. 582–94.

23 Massimiliano Bassetti, '1. Admont, Stiftsbibliothek, C–D (Bibbia di Gebhard di Salisburgo)', in *Le Bibbie atlantiche*, pp. 108–11.

24 On the history of Millstatt abbey, see Erika Weinzierl-Fischer, *Geschichte des Benediktinerklosters Millstatt in Kärnten*, Archiv für vaterländische Geschichte und Topographie, 33 (Klagenfurt: Verlag des Geschichtsvereines für Kärnten, 1951).

collection of giant manuscripts. Only a few fragments of these books are preserved: two fragments of the Bible manuscript are in the University Library in Graz,[25] and a few liturgical fragments of the *Enarrationes in Psalmos* by Saint Augustine and the *Moralia in Job* by Saint Gregory the Great are now preserved in the Klagenfurt archives.[26]

Giant Bible of Hirsau abbey

Before the conflicts with Pope Gregory VII about the Investiture Controversy, Emperor Henry IV, when still King Henry III, supported ecclesiastical renewal, while Cardinal Bishop Humbert of Moyenmoutier and Saint Peter Damian carried on the momentum for a moral and spiritual reform of the clergy. Shortly before 1075, King Henry III presented a Giant Bible to Hirsau abbey; this manuscript is now preserved in the Bavarian State Library in Munich.[27] Hirsau abbey was founded in the Nagold river valley in about 830 by Count Erlafried of Calw, and it was re-founded in 1059 after a period of collapse.[28] The abbey was brought to international prominence by William of Hirsau, abbot from 1069 to 1091, and author of the *Constitutiones Hirsaugienses* based on the customs of Cluny.[29] Abbot William is famous for being the father of the Hirsau Reform, which influenced many Benedictine monasteries in Germany.[30] In 1075, Abbot William went to Rome. On this occasion he became acquainted with Pope Gregory VII, with whose reforming efforts he sympathised and whom he strongly supported afterwards during the Investiture Controversy against

[25] Graz, Universitätsbibliothek, MS 1703/1, MS 1703/2, MS 1703/3.

[26] Klagenfurt, Kärntner Landesarchiv, Fragment 13/42.

[27] Munich, Bayerische Staatsbibliothek, Clm 13001. On this manuscript, see Larry M. Ayres, 'The Bible of Henry IV and an Italian Romanesque Pandect in Florence', in *Studien zur mittelalterlichen Kunst 800–1250: Festschrift für Florentine Mütherich zum 70. Geburtstag*, ed. by Katharina Bierbrauer, Peter K. Klein and Willibald Sauerländer (Munich: Prestel-Verlag, 1985), pp. 157–66; Larry M. Ayres, '3. München, Bayerische Staatsbibliothek, Clm 13001 (Bibbia di Enrico IV)', in *Le Bibbie atlantiche*, pp. 114–20.

[28] About the history of Hirsau abbey, see Klaus Schreiner, 'Hirsau', in *Die Benediktinerklöster in Baden-Württemberg*, ed. by Franz Quarthal, Germania Benedictina (Augsburg: Kommissionsverlag Winfried-Werk, 1975), vol. 5, pp. 281–303.

[29] *Willehelmi Abbatis Constitutiones Hirsaugienses*, ed. by Pius Engelbert, Corpus consuetudinum monasticarum, 15 (Siegburg: apud Schmitt successoribus, 2010).

[30] About Hirsau abbey, see Hermann Jakobs, *Die Hirsauer: ihre Ausbreitung und Rechtsstellung im Zeitalter des Investiturstreites*, Kölner historische Abhandlungen, 4 (Cologne: Böhlau, 1961).

Henry IV. On that same occasion he would have found out about the production of giant biblical and liturgical manuscripts.

Giant Bible of Füssen abbey

Finally, another Giant Bible belonged to the Benedictine abbey of Saint Mang in Füssen.[31] The manuscript is now in the Vatican Library, in the Palatini collection.[32] The abbey was founded during the first half of the ninth century as a proprietary monastery of the bishops of Augsburg. It was built on the important medieval road from Augsburg across the Alps to Upper Italy, in the Füssen Gap where the Lech river breaks out of the Alps. The monastery's key position gave it an immense strategic value, which made it of political concern both to the bishops of Augsburg and to the Holy Roman Emperors. In the eleventh and twelfth centuries, the religious community made efforts to maintain a life true to the Rule of Saint Benedict amidst the various pressures caused by external social developments. The monks embraced the Roman reforming movement intended to bring about a return to the essentials of the Benedictine lifestyle. This historical context explains the presence of a Giant Bible in the choir of Füssen abbey at the end of the eleventh century.

The region of Umbria in Italy

In the eleventh century, the region now called Umbria in the centre of Italy belonged to the *Patrimonium Sancti Petri*, which would become the Papal States. Analysis of book circulation reveals that a number of Giant Bibles and liturgical manuscripts were allocated to monastic institutions in the Umbrian region. The most important and powerful monasteries in this area owned collections of giant manuscripts, which were used daily during divine offices and were preserved in the choir or in the sacristy. The Umbrian monasteries that owned a Giant Bible, sometimes along with giant liturgical manuscripts, at the end of the eleventh century were: Saint

---

[31] About Füssen abbey, see Josef Hemmerle, *Die Benediktinerklöster in Bayern*, Germania Benedictina, 2 (Augsburg: Kommissionsverlag Winfried-Werk, 1970), pp. 109–14; Thomas Riedmiller, 'Das ehemalige Benediktinerkloster St. Mang in Füssen', in *Klosterland Bayerisch Schwaben. Zur Erinnerung an die Säkularisation der 1802/1803*, ed. by Werner Schiedermair (Lindenberg: Fink, 2003), pp. 220–22.
[32] BAV, MS Pal. lat. 3, 4, 5. For description of manuscript, see Lucinia Speciale, '4. Città del Vaticano, Biblioteca Apostolica Vaticana, Vat. Pal. lat. 3–4–5 (Bibbia Palatina)', in *Le Bibbie atlantiche*, pp. 120–26; Charles Buchanan, 'The Palatine Bible (Città del Vaticano, BAV, MS Pal. lat. 3, 4, 5): A Visual Assault Against a Two-Headed Monster', in *Les Bibles atlantiques*, pp. 91–103.

Peter in Perugia, Saint Fortunatus in Todi, Saint Pontianus in Spoleto, Saint Eutizio in Val Castoriana, not far from Norcia, and Saint Valentine in Piano, near Alviano. To these monasteries can be added the famous Fonte Avellana abbey that, until the nineteenth century, belonged to the diocese of Gubbio in Umbria; Fonte Avellana is now in the diocese of Cagli, in the Marche region. The community of Fonte Avellana had a Giant Bible made in 1146, which is now preserved in the Vatican Library.[33]

Giant Bibles and liturgical manuscripts of Saint Peter's abbey
in Perugia
Saint Peter's abbey, founded in 966 by Abbot Peter over the first cathedral church in Perugia, was a very powerful institution in the centre of Italy.[34] During the Middle Ages, the abbey formed a very big property along the Tiber river valley and became an important pastoral, political, economic and cultural centre from the beginning of the eleventh century. During this time, abbots of Saint Peter obtained confirmations of its privileges and goods from emperors and popes. These precious documents are still preserved in the monastic archives. The presence of a collection of giant manuscripts in the choir of this abbey demonstrates the very strong relationship between Saint Peter's, the circle of Roman reformers and the papal court. Saint Peter's abbey was so important and powerful that it even had three specimens of Giant Bibles.[35] In fact, we know well two Giant Bibles from this abbey: the 'Bibbia di San Pietro', preserved in the monastic archives,[36] and the 'Bibbia dell'Augusta', preserved in the city library, the Biblioteca comunale Augusta.[37] In the abbey book collection, we can include a third Giant Bible that I have termed the 'Terza

---

33 BAV, MS Vat. lat., 4216.
34 On the history of Saint Peter's abbey in Perugia, see Giustino Farnedi, *L'Abbazia di San Pietro in Perugia e gli studi storici*, Italia Benedettina, 35 (Cesena: Centro Storico Benedettino Italiano, 2011); Nadia Togni, 'Repertorio dei monasteri in Umbria, 50. Perugia, San Pietro', in *Monasteri Benedettini in Umbria: Alle radici del paesaggio umbro*, Biblioteca del Monasticon Italiae, 1 (Cesena: Centro Storico Benedettino Italiano, 2014), pp. 180–85.
35 See Nadia Togni, 'Le Bibbie atlantiche dell'Umbria', in *Umbria e Marche nell'età romanica: arti e tecniche a confronto tra XI e XIII secolo*, ed. by Enrica Neri Lusanna (Todi: Ediart, 2014), pp. 157–70 (pp. 161–66); Nadia Togni, 'Les manuscrits atlantiques de l'abbaye bénédictine de San Pietro de Pérouse', in *Les Bibles atlantiques*, pp. 325–62; Giustino Farnedi, 'Bibbia e liturgia nelle espressioni documentarie e artistiche di San Pietro di Perugia', in *Les Bibles atlantiques*, pp. 363–402.
36 Perugia, Archivio storico di San Pietro, MS C.M. 1.
37 Perugia, Biblioteca comunale Augusta, MS L 59.

Bibbia di San Pietro', of which I discovered sixteen fragments, preserved in the monastic archives and in the city library. Moreover, the monks of Saint Peter's owned a complete set of liturgical manuscripts in the same monumental format: homiliaries, passionals, lectionaries and works of the Church Fathers, such as Augustine, Gregory the Great, Bede, Sulpicius Severus, Odo of Glanfeuil and Bruno of Segni. I was able to track down twenty-one fragments representing a collection of twelve liturgical manuscripts that the monks used in the choir of their magnificent basilica.[38]

Giant Bibles and liturgical manuscripts of Saint Fortunatus' abbey in Todi

In the centre of Todi, the Benedictine abbey of Saint Fortunatus was founded at the beginning of the tenth century. In 1192 it was transferred to the Camaldolese monks of Fonte Avellana and ultimately, in 1254, the bishop of Todi granted it to the Franciscan order.[39] From the Benedictine abbey of Saint Fortunatus comes a Giant Bible known as the 'Bibbia di Todi'; this manuscript can be dated to the end of the eleventh century. This Giant Bible belonged to the Saint Fortunatus community until 1860, when it was given to the pope and entered the collections of the Vatican Library, where it is still preserved.[40] The Benedictines of Todi also had a giant liturgical manuscript, namely Saint Gregory's *Moralia in Job*, in two volumes.[41] As in Saint Peter's abbey in Perugia, the Giant Bible manuscript

---

[38] In the sixteenth century, these fragments were used to cover some of the abbey's books. The Giant Bibles and some fragments of liturgical manuscripts of Saint Peter's abbey were on display in September 2011; the exhibition, organised by Nadia Togni, was preceded by a conference about the Italian Giant Bibles and liturgical manuscripts in Umbria, entitled: 'Bibbie e manoscritti atlantici in Umbria'.

[39] On Saint Fortunatus' abbey, see *Il Tempio di San Fortunato a Todi*, ed. by Guglielmo De Angelis d'Ossat (Milano: Silvana, 1982); *Il Tempio del Santo Patrono:. Riflessi storico-artistici del culto di San Fortunato a Todi*, ed. by Marcello Castrichini (Todi: Ediart, 1988); Nadia Togni, 'Repertorio dei monasteri in Umbria, 64. Todi, San Fortunato', in *Monasteri benedettini in Umbria*, pp. 243–48.

[40] BAV, MS Vat. lat. 10405; for a description of the manuscript, see Lucinia Speciale, '13. Città del Vaticano, Biblioteca Apostolica Vaticana, Vat. lat. 10405 (Bibbia di Todi)', in *Les Bibles atlantiques*, pp. 158–62.

[41] Todi, Biblioteca Comunale Lorenzo Leoni, MS 1 and MS 2. For a description of the manuscripts, see *I manoscritti medievali della biblioteca comunale 'L. Leonii' di Todi. Catalogo*, ed. by Enrico Menestò and others, 2 vols (Spoleto: Centro italiano di studi sull'Alto Medioevo, 2009), I, pp. 184–91; see also Massimiliano Bassetti, 'Per la storia dei manoscritti atlantici: scritture ai margini dei *Moralia in Iob* di Todi', *Bollettino della deputazione di storia patria per l'Umbria*, 93 (2001), 275–364.

would have been commissioned from a Roman *scriptorium* along with its own set of liturgical books of the same size and format, to be used by the monks of Saint Fortunatus' during celebrations that took place in the choir of the basilica.[42]

Giant Bible of Saint Pontianus' abbey in Spoleto
In the south of Umbria, the town of Spoleto occupied a strategic geographical and historical position during Antiquity and the Early Middle Ages.[43] Before the end of the tenth century, a women's monastery was built on the spot where, according to tradition, Saint Pontianus, the patron saint of Spoleto, was martyred. In the second half of the eleventh century, Saint Pontianus' abbey owned a Giant Bible in two volumes, now preserved in San Daniele del Friuli.[44] In this manuscript we can still read the obituary of Gerlenda, abbess of Saint Pontianus, who died in 1078: 'MLXXVIII obiit reverentissima abbatissa Gerlenda huius coenobii domina, VI idus martii' (MS II, fol. 145r).[45] Documents from Umbrian female monasteries in the Middle Ages are very rare;[46] accordingly, the possession of this biblical manuscript, with its strong symbolic value, gives a rare glimpse of the liturgical life led by the community of nuns at Saint Pontianus' abbey during the eleventh century.

Giant Bibles of Saint Eutizio's abbey near Preci
During the sixth century in Val Castoriana, not far from Norcia, where Saint Benedict was born, a group of Syrian monks founded Saint Eutizio's abbey.[47] Located along the Via Flaminia, which connects Rome to the

---

[42] Togni, 'Le Bibbie atlantiche dell'Umbria', p. 166.

[43] Mario Sensi, *'Mulieres in Ecclesia'. Storia di monache e bizzocche*, 2 vols (Spoleto, Centro italiano di studi sull'Alto Medioevo, 2010), II, pp. 897–910; Nadia Togni, 'Repertorio dei monasteri in Umbria, 63. Spoleto, San Ponziano', in *Monasteri benedettini in Umbria*, pp. 239–42.

[44] San Daniele del Friuli, Biblioteca Guarneriana, MS I–II. For a description of the manuscript, see Cesare Scalon, '8. San Daniele del Friuli, Biblioteca Guarneriana, I-II', in *Le Bibbie atlantiche*, pp. 139–44.

[45] Togni, 'Le Bibbie atlantiche dell'Umbria', p. 166.

[46] Giovanna Casagrande, 'Monaci e ordini mendicanti nell'Umbria del secolo XIII', in *L'Umbria nel XIII secolo*, ed. by Enrico Menestò (Spoleto: Centro italiano di studi sull'Alto Medioevo, 2011), pp. 45–71 (p. 51).

[47] On Saint Eutizio's abbey, see *Castella et Guaita abbatie: tracce di un itinerario storico e artistico da S. Eutizio a Preci (secc. XI–XIX)*, ed. by Alessandro Bianchi, Luca Pistelli and Carlo Rossetti (Pistrino: Comune di Preci, 2002); Nadia Togni, 'Repertorio dei monasteri in Umbria, 54. Preci, Sant'Eutizio', in *Monasteri benedettini in Umbria*, pp. 199–204.

Adriatic Sea, this abbey enjoyed great prosperity during the Middle Ages, which allowed the monks to build a great monastery with a library and a *scriptorium*. Professional scribes and illuminators worked in Saint Eutizio and produced a large number of manuscripts that, since the beginning of the seventeenth century, have been preserved in the Vallicelliana Library in Rome. Two specimens of Giant Bibles came from this rich and powerful abbey: the first one dates from between 1090 and 1110,[48] while the second one dates from the early twelfth century.[49] An annotation dated to 1317, at fol. 1r of the Giant Bible Biblioteca Vallicelliana, MS A 2 states that at that time the manuscript belonged to Santa Croce di Pupaggio, a priory of Saint Eutizio.[50]

Giant Bible of Saint Valentine in Piano, near Alviano
The monastery of Saint Valentine in Piano is in the south-west of Umbria, not far from the River Tiber. Unfortunately, few archival documents about this Benedictine institution survive; the oldest one dates back to 1276 and it is the registration of tithe due to the Papal States: 'Eodem mense die IIII exeunte invenerunt in ecclesia S. Valentini in Plano XXVII sol. cort. I flor. argenti XVI pap. et III proves'.[51] A Giant Bible dating from the end of the eleventh century, now preserved in the Palatine Library in Parma,[52] allows us to know another element of this monastery's history. In the margins of a few pages are annotations written in the middle of the thirteenth century; most of these annotations concern various estates of

[48] Rome, Biblioteca Vallicelliana, MS A 1. Manuscript description by Valentina D'Urso, 'Roma, Biblioteca Vallicelliana, Manoscritti, ms. A 1 primo', in *Manus: censimento dei manoscritti delle biblioteche italiane* <http://manus.iccu.sbn.it//opac_SchedaScheda.php?ID=16613> [accessed 22 March 2014].

[49] Rome, Biblioteca Vallicelliana, MS A 2. Manuscript description by Patrizia Formica, 'Roma, Biblioteca Vallicelliana, Manoscritti, ms. A 2', in *Manus: censimento dei manoscritti delle biblioteche italiane* <http://manus.iccu.sbn.it//opac_SchedaScheda.php?ID=186284> [accessed 22 March 2014].

[50] Togni, 'Le Bibbie atlantiche dell'Umbria', pp. 166–67.

[51] Pietro Sella, *Rationes decimarum Italiae nei secoli XIII e XIV. Umbria*, 2 vols, Studi e Testi, 161–62 (Vatican City: Biblioteca Apostolica Vaticana, 1952), I, p. 568, No. 8011.

[52] Parma, Biblioteca Palatina, MS 386. Manuscript description by Larry M. Ayres, '9. Parma, Biblioteca Palatina, 386 (Bibbia di San Valentino in Piano)', in *Le Bibbie atlantiche*, pp. 144–48; Giuseppa Zanichelli, 'Scheda n. 13', in *Cum picturis ystoriatum: codici devozionali e liturgici della Biblioteca Palatina*, ed. by Stefano Calzolari, Il giardino delle Esperidi, 14 (Modena: Il Bulino, 2001), pp. 76–79.

the monastery, located along the banks of the Tiber and often subject to river flooding. At fol. 268v we can also read the act by which the '*presbiter*' Vitale, from the hermitage of Saint Fortunatus, promised obedience to the abbot of Saint Valentine: 'Domino Gregorio, abbati Sancti Valentini in Plano Ameliensis diocesis'.[53] Once again, the presence of a Giant Bible in the choir of Saint Valentine is evidence of the liturgical life of a community of monks and of their ideological support for the Roman ecclesiastical reform.

Kingdom of Croatia and Dalmatia

In the eleventh century, strong relationships were established between the Roman Church and the kingdom of Croatia and Dalmatia, which stretched from the Adriatic coasts to Pannonia. At this time, the region was under the pope's influence and the local clergy provided important political leadership in the creation of an autonomous Croatian nation. The kingdom of Croatia and Dalmatia was placed at the crossroads of the interests of German princes, the Byzantine Empire, Venice and the Normans in the south of Italy; it acted as a cultural link between East and West, between the Roman Church and the Holy Roman Empire. After the Great Schism of 1054, a papal ally in the Balkans was a necessity. King Peter Krešimir IV, called the Great, and the Croatian upper nobility lent their support to the pope. Under his rule, the kingdom of Croatia and Dalmatia was finally connected to the Roman Church. Pope Nicholas II immediately commanded King Peter Krešimir IV to reform the Croatian Church in accordance with Roman Church rite, first in 1059 and then in 1060. At the time of Gregory VII, the kingdom of Croatia was subjected directly to the authority of the pope and, in 1076, the Croatian King Demetrius Zvonimir donated the city of Vrana with its Benedictine monastery of Saint Gregory, as a sign of loyalty to the pope, as we can read in the *Collectio Canonum* of Cardinal Deusdedit, written in 1087 and dedicated to Pope Victor II.

In this political and pastoral context, the kingdom of Croatia and Dalmatia was necessarily involved in the ecclesiastical reform promoted by the Roman Church in the second half of the eleventh century. A very important role in promoting reform was played by the Benedictine Order, which fostered the use of Roman liturgy first in the Dalmatian coastal areas and in Istria, then in the whole Croatian kingdom. The first Benedictine monks came to Croatia and Dalmatia around the tenth century, and they

---

53 Togni, 'Le Bibbie atlantiche dell'Umbria', p. 167.

founded more than thirty monasteries between Krk and Kotor.[54] As a means of expression of the Gregorian Reform, Italian Giant Bibles and liturgical manuscripts also reached the Adriatic shores of Croatia and they were soon commissioned and acquired by new monastic and canonical institutions. Between the eleventh and twelfth centuries, relationships with the Roman curia were so strong and continuous that Croatian prelates necessarily knew the editorial project of the Giant Bibles. In fact, they commissioned some of these manuscripts to equip the monasteries and churches of their dioceses.

Giant Bible and liturgical manuscript of Split cathedral chapter
Two giant manuscripts can be linked to the cathedral of Split: the Bible preserved in the Dominican monastery library of Dubrovnik[55] and the Passional now preserved in the library of the Zagreb cathedral chapter.[56] The Zagreb Passional might come from Split, like the fragment of Beneventan script which is bound within it. We know that Maio, the deacon of the cathedral of Split from 1015 to 1030, during Paul's episcopate, wrote this Beneventan fragment. Like this fragment, the Passional should also be linked to the cathedral of Split. We do not have any evidence regarding the origin of the Dubrovnik Giant Bible, dated to the second half of the eleventh century and preserved in the Dominican monastery since 1225,

---

[54] In 986, the monastery of Saint Chrysogonus in Zadar, the most ancient Benedictine monastery in Croatia, was entrusted to Madius, a monk from Monte Cassino abbey. At the beginning of the eleventh century, Benedictine monks founded four monasteries near Osor and Susak. In 1059, Theodoric, bishop of Zadar, founded the monastery of Saint Cosmas and Saint Damian in Pašman Island. Also in 1059, King Peter Krešimir IV built the monastery of Saint Euphemia in Split. In 1066, he granted a charter to the powerful monastery of Saint Mary in Zadar, whose founder and first nun was his cousin, the abbess Čika. A few years later, King Peter Krešimir IV founded the monastery of Saint John the Evangelist in Biograd na Moru, and in 1070 he gave the monastery of Saint Michael on the island of Susak to Desiderius, the abbot of Monte Cassino. Finally, in the second half of the eleventh century, other monasteries were founded: Saint John the Evangelist in Trogir, Saint Peter in Rab Island, the Lokrum abbey not far from Dubrovnik and Saint Mary in Rožat, near Dubrovnik.

[55] Dubrovnik, Dominikanski samostan, MS MR 58. On this manuscript, see Nadia Togni, 'Un esemplare di Bibbia gigante italiana dell'XI secolo conservato in Croazia: la Bibbia atlantica di Dubrovnik', Segno e testo, 4 (2007), 341–93.

[56] Zagreb, Metropolitanska knjižnica, MS MR 164. On this manuscript, see Nadia Togni, 'Un Passionario atlantico umbro-romano a Zagabria', in Hagiologica: Studi per Réginald Grégoire, ed. by Alessandra Bartolomei Romagnoli, Ugo Paoli and Pierluigi Piatti, Bibliotheca Montisfani, 31 (Fabriano: Monastero San Silvestro Abate, 2012), pp. 35–59.

when it was founded. However, it is possible to think that this biblical manuscript was intended for the cathedral of Split, before being transported south to Dubrovnik, where new Dominican communities would have acquired it. In this case, the chapter of the cathedral of Split might have had a Giant Bible and a set of giant liturgical manuscripts produced in Rome in the second half of the eleventh century.

Conclusion

The research I have presented in this chapter proves that, in the second half of the eleventh century and at the beginning of the twelfth, the provenance of Italian Giant Bibles and liturgical manuscripts in Italy and in Europe overlaps with monastic and canonical institutions that received Roman ecclesiastical reform and became themselves the most important centres of diffusion of moral and spiritual renewal of the clergy. The circulation and the use of this new type of manuscript conceived by the Roman Reformers, with its strong ideological and representative value, coincide with places and chronological terms of the Gregorian Reform.

Comparing bibliographical data with historical information in connection with a geographical basis allows the identification of new relationships between manuscript circulation and the network of monasteries and cathedral churches, and their abbots and bishops in the Middle Ages. Therefore, the analysis of the circulation and use of a specific type of book, such as Italian Giant Bibles and liturgical manuscripts, is fundamental to our understanding of the dynamics of book dissemination in the eleventh and twelfth centuries in Italy and in Europe.

Investigation of relationships between manuscript production, purchasers and recipients is the innovative element of this research. In this paper, I propose to study mediaeval manuscripts not only as material objects or textual supports, but also as a book with a concrete use in its historical context. In this case, we have analysed Italian Giant Bibles as liturgical manuscripts, employed every day in church by the canonical and monastic communities for which they were produced in the eleventh century. This study of Italian Giant Bibles could be an exemplar for research on the circulation of graphic and written culture in Europe during the Middle Ages.

Isolation or Network? Arengas *and Colophon* Verse in Frisian Manuscripts around 1300

ROLF H. BREMMER JR

LITERACY CAME RATHER late to Frisia, a narrow stretch of land no deeper than some 25 kilometres and running along the coast of the North Sea between the estuaries of the Rhine and the Weser.[1] Although the Frisians had been converted to Christianity from the late seventh century to the end of the ninth, very few centres of learning, if any at all, had come about in the centuries immediately following their conversion, due to various circumstances. First of all, the missionaries who evangelised amongst the Frisians had their bases far away from the coast: Willibrord's home abbey was in Echternach (Luxembourg), Boniface worked from Fulda (Hessen), Liudger resided in Werden (Ruhr area), while also from Corvey abbey on the lower Weser anonymous monks had worked in the Frisian lands. As a result, when newly converted pious Frisians wanted to donate land in honour of God and for the benefit of their souls, they did so to these monasteries rather than seeing to it that such pious communities were founded within the confines of Frisia itself to which they could relate.

A second factor frustrating the foundation of centres of Christian literacy was the arrival of the Vikings. Shortly after Charlemagne had completed the conquest of Frisia and its incorporation into his empire, the coastal districts started to become a target for increasingly frequent Scandinavian raids. These plundering activities were only temporarily brought to a halt when Charlemagne's grandson Hlothar appointed the Dane Rorik as count of Frisia in 850. For more than twenty-five years successive Danes ruled the Low Countries not unlike a kind of Normandy or Danelaw, but eventually they failed to settle permanently and establish

---

[1] The coming of literacy to Frisia is the subject of my *'Hir is eskriven'. Lezen en schrijven in de Friese landen rond 1300* (Hilversum: Verloren, 2004). Parts of the present article elaborate on information to be found there; see also Marco Mostert, 'The Early History of Written Culture in the Northern Netherlands', in *Along the Oral-Written Continuum. Types of Texts, Relations and Their Implications*, ed. by Slávica Rankovic, with Leidulf Melve and Else Mundal (Turnhout: Brepols, 2010), pp. 449–88 (pp. 473–88). I would like to express my gratitude to both Jenny Weston and an anonymous reviewer for their insightful suggestions that helped improve my contribution.

a duchy or county there. Only around 950 did the coast see a nunnery in the dunes of Egmond (about 30 km north-west of Amsterdam), founded at the invitation of Count Dirk I, by Benedictines of the abbey of St Bavo in Ghent and hence oriented more to the south than to the north.

A third factor thwarting the rise of literacy was the ecclesiastical administration. Frisia never received its own bishopric, but the Frisian lands subsisted under the successors of whichever missionary had been responsible for their conversion. Hence, the Frisian lands became divided between four different bishoprics: Utrecht (Willibrord), Münster (Liudger), Paderborn (successor to Corvey abbey) and Bremen (Willehad), all of them situated outside Frisia.

Finally, in the course of the eleventh century, the affluent Frisian lands had started to withdraw themselves from the empire to such an extent that dukes and counts were no longer recognised as having any authority over them, except for the king/emperor himself to whom they considered themselves to be directly subordinated (German *reichsunmittelbar*). Whatever feudal officials – some of them belonging to the most powerful noble families in Germany – had been enfeoffed with parts of Frisia, none of them ever settled in their Frisian fiefs nor did they erect any castles there. As a result, no opportunities were created for the development of centres of comital administration and courtly culture.[2]

The situation of underdeveloped literacy changed with the so-called 'second conversion' of the Frisians.[3] This movement refers to the building of stone churches and the foundation of monasteries in Frisia from the middle of the twelfth century onwards, beginning in Frisia west of the River Lauwers and proceeding from there in an easterly direction. The founders of these monasteries usually linked up with the new monastic orders, such as the Cistercians and Premonstratensians, although occasionally monasteries and nunneries following the traditional mode of Benedictine monasticism were instituted too. It was the infrastructure created by these new monastic houses that at least partly filled the cultural vacuum that had come about through the absence of ecclesiastical and secular centres of administrative power. Abbots, for example, frequently

---

[2] For a concise overview of the early medieval history of Frisia, see Oebele Vries, 'Geschichte der Friesen im Mittelalter: West- und Ostfriesland', in *Handbuch des Friesischen/Handbook of Frisian Studies*, ed. by Horst H. Munske (Tübingen: Niemeyer, 2001), §51.

[3] Heinrich Schmidt, 'Kirchenbau und "zweite Christianisierung" im friesisch-sächsischen Küstengebiet während des hohen Mittelalters', *Niedersächsisches Jahrbuch für Landesgeschichte*, 59 (1987), 63–93.

fulfilled the judicial roles that elsewhere were played by counts. The newly founded monasteries also provided an alternative for advanced education and at least partly replaced the role that the cathedral schools of Utrecht, Münster and Bremen had played.

Until very recently, little attention had been paid to the rise of literacy in Frisia, the focus of scholarly interest being directed rather to the demise of writing in the Frisian vernacular at the end of the Middle Ages. The general opinion, as expressed by Oebele Vries, was that Frisian society until 1300 had only marginally been influenced by literacy. Of course, Vries concedes, the monks must have been skilled in the art of writing, but because until now no early *scriptoria* going back to 1300 have been identified in Frisia, Vries concludes that writing must have enjoyed little priority. Furthermore the near absence of thirteenth-century charters would point to a minimal use of pragmatic literacy. According to Vries, around 1300 the monks' interest was more directed towards reclaiming land for farming than cultivating the art of writing.[4]

In one respect Vries is undeniably right: we have little manuscript evidence from the thirteenth century to help us form a well-founded idea about the state of literacy in Frisia. However, a great amount of handwritten material was lost in the course of time, through fire, water, neglect, war, the art of printing and the Reformation, for there is sufficient evidence to suggest there were plenty of books available in Frisia at this time. To give just an idea: the quite sizeable *Chronicle of Bloemhof Abbey*, written between 1200 and 1300 by the first four abbots of a modest Premonstratensian monastery in Fivelgo, makes reference to or quotes from almost one hundred different works, ranging from the Vulgate to Virgil's *Aeneid* and *Georgics*, and from Isidore of Seville's *Etymologiae* to the *Sermones* of Pope Innocent III.[5] Nevertheless, the autograph chronicle itself is the only book from the abbey's well-stocked library to have survived.[6] However, – and this is typical for the Frisian situation – some charters written by Bloemhof abbots have escaped the fate of destruc-

---

4   Oebele Vries, *'Naar ploeg en koestal vluchtte uw taal'. De verdringing van het Fries als schrijftaal door het Nederlands (tot 1580)* (Leeuwarden: Fryske Akademy, 1993), pp. 14–16.

5   Bremmer, *'Hir is eskriven'*, Appendix I, pp. 155–56. Some quotations may have been culled from *florilegia*, but this possibility does not really diminish the impression of the abbots having access to a wide range of books.

6   Groningen, Universiteitsbibliotheek, MS 116; for an excellent dual-language edition (Latin-Dutch), see *Kroniek van het klooster Bloemhof te Wittewierum*, ed. by H. P. H. Jansen and A. Janse (Hilversum: Verloren, 1991).

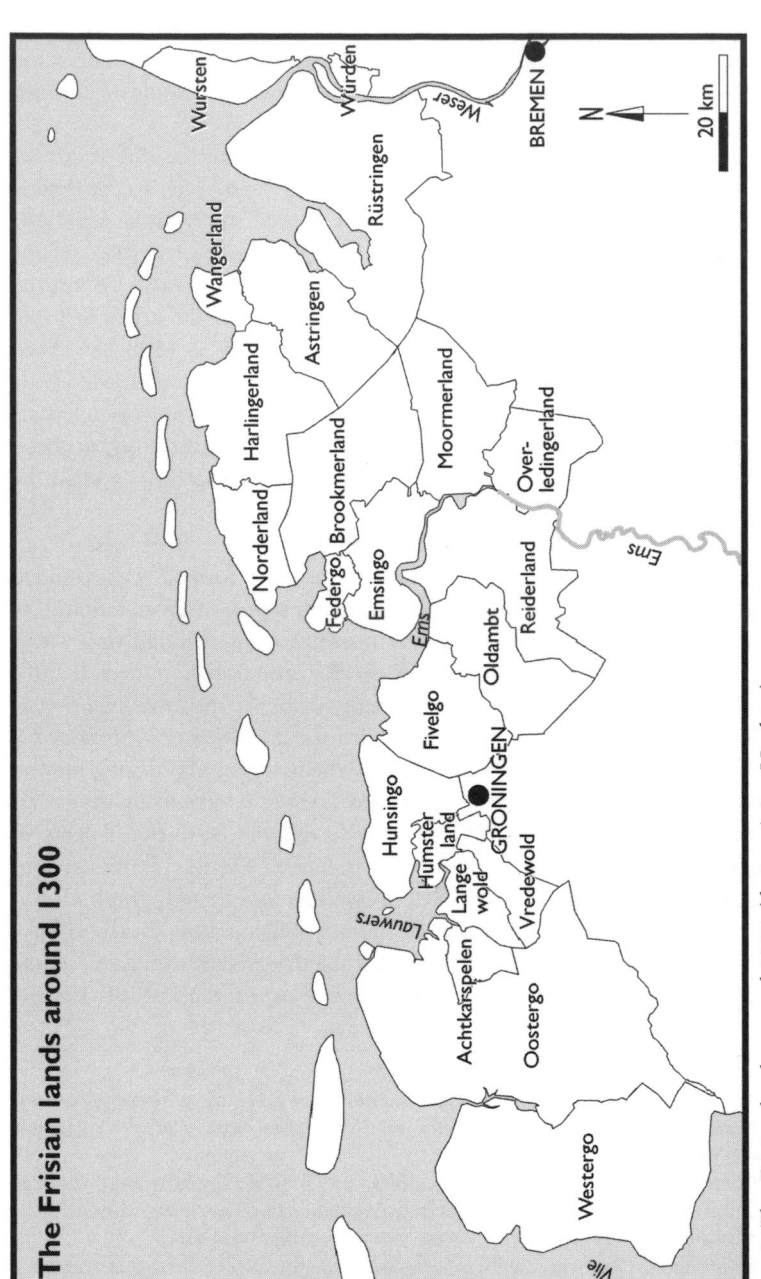

Map 1: The Frisian lands around 1300 (design Arjen Versloot).

tion, in all likelihood because they were kept outside the abbey when flames consumed its library in the sixteenth century. Such dramatic losses notwithstanding, it is my intention to demonstrate that despite their geographically and politically marginal position and despite Vries's claim that literacy had barely touched Frisia before 1300, products of pragmatic literacy in the Frisian lands from around 1300 reveal an active participation in international diplomatic fashions and scribal customs. I will base my arguments on *arengas* and scribal verse.

Arengas *and the world outside*

One of the most important items of pragmatic literacy is the charter, 'a legal deed, written as a separate text which by itself may serve as evidence of the right or grant it contains';[7] for the Frisian context I would like to add to this definition that many charters serve as evidence of peace agreements concluded. Initially, charters and writs were issued only by the highest secular and ecclesiastical authorities, such as kings and counts, popes and bishops.[8] The mere position of these dignitaries at the top of society inspired the necessary authority into these judicial documents. Things were different, though, for issuers of charters who occupied positions of lesser status. Especially when important decisions were concerned, the issuers felt obliged to declare in an introductory statement why the judgment that followed was put down in writing.[9] Usually such a statement, called an *arenga* or preamble (or proem), expresses a general truism, related above all to religion, but also to law and the human condition. In their generalisations, such statements resemble proverbs and maxims. A reason that is often adduced to justify the recording of a judicial agreement is the *fragilitas* of human *memoria*,[10] a striking example of which is provided by Frederic, abbot of the Benedictine monastery of St Juliana in Rottum (Hunsingo), after he had successfully arbitrated in a conflict that

---

[7] J. W. J. Burgers, 'Trust in Writing: Charters in the Twelfth-Century County of Holland', in *Strategies of Writing. Studies on Text and Trust in the Middle Ages*, ed. by Petra Schulte and others (Turnhout: Brepols, 2008), pp. 111–31 (p. 111).

[8] For a recent survey of scholarship on charters, see *Problems and Possibilities of Early Medieval Charters*, ed. by Jonathan Jarrett and Allen S. McKinley (Turnhout: Brepols, 2013).

[9] Heinrich Fichtenau, *Arenga. Spätantike und Mittelalter im Spiegel von Urkundenformeln* (Graz and Cologne: Böhlaus, 1957), pp. 131–35.

[10] Fichtenau, pp. 125–28.

took place in 1254. No fewer than four times in this pious *arenga* does
Frederic use a term that is connected to writing:

> Cum testante <u>Scriptura</u> labilis sit hominis scientia et instabile sit cor
> hominis, pene omnia dicta et facta ad hoc precipue et maxime redi-
> gantur in <u>scripto</u>, ut ea postmodum a memoria hominum elabi non
> contingat, nec aliquorum improbitate vel malicia prohibente <u>scripto</u> ea
> possint eciam successu temporis violari, universis hoc <u>scripto</u> declar-
> amus et innotescimus, quod [...].[11]

> [Because, according to the testimony of Scripture, man's knowledge
> is erratic and man's heart unstable, almost everything that has been
> said and done in this case must be put down in writing, especially
> and particularly, so that it does not happen that these things escape
> the memory of men afterwards and because the written word may
> prevent that through the degeneration or malice of others (the agree-
> ment) might be violated in the passing of time, (therefore) we declare
> with this document to all and make known that (...).]

Just as witness goes forth from Scripture (*Scriptura*), thus following Frederic's train of thought, witness emanates from the present writ (*scripto*).
The charter therefore especially aims at guaranteeing the validity of the
outcome of the arbitration for the future, now that the problem has been
solved. What Frederic has so eloquently formulated is in reality a skilful
assemblage of words and phrases which he had found elsewhere or which
inspired him to create a variant: 'testante Scriptura' is a set collocation;[12]
'labilis sit hominis scientia' is found in almost similar words in other
charters;[13] 'dicta et facta' is another set phrase,[14] as is 'pr(a)ecipue et

---

[11] P. J. Blok and others, *Oorkondenboek van Groningen en Drenthe*, 2 vols
(Groningen: Wolters, 1896–1899) (henceforth *OGD*), no. 120 (1254). Unless
otherwise noted, all translations are mine.

[12] The phrase yields dozens of hits in the digital *Library of Latin Texts – Series
A*. Brepolis (Turnhout: Brepols, 2014). Authors using the phrase include Adso of
Montier-en-Der (d. 992), Peter Damian (c. 1007–1072/3), Peter the Venerable
(c. 1092–1156) and Aelred of Rievaulx (1110–1167).

[13] See 'Cum humana memoria labilis sit', e.g., *Digitaal Oorkondenboek Noord-
Brabant*, ed. by Geertrui Van Singhel, ONB II, no. 1034 (August 1260) <http://
www.donb.nl/> [accessed 17 December 2014]; Thomas a Kempis (c. 1380–1471),
Doctrinale iuvenum, iv. I: 'cor hominis est instabile et memoria multum vaga et
labilis' (*Library of Latin Texts – Series A*).

[14] For example, Mary Carruthers, *The Book of Memory. A Study of Memory in
Medieval Culture*, 2nd edn (Cambridge: Cambridge University Press, 2008), 9–10.

maxime'. In other words, Frederic was well attuned to the international genre of diplomatic.

An introduction similar to that of Abbot Frederic was used by Thiade and Ludolf, parish priests of Fransum and Wiewerd, two villages in the district of Fivelgo, respectively:[15]

> Quoniam secundum Boetium de Consolatione Philosophiae cor humanum inter omnia mobilia mobilius fere dignoscitur et ideo naturaliter obliviosum, idcirco solemniter acta necesse est literarum caractere roborari et confirmari.
>
> [Because, according to Boethius' *Consolation of Philosophy*, the human heart is commonly known to be the most mobile of mobile things and is hence by nature forgetful, it is therefore on this account necessary for the agreement to be corroborated and confirmed in the form of a written document.]

In contrast to the previous charter, in which Frederic appeals to the divine authority of the Bible – the Writ *par excellence* – here the late-antique author Boethius is invoked for authority, something which is very unusual in *arengas*.[16] The appeal becomes even more curious once we realise, at least insofar as I have been able to ascertain, and contrary to what the two priests wanted the recipients of the charter to believe, that Boethius never wrote such a thing in his *Consolation*. Indeed, the appeal to Boethius would have offered a fine opportunity for calling Thiade and Ludolf's bluff and they would have admitted their mistake: *cor omni mobile mobilius* was a phrase coined by or at least attributed to St Bernard of Clairvaux.[17] By quoting an authority, even though the attribution is erroneous, the drafters demonstrate, like Frederic, that such *arengas* were rarely original compositions, but were often pieced together from various sources.

My last example of an *arenga* is taken from an agreement that was concluded after years of violent clashes between representatives of Emsingo and Brokmerland around 1250 – the document itself does not mention a date but emphasises the necessity of written documentation. In a convoluted sentence to which there seems to come no conclusion, the reasons are given for why the pact is to be recorded in writing: man's sinfulness

---

[15] *OGD*, no. 225 (1306).

[16] I owe this information to Jan Burgers.

[17] Bernardus Claraevallensis (Incertus), *Meditationes de humanae conditione*, cap. ix 'De instabilitate cordis humani', *PL* 184 499B, and *De interiori domo*, cap. xiii 'De mobilitate cordis', *PL* 184 518C.

and his forgetfulness. At the same time, the exposition offers us a welcome insight into the way in which these two neighbouring Frisian lands were successful in restoring peace amongst themselves:

> Deficiente enim ubique iusticia, et veritate a filiis hominum diminuta, inimico generis humani instigante, qui primos parentes ad peccandum incitavit, ita ut nullus alii quod suum esset tribuet nichilominus solet provocare, quare igitur placuit judicibus utriusque terre in unum convenientibus constitutiones conscribere, quibus iusticia et pax propagetur et iniusticia eliminetur, statutis ad hoc ex utraque terra sex judicibus, Emboni placitatori et suis sociis et Onnoni Bettamonna et suis sociis, qui hiis negociis interessent ad hoc statuimus; hii vero has constitutiones, que hic infra habentur, conscribere decrevere, ne aliquorum temporum labente curriculo ab humana evanescerent memoria.[18]

> [Since justice is defective everywhere and truth diminished by the children of men at the instigation of the enemy of the human race, who incited our first parents to sin and is still wont to provoke that nobody adjudges to another one what is his, for this reason it has pleased judges from both lands, having come together, to write down statutes, through which justice and peace may be promoted and injustice annulled, six judges from either land have been appointed, (viz.) Embo the arbiter with his men and Onno of the Bettamen with his men, whom, to this end, we have appointed to take part in these matters; and they have decided to write down the settlements which are contained herein below, lest with the wavering course of whatever time they vanish from human memory.]

The opening words are hardly original: 'Deficiente enim ubique iusticia' goes back all the way to Pope Leo I (c. 400–461);[19] 'veritate a filiis hominum diminuta' is quoted from Ps 11.1; the phrase 'inimico generis humani instigante' finds its origin in Pope Gregory IX's *Liber Extra*, a collection of decretals edited by Raymond of Pennaforte and issued in 1234.[20] The *arenga* also closes with borrowed words: 'temporum labente curriculo' is

---

[18] Wybren Jan Buma, *Die Brokmer Rechtshandschriften*, Oudfriesche Taal- en Rechtsbronnen, 5 (The Hague: Nijhoff, 1949), p. 139.

[19] Leo Magnus, *Sermo 33*, *PL* 54 240C.

[20] *Corpus iuris canonici*. Pars I. *Decretum magistri Gratiani*. Pars II. *Decretalium collectiones*, ed. by Emil Friedberg and Emil L. Richter (Leipzig: Tauchniz, 1879–1881), X (= *Liber extra*) .5.6.8, but also found in many other charters.

a set phrase,[21] as is 'ab humana evanescerent memoria'.[22] After this *tour de force*, the drafters of the charter come down to earth and proceed to fill four leaves with all kinds of stipulations for the payment of *wergild* and the compensation of misdeeds and injuries – *terra cognita* for the Frisians –, to conclude this listing abruptly with a call for approval that is derived from the liturgy: 'Amen dicant omnia' [Let all things/creatures say 'amen'].[23] In this way, by beginning the *arenga* with calling to mind human sinfulness and by ending with a liturgical invitation, the material content of the pact is placed within an elevated, devotional setting, a tactical move in which we may unquestionably recognise the hand of a diplomatically oriented clergyman. His learning is revealed by his use of no fewer than six phrases and collocations that he found elsewhere – assuming that he did not borrow the *arenga* in its entirety.

Sometimes we find a phrase at the end of a charter which elsewhere is used in the *arenga*. For example, an agreement that recorded the reconciliation between the land of Fivelgo and the city of Groningen in 1258 after a period of hostilities has the following conclusion:

> Ne autem que geruntur in tempore labantur cum tempore, decretum est hanc formam pactorum singulis annis Dominica 'Vocem jocunditatis' sollempniter recitari. Pax servetur, pacta custodiantur.[24]

---

[21] Thus, for example, Sulpicius Severus, *Dialogus* I.xix, but also in thirteenth-century charters ranging from Hungary to Prussia, from France to England, and in chronicles and sanctorales, as a quick search on the internet will reveal, including William Stubbs, *Select Charters and Other Illustrations of English Constitutional History*, 2nd edn (Oxford: Clarendon Press, 1877), p. 132, l. 6 (1179); *Codex diplomaticus Prussicus. Urkunden-Sammlung zur älteren Geschichte Preussens*, ed. by Johannes Voight, 6 vols (Königsberg: Bornträger, 1842), II, p. 29, l. 11 (1292); Godfrid E. Friess, 'Geschichte des einigsten Collegiat-Stiftes Ardagger in Nieder-Oesterreich', *Archiv für österreichische Geschichte*, 46 (1871), 419–561, no. VIII (472, l. 3) (1198).

[22] For example, *Oorkondenboek van het Sticht Utrecht tot 1301*, ed. Samuel Muller and A. C. Bouman, 5 vols (Utrecht: Oosthoek, 1920–1959), IV, no. 2027, p. 259, ll. 2: 'ne ab humana evanescant memoria' (1280); *Hamburgisches Urkundenbuch*, ed. by J. M. Lappenberg and others (Hamburg: Pethers and others, 1842), I, no. 786, ll. 3 (1280).

[23] See Brian Møller Jensen, '*Beata Maria semper virgo* in Piacenza, Biblioteca Capitolare c. 65', in *Liturgy and the Arts in the Middle Ages: Studies in Honour of C. Clifford Flannigan*, ed. by Eva L. Lillie and Nils Holger Petersen (Copenhagen: Viborg Press, 1996), pp. 134–67 (p. 147, n. 42).

[24] *OGD*, no. 127.

[However, lest what is done in time should decay with time, it has been decreed that the text of this treaty will solemnly be recited each year on the fifth Sunday after Easter. May peace be preserved and pacts be respected.]

The *topos* of the passing time that causes oblivion and hence requires an act of recording has been expanded here with the call for an annually returning ritual intended to keep the contents of the agreement vivid by reading them aloud on Rogation Sunday.[25] Where this reading performance had to take place – in only one or in several places at the same time – and in whose presence is left unmentioned. Nor is it stated that the text has to be read in Latin or in the mother tongue, although I assume the latter to have been the case. The beginning of the *eschatol*, or concluding remark, and the call for peace and respect for agreements betray the hand of someone who must have been well at home in the world of charters and pacts, for the phrase 'que geruntur in tempore labantur cum tempore' circulated widely, with minor variations, throughout Europe, in *arengas*.[26] Moreover, the concluding wish for peace and respect for pacts is a quotation lifted verbatim from the first chapter on pacts in Pope Gregory IX's *Liber extra*.[27]

Such wonderful *arengas* and *eschatols* as have been foregrounded above were clearly not invented by the issuers on the spot, hence their compo-

---

[25] On Rogation Sunday people would come to church to ask for God's blessings for the newly sown crops and for a bountiful harvest in the autumn. The words 'Vocem jocunditatis' (Isaiah 48.20) refer to the opening words of the Introit for the service. Usually prayers were said (or sung) as the clergy and the parishioners processed around the boundary lines of the parish.

[26] For example: '*Que geruntur in tempore, ne labantur cum tempore*, poni solent in lingua testium et scripture perhennari', *Westfälischen Urkundenbuch. Vol. 7: Die Urkunden des kölnischen Westfalens vom Jahre 1200–1300*, ed. by Staatsarchiv Münster (Münster: Regensberg, 1908), no. 291 (p. 122) (1226; Westphalia); '*Ne labantur cum tempore, que geruntur in tempore*, perennari solent litteris ac testibus roborari', *Latvijas vēstures avoti*, ed. by A. Švābe (Rīga Latvijas Vēstures institūta apgādiens, 1940), no. 242 (1241; Latvia) <http://www.historia.lv/dokumenti/ligums-starp-samsalas-un-vikas-biskapu-heinrihu-un-livonijas-ordena-mestru-andreju-no> [accessed 23 January 2015]; '*Ne ea que geruntur in tempore simul labantur cum tempore* provida hominum sagatitas adinvenit, ut rerum gestarum series redigatur inscriptis pro rei memoria sempiterna'. This last example, from 1336, is to be found in the National Archives of Hungary, Budapest, *Collectio Antemohacsiana*, signature Dl.2999. I owe these details to Dr Zsolt Hunyadi, University of Szeged. See also <http://www.staff.u-szeged.hu/~capitul/kookl.htm> [accessed 23 January 2015].

[27] *Corpus iuris canonici*, ed. by Friedberg and Richter, X.1.35.1.

sition must have been learned at school or during some advanced stage of education. It is on record that the village of Farnsum, where Thiade was parish priest, had a parish school as early as the beginning of the thirteenth century,[28] and the inappropriate appeal to it notwithstanding, Boethius' book on the consolation of philosophy was a set text in the school curriculum. For the sermons of St Bernard, perhaps a monastic environment has to be envisaged. Remarkably, the latest additions to canon law, collected in the *Liber extra* in 1234, appear to have spread even to the remotest villages in Frisia. Moreover, within twenty years, this source of canon law was not only read in Frisia but its contents proved also to have been internalised and applied in practice. Alternatively, such phrases as 'Pax servetur, pacta custodiantur' had been copied and adapted from recent charters which the composers had seen or perhaps taken from canonist handbooks or maybe even from handbooks designed for the art of composition of letters and charters, the so-called *artes dictamini* and *artes notoriae*.[29] In any case, *arengas* in which the desirability of recording in writing with an eye to the passing of time and subsequent oblivion is emphasised, are found more frequently in Frisia around 1300 than just in the instances that I have discussed above.[30]

The oldest surviving charter from Frisia west of the River Lauwers, drafted in 1329, in which the vernacular is used, begins with an impressive *arenga* and a protocol in Latin and is also concluded by a Latin *eschatol*. The issuers of this charter justify their use of the Frisian vernacular with an appeal to a better understanding of its contents.[31] The opening of this charter is as follows:

> Cum ob hominum labilem memoriam et caducam, quae nube oblivionis de facili obfuscatur, ac humanae conditionis inconstantiam, quam

---

[28] Bremmer, '*Hir is eskriven*', p. 42.

[29] Stephen M. Wight, *Medieval Diplomatic and the 'Ars dictandi'*. <http://scrineum.unipv.it/wight/wight.htm> [accessed May 2014].

[30] For example, *OGD*, no. 168 (1285; arbitration between Aduard abbey and the inhabitants of Oosterwold, drafted by Egbert, prefect of the city of Groningen, and Snelger of Scharmer), nos. 210 (1313), 254 (1317) and 255 (1317; the same *arenga* as no. 254, both composed by Hayco, abbot of Bloemhof), nos. 258 (1318), 259 (1318) and 266 (1320).

[31] See Bert Looper, '"Ta in better begryp". Latyn en folkstaal yn de oarkonden út de Fryske lannen tusken Fly en Wezer, 1200–1400', *It Beaken*, 46 (1984), 1–14. On the Latinisation of the personal names and place-names in this charter, see H. T. J. Miedema, 'Namen en latinizering in de eerste Oudfriese oorkonde', *Naamkunde*, 8 (1976), 68–86.

ab adolescentia ad dissentiendum, contradicendum, et ad malum constat esse pronam, nonnulli actus hominum legitimi in dissensionis et dissidentiae materiam et actiones deveniunt, et in antea verisimiliter valeant devenire: Ea propter nos Thitardus Presbyter [...].[32]

[Because of man's unstable and transitory memory, which is obscured the more easily by a cloud of oblivion, and because of the inconstancy of the human condition, which from adolescence is known to be prone to dissent, contradiction and evil, some legal acts of men in conflicts turn to a matter of dissension and dissidence and (violent) actions, and may most likely turn to the previous situation. For this reason we, Thithard the priest (...).]

Here too we are dealing with an *arenga* that is patched together from phrases that are likewise found in charters issued far away from Frisia: the phrase 'ob hominum labilem memoriam et caducam' is also recorded elsewhere in *arengas*;[33] the 'cloud of oblivion' proves to be popular;[34] while the tendency of adolescents to disagree and contradict and to be prone to evil is also encountered in Hungarian and Westphalian charters.[35]

In conclusion, then, what my analysis of a limited sample of *arengas* from the earliest Frisian charters composed in Latin has brought to light is that they contain not just the motives for recording the results of transactions between contesting parties. These motives were also couched in a phraseology that reflects the fashion and style found elsewhere in (near-) contemporary charters from all over Latinate Europe. Apparently, the composers of these Frisian charters, even though they lived in a geographi-

---

[32] *Oudfriesche Oorkonden*, ed. Pieter Sipma, 3 vols, Oudfriesche Taal- en Rechtsbronnen, 1–3 (The Hague: Nijhoff, 1927), I.1, p. 1.

[33] For instance, 'propter labilem memoriam hominum et caducam', *Svenskt diplomatarium*, ed. by J. G. Liljegren (Stockholm: Norstedt, 1829), vol. I, 35, no. 655, l. 3 (1276); *Codex diplomaticus et epistolaris regni Bohemiae*, ed. by Gustav Friedrich and Zdeněk Kristen (Prague: Sumptibus Comitiorum Regni Bohemiae, 1981), V/2, p. 489.

[34] For example, 'et ne etiam oblivionis nube obfuscentur', *Westfälisches Urkundenbuch*. Vol. 7: *Die Urkunden des kölnischen Westfalens vom J. 1200–1300*, ed. by T. Ilgen (Münster: Regenberg, 1901), no. 340 (1230?).

[35] For example, 'Verum quoniam omnis etas ab adolescentia in malum prona est et ad dissentiendum natura proclivis', *Pannonhalmi Bencés Főapátság Levéltára*, sign. 1210 <http://www.mom-ca.uni-koeln.de/mom/HU-PBFL/PannHOSB/1210/charter> [accessed 17 December 2014] (1210; Pannonhalma Abbey); *Osnabrücker Urkundenbuch. Die Urkunden der Jahren 1201–1250*, ed. by Friedrich Philippe and Max Bär, 8 vols (Osnabrück: Historischer Verein zu Osnabrück, 1896), II, pp. 45 (1215) and 49 (1221).

cally remote place, were not working in isolation. On the contrary, they participated in a network that shared the fruits of an increasingly flourishing production of diplomatic documents. These Frisian charters thus testify to a higher degree of pragmatic literacy in Frisia around 1300 than has hitherto been assumed.

There is an additional side to these *arengas*. They could have been copied verbatim from charters that had passed the scribes' eyes or, perhaps, from a collection of examples. The available evidence suggests, however, that the scribes did not slavishly copy and paste but rather creatively used phrases and collocations to make new *arengas*, perhaps to demonstrate to the recipients of the charter that they knew the tricks of the trade. If this suggestion is true, the corollary would be that the recipients in their turn were familiar with the convention and expected a well-crafted *arenga* for their document, another indication of a certain degree of literacy.

Scribes reveal themselves

The conclusion that literates in Frisia around 1300 participated in a widespread European set of interconnections can be further corroborated when we take the scribes of vernacular manuscripts into consideration. Scribes of the Old Frisian legal miscellanies – practically the only genre in which the Frisians engaged – it is true, only rarely reveal their identities, but curiously they appear less modest in this respect in the oldest such manuscripts than in later ones. We have about six manuscripts that were written around 1300 or shortly thereafter. They are the First Rüstring Manuscript (Oldenburg, Niedersächsisches Staatsarchiv, MS Bestand 24–1, Ab. Nr. 1; *c*.1300), the Second Rüstring Manuscript (Hanover, Niedersächsische Landesbibliothek, MS Sign. XXII, 1431; dated 1327), the First Brokmer Manuscript (Oldenburg, Niedersächsisches Staatsarchiv, MS Bestand 24–1, Ab. Nr. 3; after 1276 but before *c*.1300), the Second Brokmer Manuscript (Hanover, Niedersächsische Landesbibliothek, MS Sign. XXII, 1423; completed 1345), the First Hunsingo Manuscript (Leeuwarden, Tresoar, MS R2; *c*.1325–1350) and the Second Hunsingo Manuscript (Leeuwarden, Tresoar, MS R 3; *c*.1325–1350. Of the last two manuscripts the contents of the latter are identical with those of the former, but presented in a different order).[36]

---

[36] Rolf H. Bremmer Jr, *Introduction to Old Frisian. History, Grammar, Reader, Glossary* (Amsterdam and Philadelphia: Benjamins, 2009), §14; see Thomas S. B. Johnston, 'The Old Frisian Law Manuscripts and Law Texts', in *Handbuch des*

Five out of these six legal manuscripts conclude with a final formula, called a colophon, in which the scribe mentions the place or the date of the copy (or both, for that matter).[37] Moreover, three of them also mention the name of the scribe in a line of verse. A closer look at these colophons might therefore yield further insights into their significance.

The most important text in the two Brokmer manuscripts is the thirteenth-century *Borkmonna bref* or 'Charter of the Brookmen (i.e. marsh dwellers)', which contains the legal dos and don'ts for the inhabitants of Brokmerland, a district east of Emsingo that had recently been reclaimed from extensive marshlands. In the Second Brokmer Manuscript, this legal manifesto is concluded with a scribal notification that: 'Hec littera scripta est per manus Osbrondi anno domini M°. C°.C°.C°. XL°.V°.'[38] [This letter (i.e. charter) has been written by the hand of Osbrond, AD 1345.] 'Per manus X(+genitive)' is a common formula by which scribes reveal their identity, but a scribe named Osbrond does not appear in the largest collection of medieval colophons, compiled by the Benedictine monks of Bouveret Abbey, Switzerland.[39] The First Brokmer Manuscript, which on palaeographical evidence can be dated to almost fifty years earlier than the Second, concludes with a description of the normative nature of the text copied, preceded and followed by a line of verse:

> Qui scripsit valeat et longo tempore vivat.
> Hec est littera Brocmannorum per quam omnes cause siue excessus eorum corriguntur et iudicantur.
> Qui scripsit scripta, sua dextera sit benedicta. [40]

> [May he who copied this be well and live for a long time. This is the legal manifest of the Brookmen, according to which all their legal cases and trespasses should be rectified and judged. May the right hand of him who copied this writing be blessed.]

The rhyming lines consist of leonine verse, i.e. the last word of the line rhymes with the last word before the caesura. Would the anonymous scribe have been the inspired inventor of these lines? Even though his

---

Friesischen/Handbook of Frisian Studies, ed. by Horst H. Munske (Tübingen: Niemeyer, 2001), §54.

[37] Lucien Reynhout, *Formules latines de colophons*. I: *Texte*. II. *Annexes* (Turnhout: Brepols, 2006), I, p. 20.

[38] Buma, *Die Brokmer Rechtshandschriften*, p. 130.

[39] *Colophons*.

[40] Buma, *Die Brokmer Rechtshandschriften*, p. 129.

first line is listed only once by the Benedictines of Bouveret, in a Bavarian manuscript, the suggestion seems unlikely to me in view of the peripheral position of Frisia. The scribe's second rhyming line, however, with a popular variant in which *dextera* is replaced by *manus*, was more widely spread.[41]

The First Rüstring Manuscript is even concluded by a four-line poem in leonine verse:

> Explicit expliceat, ludere scriptor eat.
> Est liber hic scriptus, qui scripsit sit benedictus.
> Qui me scribebat, Ricmarus nomen habebat.
> Non videat Christum, qui librum subtrahat istum.[42]

> [It is finished and let it be finished, let the writer go and play. This book here is written, may he who copied it be blessed. The one who wrote me, was called Ricmar. May he who steals this book not see Christ.]

Having heaved the familiar sigh of relief in line one, and pronounced a blessing for himself for his job in the second line, the scribe proceeds to reveal his name. He finishes his composite poem with the opposite of a blessing by uttering a heartfelt curse for the one who dares steal the product of his strenuous labour.[43] Not to see Christ – such a horrible fate is possible only for those who will reside in hell, the proper place for book thieves.

The scribe of the Second Rüstring Manuscript, on the other hand, concludes with a kind metrical wish both for the reader and himself and leaves it at that. A precise date for the completion of his scribal activity follows, but he refrains from revealing his name:

> Sit tibi tale vale,
> Michimet desidero quale.
> Anno Domini MCCXVIJ in die Thome apostoli. (R2 VIII.15)[44]

---

[41] For the two verses, see respectively *Colophons*, no. 23235, only one occurrence (twelfth century, Bamberg) and *Colophons*, nos. 23206–24, ca. 10 occurrences, all later than thirteenth century.

[42] Buma, *De Eerste Riustringer Codex*, p. 134.

[43] *Colophons*, no. 20393, 42x, between twelfth and fifteenth centuries; *Colophons*, no. 20751, 8x, twelfth–fourteenth century; *Colophons*, no. 23093–94 (popular with names of scribe); *Colophons*, no. 22635–39, common eleventh to fourteenth century.

[44] Wybren Jan Buma, *De Tweede Rüstringer Handschrift* (The Hague: Nijhoff, 1954), p. 44.

[May things go as well for you as I wish them for myself. In the year of Our Lord 1327, on the day of the Apostle Thomas (21 December).]

Colophons does not list this verse amongst its many thousands, so that for once it would seem that we are dealing with a Frisian scribe who dared compose his own rhyming colophon lines instead of copying or adapting them from some exemplar.

The scribe of the First Hunsingo Manuscript, finally, needed only one line to eternalise his name. Because he had the space to do so, he seized the opportunity to write the colophon in big letters, telling us with the stock formula 'Acta sunt hec' that the text he had just finished copying was recorded in 1252 in the presence of three abbots and the most important men of Hunsingo. At the same time he managed to upgrade the initial letter Q of the popular name-revealing rhyme[45] by ornamenting it with what might have been intended as a self-portrait:

Qui me scribebat, Elbertus nomen habebat.[46]

[He who copied me, was called Elbert.]

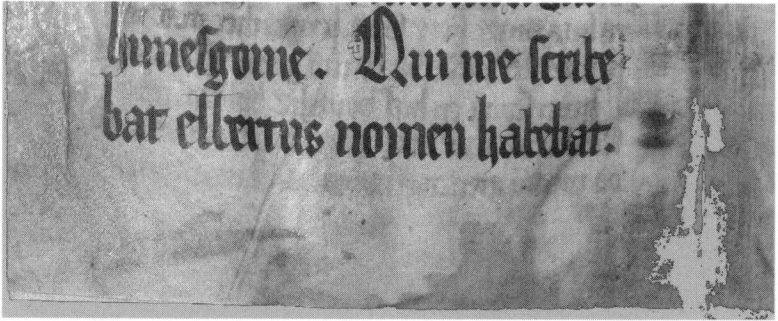

Figure 1: Leeuwarden, Tresoar, MS R2, p. 135 (detail, enlarged).

Even though the scribes of the five manuscripts under discussion were active in different parts of Frisia, the Latin colophon verses of four of them clearly suggest that they were not working in a culturally isolated

---

[45] For example, *Colophons*, nos. 8431, 8433, 8436, 8439, 8441.
[46] Jelle Hoekstra, *De Eerste en de Tweede Hunsingo Codex* (The Hague: Nijhoff, 1950), p. 172.

environment at the edge of Europe. One by one, the scribes appear to be standing with both their feet in the contemporary fashions of the international writing culture. Originality was not their aim, for they had faithfully copied their verse lines from other documents, only making such adaptations as was sometimes required, like substituting the names of other scribes for their own. Ricmar, who completed the First Rüstring Manuscript, takes the laurels with his four-line poem. Only for the two-line verse that finishes the Second Rüstring Manuscript have I been unable so far to find any parallels, which would suggest that, for once, a Frisian scribe was original. However, given the borrowed nature of the lines of his Frisian colleagues, I assume that these lines will be derivative, too, but for some reason or other they have not yet been recorded in any collection such as that of the Swiss Benedictines. Despite their massive work, the Swiss monks must have missed many colophon verses, if only because they did not include the Frisian manuscripts into their corpus. Ricmar, Elbert, Osbrond and the anonymous scribe of the First Brokmer Manuscript must have set their eyes on quite a number of manuscripts to be able to write their rhymes or to make up new poems out of existing lines.

None of the abovementioned scribes explicitly mentions in his colophon whether he is a layman or a clergyman. This is the case, however, for the anonymous scribe of a version of the two most important pan-Frisian law codes, the *Seventeen Statutes* and the *Twenty-Four Landlaws*, as found in the First and the Second Hunsingo Manuscripts.[47] This scribe can boast of an innovation, for he was the first Frisian, for all we know, to have composed a vernacular colophon rhyme. The awkwardly superfluous syllables in the second line show the man to be still in an experimental phase, but the desire to end his copying work with a rhyme must have been stronger than an awareness of metric inadequacy on his part:

Ut sendta riucht
and ik bem self twera en Godes kniucht.[48]

[Finished are the laws, and I myself am truly a servant of God.]

A 'servant of God' (*famulus* or *servus Dei*) – this is a well-known and popular term for a clergyman. Whether a monk or a secular priest, by the

---

[47] These two early to mid fourteenth century manuscripts were copied by the same scribe and have the same contents, though presented in a different order of sequence.
[48] Hoekstra, *De Eerste en Tweede Hunsingo Codex*, p. 56.

first half of the fourteenth century the growing international fashion of writing colophon verse had affected Frisian scribes in such a way that they even started applying it in the vernacular.

In conclusion, then, my analysis of a select number of *arengas* in charters and of the colophon verses of five vernacular manuscripts has shown that Frisian scribes are fully in touch with the international conventions of the period. Their active participation gives support to the hypothesis that pragmatic literacy in (a number of) Frisian lands around 1300 had advanced further than has hitherto been realised. The outcome is the more surprising in view of the limited handwritten material that survives from this medieval European borderland and shows that in this respect at least the formal aspect of these documents counts as much as does their number.

Writing the Germanic Languages: The Early History of the Digraphs <th>, <ch> and <uu>

ANNINA SEILER

THIS PAPER TRACES the origin and early history of the three digraphs <th>, <ch> and <uu> in early Old English and in some of the Continental Germanic languages.[1] Today, the digraphs form part of the graphemic systems of various European languages. Their creation and application in the Early Middle Ages hence represents an important graphemic innovation, which has permanently solved some of the problems arising in the process of creating orthographic systems for the vernacular languages with the Latin alphabet – despite the fact that the transmission of the digraphs from the Early Middle Ages to the Modern Era did not proceed in a straightforward line. By way of an introduction, I will briefly describe the distribution and use of the three digraphs in the orthographies of modern European languages, which, to some extent, still reflect the areas in which the digraphs were used in the Early Middle Ages. I will then provide a detailed account of their use in Old English of the eighth century. It has been suggested that Irish influence is responsible for the use of <th> for a dental fricative and of <ch> for a palatal/velar fricative in Old English. While Irish influence should certainly not be underestimated, there is stronger evidence, as I argue, for attributing the origin of the digraphs to the Merovingian Franks or, more precisely, to the spellings used for Frankish names in Latin charters. The Merovingian hypothesis is strengthened by the fact that the same graphs were also adopted into Old High German writing. The adoption of the digraphs, however, should not be envisaged as a process of straightforward borrowing, but rather as an independent reinterpretation and extension based on a perception of the graphs as essentially Latin spellings. Thus, the paper highlights the

---

[1] I would like to express my sincere thanks to the editors of this volume for their efforts to produce this book, to the anonymous reader for many excellent suggestions on an early draft of this paper, and to Viviane Bergmaier, Roland Zingg and Ludwig Rübekeil for their help with tricky details concerning Latin, history and etymology, respectively. All mistakes are of course my own.

complex relationship of the spelling systems of the early medieval vernaculars and Latin, the 'father tongue' of the Middle Ages. On a theoretical
level, it yields some insights into the general mechanisms of graphemic
change in non-standardised *scriptae*.[2]

The digraphs <th>, <ch> and <w> form part of the writing systems
of various modern European languages. In some instances, the boundaries of their use – so-called is(orth)ographs[3] – coincide with those of
language families, but very often they do not correlate with them since
spelling traditions are influenced by historical and cultural factors rather
than linguistic ones.[4] Yet the absence or presence of certain sounds in the
phonology of a given language has an impact on the graphemic inventory
in so far as it determines the use, or non-use, of certain graphs. As a result,
the distribution of <th>, <ch> and <w> in modern orthographies reflects
the pathways of graphemic change as well as the graphemic 'need' prevalent in groups of related languages with similar phonological systems. The
use of <th> for native vocabulary is concentrated in the British Isles: the
digraph represents an interdental fricative in English, Welsh and Jèrriais.[5]
It used to stand for the same sound in Old Irish, but today expresses [h],
the lenition of /t/, in Modern Irish and Scottish Gaelic. The digraph <ch>
is grouped into two different areas of use, a Romance type where <ch>
denotes a post-alveolar affricate [ʧ]or fricative [ʃ], which also includes

---

[2]   The term *scriptae* is defined by Kabatek as referring to 'supra-individual
orthographic conventions' and corresponds to German 'Schreibsprachen'; see
Johannes Kabatek, '*Koinés* and *scriptae*', in *The Cambridge History of the Romance
Languages II: Contexts*, ed. by Martin Maiden, John Charles Smith and Adam
Ledgeway (Cambridge: Cambridge University Press, 2013), pp. 143–86.

[3]   On the term *isograph* or *isorthograph*, see Otto Back, 'Towards a Diatopic
Approach to Orthographic Phenomena of European Languages', in *New Trends
in Graphemics and Orthography*, ed. by Gerhard Augst (Berlin: de Gruyter, 1986),
pp. 155–63.

[4]   This issue has been addressed, for example, by Herbert Penzl, 'Zur alphabetischen
Orthographie als Gegenstand der Sprachwissenschaft', in *Orthography and
Phonology*, ed. by Philip A. Luelsdorff (Amsterdam: Benjamins, 1987), pp. 225–38
(p. 325) or, more recently, by Anja Voeste, 'Die Orthographien Europas zu Beginn
der Frühen Neuzeit – ein vergleichender Blick', in *LautSchriftSprache: Beiträge zur
vergleichenden historischen Graphematik*, ed. by Elvira Glaser, Annina Seiler and
Michelle Waldispühl (Zürich: Chronos, 2011), pp. 185–95 (p. 185).

[5]   It is also used in Albanian orthography, where <th> represents a transliteration
of Greek theta, see Florian Coulmas, *The Blackwell Encyclopedia of Writing Systems*
(Oxford: Blackwell, 1999), s.v. 'Albanian writing'. Apart from that, <th> is used
for Greek loanwords in many European languages, see German *Theater*, French
théâtre.

English, and a German type with <ch> for a palatal/velar fricative [ç]/ [χ], which extends to the West Slavic languages scripted with the Latin alphabet.[6] The digraph <uu> spelled as a ligature gave rise to the character <w> and represents the latest addition to the Roman alphabet so far.[7] It is used in several West Germanic languages (English, German, Dutch etc.), in some West Slavic varieties, and in the Celtic languages Welsh, Cornish and Breton. While it started out as a representation of the bilabial approximant [w] and still stands for this sound value in most languages, it came to represent [v] in German when the sound changed from a bilabial to a labiodental fricative. The letter is nevertheless retained as a spelling for this sound since <v> for [v] appears only in foreign words. The character <w> is not used in the Romance languages with the exception of native place and personal names in some northern French dialects (e.g. in Walloon).

In the Germanic languages, the three digraphs can be traced back as far as the eighth century – to texts that were among the very first to be written in Old English and Old High German. In both languages the three digraphs express roughly the same sounds: <th> represents a dental fricative [θ] or [ð], <ch> renders a palatal/velar fricative [χ] deriving from Gmc. */h/ or from Gmc. */k/ (by the Second Consonant Shift) in Old High German, and <uu> stands for the bilabial approximant [w]. There is, however, no uninterrupted line of transmission from Old English and Old High German to the modern languages, except for <uu>/<w> in German, as has been pointed out above. The digraph <th> is no longer used in High German; it became obsolete when the dental fricative [θ] changed to a stop [d] and disappeared quickly. The digraph <ch>, on the other hand, has been used throughout for the representation of a palatal/ velar obstruent, but there is considerable variation concerning the exact sound position it was employed to represent. The current use of <ch> in

---

6   The digraph <ch> represents the palatal fricative [ʃ] or affricate [ʧ] in French, Portuguese and Spanish. In Italian and Rumanian, on the other hand, <ch> stands for [k] before palatal vowels, e.g. Ital. *chiave* 'key'; see Heinrich Lausberg, *Romanische Sprachwissenschaft, I: Einleitung und Vokalismus*, Sammlung Göschen vol. 128/128a, 3rd edn (Berlin: de Gruyter, 1969), p. 24. In English, <ch> representing the affricate [ʧ] occurs in native words (e.g. *chin, chill*) or in early borrowings from French (*charter, Charles*); <ch> representing [ʃ] appears in more recent borrowings from French (*champagne, Charlotte*); in words of ultimately Greek origin, <ch> stands for [k] as in *chorus, archive*. See Donald George Scragg, *A History of English Spelling* (Manchester: Manchester University Press, 1974), p. 45, n. 2.

7   See Coulmas, s.v. 'Roman alphabet', 'W, w'.

words like *Eiche* 'oak' (< **aik-*), *Nacht* 'night' (< **naht-*) roughly dates to the Middle High German period.[8]

In Old English, the digraphs <uu> and <th> were only used in some very early sources and were replaced by the runic characters *wyn* <ƿ> and *thorn* <þ>, or the letter *eth* (called *that* in Anglo-Saxon sources) <ð>, which was created from an insular, round-backed shape of the letter *d* with a diacritic dash through the stem. When the new characters came to be used, the digraphs went underground, in a manner of speaking, rather than dying out; throughout the Old English period, they remained in use for Anglo-Saxon names in Anglo-Latin texts and it is from there that they resurfaced after the Norman Conquest of England.[9] The digraph <ch> was used to represent a velar fricative only for a very short period of time; in later Old English, together with <k>, it occurs as a variant spelling of <c> to distinguish velar [k] from palatalised [ċ]. Yet it was only properly established in the spelling system during the Middle English period and then with a different sound value [ʧ]. The general assumption is that the new use of <ch> represents a spelling tradition borrowed from French. Dietz, however, has argued that the use of <ch> for [ʧ] in Middle English is based on a functional reinterpretation of the Anglo-Latin digraph, which is later paralleled in French.[10] The modern use of <ch> in English consequently may well be a direct continuation of the use of the digraph from early Old English.

---

[8] See Wilhelm Braune, and Ingo Reiffenstein, *Althochdeutsche Grammatik I: Laut- und Formenlehre*, 15th edn (Tübingen: Niemeyer, 2004), §102a; Hermann Paul and others, *Mittelhochdeutsche Grammatik*, 25th edn (Tübingen: Niemeyer, 2007), at §L107–109. Most – but not all – Old High German sources use <h> or <hh> for the fricatives deriving from both Gmc. */h/ and */k/ (by the Second Consonant Shift). The graphemic change towards <ch> probably reflects the merger of the fricative allophones of both sources and the subsequent reorganisation of the palatals/velars from pre-OHG */k/ vs. */h-χ/ into OHG /k/ vs. /χ/ vs. /h/. See Annina Seiler, *The Scripting of the Germanic Languages: A Comparative Study of 'Spelling Difficulties' in Old English, Old High German and Old Saxon* (Zürich: Chronos, 2014), p. 148.

[9] See Scragg, p. 2; Michael Benskin, 'The Letters <þ> and <y> in Later Middle English, and Some Related Matters', *Journal of the Society of Archivists*, 7 (1982), 13–30 (p. 18). The same applies to <ch> for [k] in late OE/early ME texts; see Klaus Dietz, *Schreibung und Lautung im mittelalterlichen Englisch: Entwicklung und Funktion der englischen Schreibungen ch, gh, sh, th, wh und ihrer kontinentalen Entsprechungen* (Heidelberg: Winter, 2006), pp. 42, 212.

[10] Dietz, pp. 51–53; the change in the graph-sound correlation in English takes place in the twelfth century, i.e., at a time when <ch> still represents [k] in Northern French sources (p. 51).

The use of the three digraphs in Old English predates the one in Old High German by almost a century; therefore, a search for the origin of the three graphs should start there. A look at the standard handbooks of Old English reveals that Irish orthography is often cited as a model for Old English spelling practice since <th> and <ch> are used in Old Irish for similar sounds. Campbell in his *Old English Grammar* (§54–55) provides the following table as an illustration of early Old English consonant spellings:

Table 1: Campbell's account of early Old English spelling

Labials:	p	f	b	u	hu	m	
Dentals:	t	th	d	s		n	hn
Palatals/velars:	c	ch	g			n	
Glottal:		h					
Liquids:	l	hl	r	hr			

Campbell's table includes <th> and <ch> as well as digraphs for aspirated resonants (which may or may not have been bi-phonemic units), but omits <uu> in favour of the single graph <u> for /w/. According to Campbell, '[t]he model for this system was clearly the Latin one as preserved in grammatical tradition. The use of *th* and *ch* to represent voiceless spirants, respectively dental and velar (or palatal), appears, however, to have been suggested by OIr. spelling' (§55). Campbell provides the reason for this interpretation in a footnote: 'In Latin, words with *th*, *ch* seem normally to have been pronounced with *t* and *c*; *ph*, however, was equated with *f* (§57, n.3). In other words, Campbell claims that though the digraphs <th> and <ch> are based on Latin orthography, the sound value they represent in Old English is modelled on Old Irish pronunciation as it diverges from Latin. In more recent works, similar claims concerning Irish influence have been made; for example, Hogg's chapter on 'Phonology and Morphology' in the *Cambridge History of the English Language* provides a section on 'Orthography', in which he discusses the use of various early Old English graphs. With respect to <th>, he comes to the conclusion that '<th> appears to have been borrowed from Irish' (p. 77). Again this probably does not relate to the graph, which is well known in Latin orthography, but to its sound value as a dental fricative, which it did not have in Latin spelling.[11]

---

[11] Alistair Campbell, *Old English Grammar*, 2nd edn (Oxford: Clarendon Press, 1959, repr. 2003); Richard M. Hogg, 'Phonology and Morphology', in

It needs to be stressed that the use of <th> and <ch> for fricative sounds is by no means obvious – even though it might be so for speakers and writers of Modern English and German. In Latin the digraph <th> was considered an alternative of <t>, which was used in foreign, mainly Greek, words and names. The digraph was coined as a rendering of theta in Greek loanwords, which stood for an aspirated stop [t^h] in Classical times. Since Greek loanwords were quickly assimilated to Latin phonology, the aspiration was not preserved in pronunciation. The sound change from an aspirated dental stop to a fricative in Greek only took place in the post-Classical period and apparently did not affect Medieval Latin pronunciation in Western Europe. Similarly, <ch> did not represent a fricative in Latin, but was used as a variant of <c> in loanwords from Greek containing chi. There is ample evidence from Medieval Latin that <th>/<t> and <ch>/<c> were virtually considered interchangeable variants.[12]

In Old Irish sources, on the other hand, the digraphs <ch> and <th> render the voiceless fricatives /χ/ and /θ/ as, for example, in OIr. *sechitir* 'they follow', Lat. *sequuntur*, or OIr. *bráthir* 'brother', Lat. *frater*. Evidence for the sound value of the digraph <th> is provided by the fact that there is alternation of <th> with <d>, which represents [ð], i.e. lenited /d/. Furthermore, Old Norse transliterations apparently use <þ> or <ð> for Old Irish <th>, so the sounds were considered more or less equivalent.

The Cambridge History of the English Language, I: The Beginnings to 1066, ed. by Richard M. Hogg (Cambridge: Cambridge University Press, 1992), pp. 67–167. On Irish influence on Old English spelling, in particular vowels, see David L. White, 'The Case for Irish Influence in Some Odd Consonantal Spellings of Old English' (unpublished paper presented at the 3rd annual conference on Studies in the History of the English Language, 6–7 May 2004, Ann Arbor, Michigan, 2004); David L. White, *Irish Influence and the Interpretation of Old English Spelling* (unpublished thesis, University of Texas, 2000); Lisi Oliver, 'Irish Influence on Orthographic Practice in Early Kent', *NOWELE*, 33 (1998), 93–113; Marjorie Daunt, 'Old English Sound-Changes Reconsidered in Relation to Scribal Tradition and Practice', *Transactions of the Philological Society*, 38 (1939), 108–37.

[12] Anthony Harvey, 'Reading the Genetic Code of Early Medieval Celtic Orthography', in *LautSchriftSprache: Beiträge zur vergleichenden historischen Graphematik*, ed. by Elvira Glaser, Annina Seiler and Michelle Waldispühl (Zürich: Chronos, 2011), pp. 155–66 (p. 160); Maria Bonioli, *La pronuncia del Latino nelle scuole, I: dall'antichità al rinascimento* (Torino: G. Giappichelli, 1962), p. 62; Hermann Reichert, *Lexikon der Altgermanischen Namen*, ed. by Helmut Birkhan (Vienna: Verlag der österreichischen Akademie der Wissenschaften, 1987), p. xxiii; Peter Stotz, *Lautlehre: Handbuch zur Lateinischen Sprache des Mittelalters* (Munich: Beck, 1996), vol. 3, §127, 128.1; §133.

The digraphs are the regular spellings for these sounds in Old Irish.[13] Their introduction into Old Irish spelling has been investigated in detail by Anthony Harvey. Since /θ/ and /χ/ are the product of lenition of /t/ and /c/, they are morpho-phonemically related to the stops. The spelling with <th>, <ch> implies 'an insight into the synchronic structure of the language'.[14] Harvey points out that the logical spellings for the voiced fricatives would have been <bh>, <dh>, <gh>, which, however, were only used much later on. As Harvey has shown, the digraphs apparently replaced a spelling system in which the voiceless fricatives were designated by <t> and <c>. Only traces of this orthography survive, for example, in the Codex Paulinus (Würzburg, Universitätsbibliothek, MS M. p. th. f. 12) from Würzburg. Harvey assigns the introduction of <th> and <ch> as graphs for fricatives to a 'deliberate act of language-planning by some now unknown but clearly farsighted and ultimately very influential scribe'.[15]

The unexpected fricative sound values for <th> and <ch> in both early Old English and Old Irish orthography seem to suggest that there is indeed a connection between the two. This assumption is strengthened by what appears to be a general belief that, in Old English, the digraphs were more prevalent in the north of England than in the south.[16] Since Ireland played an important role in the Christianisation of the Anglo-Saxons and in introducing literacy to Anglo-Saxon England, the historical context of transmission also seems to be clear, namely the Irish mission in Northumbria. The problem with this conclusion is that Old English orthography in general and early Old English spelling in particular are areas in which little research has been undertaken. Consequently, we are still very much in the dark when it comes to the distribution and currency of certain spellings. Yet, in order to evaluate the probability of possible Irish influence, we need to know what exactly we are trying to explain.

---

[13] Rudolf Thurneysen, D. A. Binchy and Osborn Bergin, *A Grammar of Old Irish* (Dublin: Dublin University Press, 1949, repr. 1998), §§30, 122.

[14] Harvey, 'Reading the Genetic Code', p. 163.

[15] Harvey, 'Reading the Genetic Code', p. 162. See also Anthony Harvey, 'Some Significant Points of Early Insular Celtic Orthography', in *Sages, Saints and Storytellers: Celtic Studies in Honour of Professor James Carney*, ed. by Donnchadh Ó Corráin, Liam Breatnach and Kim McCone (Maynooth: An Sagart, 1989), pp. 56–66.

[16] For example, Harvey, 'Reading the Genetic Code', p. 162, or Crystal's comment on early Old English spelling in *Spell it Out: The Singular Story of English Spelling* (London: Profile Books, 2012), p. 2. 'Some scribes, especially in the north of England, went for the two-letter solution, using *th*. Some simply used a *d*.'

In other words, it is necessary to ascertain when and where the digraphs were actually used.

The most detailed account of early Old English spelling that I am aware of is an unpublished thesis by Joan Blomfield from 1935. Her account is based on an analysis of Old English material from the eighth century as presented in Sweet's *Oldest English Texts* (1885), as well as some Old High German sources.[17] While her thesis is not up to date from a methodological point of view and sometimes relies on research that is no longer accepted today, Blomfield's study provides a thorough analysis of the material. Yet, as it has never been published, it is not widely known, even though Campbell's account of early Old English orthography cited above is, to some extent, based on Blomfield's.[18] Unfortunately, Campbell clearly conflated the results of her study, as Blomfield identified two stages of early Old English spelling, including digraphs in the first stage and some single graphs in the first and the second. The following table illustrates Blomfield's stages:

Table 2: Blomfield's stages of Old English spelling[19]

Sounds	Earliest symbols	Modifications (those finally eliminated are bracketed)	
[x]	ch	(c)	h
[θ]	th, d	ð	þ
[w]	uu	(u)	ƿ

Blomfield interprets the existing spellings as representing a transition from a spelling system with the digraphs <ch>, <th> (alongside <d>), <uu> to one with the single graphs <c>, <ð>, <u> and in a third step to a spelling system making use of <h>, <þ>, <ƿ> to represent the same sounds. The single graphs <c> and <u> disappear completely, whereas the other early spellings survive as minority variants.

---

[17] Joan E. Blomfield, 'The Origins of Old English Orthography, with Special Reference to the Representation of the Spirants and W' (unpublished B. Litt. thesis, Oxford University, 1935). I am grateful to Dr Patrick V. Stiles for helping me to gain access to Blomfield's unpublished thesis. Copies can be found in Oxford and Nottingham; for details, see Patrick Stiles, 'Joan Turville-Petre: A Bibliographical Appreciation', *Old English Newsletter*, 40 (2007), 24–26. Henry Sweet, *The Oldest English Texts*, repr. 1957 (London: Trübner, 1885).

[18] Campbell, pp. v, 18, n. 2.

[19] Blomfield, p. 114, omitting details not relating to the digraphs under discussion here.

While I agree with most of the details of Blomfield's analysis, the general development outlined in this table is problematic for several reasons. First of all, it is misleading to present eighth-century spelling as part of a continuous graphemic history. The extant evidence for early Old English is heterogeneous in nature, which is in part due to the survival rate of manuscripts from that period, but also results from the fact that literacy did not appear in all places at the same time. As a consequence, the extant sources for early Old English orthography are spread out very unevenly as regards diachronic, diatopic as well as diastratic distribution. West Saxon evidence, for example, appears only at the very end of the eighth century. Northumbrian evidence consists solely of *Caedmon's Hymn* and the vernacular names transmitted in the Moore and St Petersburg manuscripts of Bede's *Ecclesiastical History* from the mid eighth century. Furthermore, we are dealing with very different text types as the vernacular material consists of names in Latin charters, names in Latin writing, a short vernacular poem, as well as Old English *interpretamenta* in bilingual glossaries.[20] A second, very important, point is that graphemic history does not develop steadily, but is often discontinuous. This aspect has been pointed out by Michael Elmentaler referring to Early Modern Low German material; it is even more true for the *scriptae* of the Early Middle Ages.[21] Change in spoken language presupposes an uninterrupted series of speech communities and progresses more or less at the same rate. Change in written language, on the other hand, is often erratic and progresses by leaps and bounds. Vernacular writing throughout the Early Middle Ages consists of more or less detached attempts, which do not form a sustained tradition of literacy; this necessitates constant processes of re-scripting on the basis of the letter-sound correlations of Medieval Latin. Apart from that, written language is often changed consciously by individuals – witness the famous attempts by Orm or Otfrid of Weissenburg.

If those aspects are taken into consideration, it becomes clear that what Blomfield presents as a diachronic development represents, in fact,

---

[20] Coins are a further source of early Old English; the data is not taken into account here since digraphs are generally avoided in inscriptions. In coins predating AD 800, there are very few exceptions to this rule, namely some instances of <uu> on Mercian coins. See Annina Seiler, 'The Scripting of Old English: An Analysis of Anglo-Saxon Spellings for *w* and *þ*', *Sprachwissenschaft*, 33 (2008), 139–72. Incidentally, digraphs are also rare in Merovingian coin inscriptions. This graphemic peculiarity may be due to issues of space and effort, which play a larger role in the production of inscriptions than in manuscript writing.

[21] Michael Elmentaler, *Struktur und Wandel vormoderner Schreibsprachen* (Berlin: de Gruyter, 2003), p. 314.

dialectal – or typological – differences, which cannot be interpreted diachronically in a straightforward way. The digraphs from Blomfield's 'earliest symbols' are attested mainly in Mercian and Kentish charters from the first half of the eighth century, and the Mercian *Épinal glossary*, whose early dating to *c.* 700 has been reaffirmed by Bernhard Bischoff.[22] The digraph spelling system also appears in an *ex libris* inscription in a Würzburg manuscript which at one time belonged to Cuðswið, abbess of the Mercian nunnery at Inkberrow, and which also dates to 700.[23] Apart from that, the digraphs are used in London, British Library, MS Cotton Tiberius C II, a Southumbrian manuscript of Bede's *Ecclesiastical History*, probably dating from the early ninth century.[24] On the other hand, the single graph spellings <d>, <c> and <u> (used for /þ/, /h/ and /w/), which mainly appear as 'modifications' in Blomfield's table, are primarily attested in the Old English elements from the two Northumbrian manuscripts of Bede's *Ecclesiastical History* dating from the mid-eighth century,[25] but also in some very early Kentish charters from the late seventh and early eighth century; they are <u> for /w/ as in *Uilfrid*, <c> for [χ] in name elements like *-berct*, and <d> for /þ/ as in *Aedil-* (alongside <th> in initial position as in *Thruidred*). The conclusion that can be drawn from the distribution is that the appearance of the digraphs coincides with Mercian influence.[26]

The only kind of evidence that lends itself to a diachronic evaluation in the early Anglo-Saxon period are Southumbrian (Kentish, Mercian and West Saxon) charters. Since we are dealing with a single text type – Latin charters including vernacular personal names – they represent a relatively homogenous corpus. Table 3 presents the spellings used for the

---

[22] Bernhard Bischoff, *The Épinal, Erfurt, Werden and Corpus Glossaries: Épinal Bibliothèque Municipale 72 (2), Erfurt Wissenschaftliche Bibliothek Amplonianus *2 42, Düsseldorf Universitätsbibliothek Fragm. K 19: Z 9/1, Munich Bayerische Staatsbibliothek Cgm. 187 III (e.4), Cambridge Corpus Christi College 144* (Copenhagen: Rosenkilde and Bagger, 1988), p. 14.

[23] The manuscript is Würzburg, Universitätsbibliothek, MS M. p. th. q. 2, a fifth-century Italian manuscript; the inscription runs *Cuthsuuithae. boec. thaerae abbatissan* 'a book of Abbess Cuðswið'; see Patrick Sims-Williams, *Religion and Literature in Western England, 600–800* (Cambridge: Cambridge University Press, 1990), p. 191.

[24] Michelle P. Brown, *The Book of Cerne: Prayer, Patronage and Power in Ninth-Century England* (London: The British Library, 1996), pp. 164, 171–78.

[25] For example, the Moore Bede (Cambridge University Library, MS Kk.5.16), AD 737, and the St Petersburg Bede (St Petersburg, National Library of Russia, MS Lat. Q. v.I.18), AD 746.

[26] This applies also to mid-eighth century charters from Kent, since Kent was under Mercian overlordship at that time.

three sounds in original charters before AD 800 grouped into twenty-five-year periods.[27] It only includes the spellings used for the most frequently occurring sound positions (that is, units that are defined by phonological context as well as sound etymology).[28]

Table 3: The digraphs in early Southumbrian charters.

Sound positions	Example	675	700	725	750	775	800
*/þ/ medially	*Æthelmund*	<d>		<th>		<ð>	
*/χ/ before /t/	*Egisberichti*	<c>	<ch>		<h>		
*/w/ before vowels other than /u/	*Uuihtredus*	<u>		<uu>			<p>

Table 3 reveals that even though there are differences in the times of appearance – and disappearance – of the three digraphs, the spellings from Southumbrian charters fall into three diachronic stages, with the digraphs in the middle. As has been mentioned, the earliest Kentish charters use single graphs and hence display a spelling system that is also found in the Northumbrian Bede manuscripts from the mid eighth century. The charters from the late eighth century (Kentish, Mercian and West Saxon) introduce the specialised single graphs <ð> and <p> as well as <h> for all sound positions of Gmc. */h/. This system appears in the texts generally labelled 'early West Saxon', for example, in the Alfredian translation of the *Pastoral Care*.

It is important to stress that the stages outlined above are broad generalisations based on the principal graphs used in the most frequently occurring sound positions. Some of the graphs that later become dominant are often already present as minority variants or, in other sound positions, in earlier stages. For example, the digraph <th> is already used in the first stage for /þ/ in initial position, but it does not appear in medial position until the second stage. Similarly, the digraph <ch> is used finally after vowels and /l/ in the first stage, but it only spreads into the more frequently attested cluster /χt/ in the second stage (the evidence for this

---

[27] The charters are Sawyer nos. 8, 19, 21, 23, 24, 31, 35, 56, 59, 65, 89, 96, 106, 114, 123, 128, 139, 153, 155, 264, 1171, 1184, 1184, 1186a, 1428b, 1861; Simon Keynes, Susan Kelly, Sean Miller, Rebecca Rushforth, Emma Connolly and Rory Naismith, 'The Electronic Sawyer: Online Catalogue of Anglo-Saxon Charters', King's College London (2013) <www.esawyer.org.uk> [accessed 24 December 2014].

[28] On the relevance of distinguishing sound positions in graphemic research, see Seiler, *The Scripting*, pp. 89, 229; Elmentaler, p. 100.

digraph is slender since it is quickly replaced by <h> in all positions).[29] Also the rune ⟨þ⟩ appears as minority variant in some of the earliest sources (e.g. the *Épinal glossary*), but it is used systematically only in tenth-century texts. Furthermore, there are texts with mixed spelling systems, displaying features from more than one of the stages.[30]

Coming back to the question of the origin of the digraphs, it has become clear that any hypothesis has to account for their use first of all in the south of England, where the digraphs are used in considerable numbers, rather than in the north. Irish influence was certainly strongest in Northumbria since the north had been converted to Christianity by Irish missionaries, whereas a Roman mission sent by Pope Gregory the Great was responsible for the conversion of Kent and for spreading Christianity to most of Southumbrian England.[31] Nevertheless, it is not impossible to attribute the use of <th> and <ch> in Southumbrian England to the Irish as well:[32] Herren has demonstrated that some Irishmen were active in the south of Anglo-Saxon England, for example, Fursa and Maeldub. According to Herren, a letter from Aldhelm demonstrates that Anglo-Saxon monks used to study in Ireland rather than in Canterbury and that Archbishop Theodore of Canterbury frequently debated with Irish scholars.[33] The presence of Irish speakers in Canterbury is also attested by the appearance of Old Irish words in the Épinal/Erfurt family

[29] The Northumbrian Bede manuscripts use the digraphs <th> and <ch> in the same sound positions: <th> initially, <ch> finally after /l/, but these sound positions represent only a small share of the total number (33 <th>: 356 <d>, 27 <ch>: 198 <c>: 48 <h> in the Moore Bede), see Seiler, *The Scripting*, p. 131, 152.

[30] For more details, see Seiler, *The Scripting*, pp. 204–10.

[31] For a detailed account of the conversion of the Anglo-Saxons, see Barbara Yorke, *The Conversion of Britain: Religion, Politics and Society in Britain, c.600–800*, ed. by Keith Robbins (Harlow: Pearson Longman, 2006).

[32] Oliver, pp. 93–98, interprets the evidence the other way round: she assumes that the early <d> spellings of the Kentish charters and other sources are attributable to Irish influence and that the introduction of <th> represents the Roman or Frankish tradition. Apart from that, the use of <c> in the name element -*berct* in Northumbrian sources has also been attributed to Irish influence, for example by Sievers and Brunner: 'In den ältesten Texten wird für letzteren [i.e. for the palatal/velar fricative] wie in kontinentalen Handschriften noch *ch* bzw. vor *t* auch *c* (also *ct* für späteres *ht*), letzteres wie im Irischen, verwendet'. Eduard Sievers, and Karl Brunner, *Altenglische Grammatik*, 3rd edn (Tübingen: Niemeyer, 1965), §4.7.

[33] Michael P. Herren, 'Scholarly Contacts between the Irish and the Southern English in the Seventh Century', *Peritia*, 12 (1998), 24–53 (p. 30).

of glossaries, which go back to a collection of glosses originally compiled in Canterbury.[34]

While such contacts provide a general historical context for a possible exchange of graphemes, sources are not detailed enough to provide information about the situations in which the Irish might have taught the fricative sound values of the digraphs <th> and <ch> to the Anglo-Saxons. This leaves us with questions that are difficult to answer: do we have to imagine bilingual writers as well as bilingual speakers on a large scale? Or was it Irish scholars who taught their Anglo-Saxon students how to write Old English?[35] Though possible, these scenarios do not strike me as being particularly convincing since the energies of all scholars involved – irrespective of their first language – were devoted to studying Latin texts. The vernacular languages only came to be written as a by-product; the nature of the vernacular evidence makes this abundantly clear. This leaves us with one plausible explanation, namely that the Irish pronounced <th> and <ch> in Latin words also as fricatives, with an Irish accent, so to speak.[36] According to Harvey, however, Latin loanwords in Irish containing <th> were treated in the same way as words containing <t>, which indicates that it was probably not the Irish pronunciation of such words that served as a trigger for adopting <th> for Old English /þ/.[37]

The Irish hypothesis has another flaw, too: though Old Irish influence might explain the use of <th> for [θ] and <ch> for [χ] in Old English, it does not provide any parallels for the third digraph <uu> for [w]. The *u consonans* inherited from Proto-Indo-European had developed into /f/, /b/ or /u/ in Old Irish, so Old Irish spelling had no graph appropriate for Germanic /w/.[38] Admittedly, the evidence from Southumbrian charters suggests that the digraphs were not introduced simultaneously, but they

---

[34] Michael Lapidge, 'The School of Theodore and Hadrian', *Anglo-Saxon England*, 15 (1986), 45–72 (pp. 53–59).

[35] This has, in fact, been suggested by White, 'The Case for Irish Influence', according to whom the Irish missionaries also worked as 'missionary linguists, not only in teaching the English Latin but also in deve[l]oping a spelling system for Old English [...]'.

[36] Blomfield, p. 60: 'The Irish had nothing to teach in the way of adapting the alphabet to a vernacular. It was their spelling of Latin compared with their pronunciation of it which must have acted as one of the chief stimuli in the evolution of Old English orthography.' Blomfield's statement, however, refers to the pronunciation of <d> as a spirant, not <th>.

[37] Harvey, 'Reading the Genetic Code', p. 162.

[38] Warren Cowgill, 'On the Fate of *w* in Old Irish', *Language*, 43 (1967), 129–38; Thurneysen, Binchy and Bergin, §§201–5.

all represent typologically similar solutions to some of the spelling problems ensuing in the scripting process; hence an explanation that accounts
for the presence of all three digraphs appears more acceptable. While I
believe that it is possible that Irish influence is responsible for the use of
<th> and <ch> in Southumbrian Old English, there is a second and, in
my view, more convincing explanation, namely that Merovingian orthography provided a model for all three digraphs.

Despite the fact that the West Frankish language died out early on
and never became a written language in its own right,[39] the Merovingian
Franks were confronted with much the same spelling problems that faced
their Insular and Eastern German neighbours when it came to rendering
the personal names of the Frankish elite. Gregory of Tours' well-known
story about the new characters invented by King Chilperic I (561–584)
implicitly reveals some of the difficulties as well as the solutions:

> He [Chilperic] also added some characters to our alphabet, namely ω
> [omega?] as the Greeks have it, *ae, the, wi*. Their letter forms are the
> following: ω Θ, *ae* ψ, *the* ȝ, *uui* Ρ. And he sent letters to all the cities
> of his realm, so that the boys should be taught [to write] like this and
> the books that had been written in the past should be re-written, after
> having been erased with a pumice stone.[40]

Chilperic's invention apparently did not meet with any success, despite
the king's order to correct ancient books, as there are no surviving sources
using comparable characters. Since the manuscripts transmitting Gregory's *History* exhibit different letter forms, the exact shapes of the characters remain doubtful.[41] Their sound values are also unclear; they probably
represented two vowels and two consonants, most likely some of the

---

[39] The language switch was probably completed by the eighth or ninth century;
Michel Banniard, 'Germanophonie, latinophonie et accès à la *Schriftlichkeit*
(Ve–VIIIe siècle)', in *Akkulturation: Probleme einer Germanisch-Romanischen
Kultursynthese in Spätantike und frühem Mittelalter*, ed. by Dieter Hägermann et
al. (Berlin: de Gruyter, 2004), pp. 340–58 (p. 351).

[40] My translation of Gregory of Tours, *Decem libri historiarum* 5, 44: *Addit autem
et litteras litteris nostris, id est ω, sicut Graeci habent, ae, the, uui, quarum caracteres
hi sunt: ω Θ, ae ψ, the ȝ, uui Ρ. Et misit epistulas in universis civitatibus regni sui,
ut sic pueri docerentur ac libri antiquitus scripti, planati pomice, rescriberentur*,
in *Gregorii Episcopi Turonensis Libri Historiarum X*, ed. by Bruno Krusch and
Wilhelm Levison, Monumenta Germaniae Historica 2, Scriptores 1,1 (Hanover:
Hahn, 1993), p. 254.

[41] Krusch and Levison, p. 255 provide an illustration of the variant letter forms
as transmitted in the different manuscripts.

specifically Germanic phonemes, for which the Latin alphabet did not provide any symbols. The passage nevertheless sheds light on the early graphemic history of West Frankish: it attests that the digraphs <th> and <uu> were firmly established in manuscript writing as early as the second half of the sixth century. This aspect has been overlooked since the interest of scholars has centred on the potential origin of the strange characters and on identifying their sound values rather than on Roman-alphabet spelling.[42] Even though both questions may never be completely solved, the letter names *the* and *uui* indicate that the sounds which Chilperic's new consonant symbols should have represented were otherwise spelled with the digraphs <th> and <uu> in Gregory's time. The names of consonants of the Roman alphabet all consist of the sound represented by the letter followed, or preceded, by *e*; in the case of stops, the vowel is added after the sound (e.g. *be, ce, de*), for fricatives and resonants it precedes the sound (e.g. *ef, el, em*). If Chilperic's letters represented Gmc. /þ/ and /w/, respectively, we would expect the names *eth* (which is in fact the letter name of the character *ð*) and *uue* (cf. the Modern German letter name [ve:] for *w*). However, as Wagner has argued, it is possible that the letter name *the* parallels that of the stop *t* (*te*) – in Latin <th> was perceived as a variant of <t> after all (447). The use of *uui* rather than *uue* may be due to the letter name *ui* for Greek upsilon (447–50), which is also applied to *w*.[43]

In any case, <th> and <uu> are well attested in Merovingian sources from the seventh and eighth century, and those texts also apply <ch> as the main rendering of Gmc. */h/ in all positions. The use of the digraphs <ch> and <gh> in Merovingian orthography has been analysed in an excellent study by Wells.[44] I have supplemented details concerning <th> and <uu>. The bulk of the evidence comes from thirty-eight original royal

---

[42] For a discussion and references, see for example, Banniard, p. 353; Norbert Wagner, 'König Chilperichs Buchstaben und andere Graphien', *Sprachwissenschaft*, 1 (1976), 434–52.

[43] Carl Darling Buck, 'The Letter *Y*', *Manly Anniversary Studies* (1923), 340–50 (p. 349). Wagner, p. 447, holds that the shape and sound value of *the* is based on Greek zeta. The shape of *uui* is commonly believed to be modelled on the rune wyn ᚹ; Wagner, however, argues that it could also have been Greek upsilon Υ (or the combined influence of both writing systems). In his view, the passage in fact represents the first use of the letter name *ui* for upsilon in the Latin alphabet, which is used in several Germanic languages (see also Modern English [waɪ]). For a different opinion, see Buck, p. 350.

[44] Christopher Wells, 'An Orthographic Approach to Early Frankish Personal Names', *Transactions of the Philological Society*, 71 (1972), 101–64.

diplomas dating from 625 to 717.[45] An overview of how the digraphs are employed in these documents is presented in Table 4.

Table 4: The digraphs and their alternatives in
Merovingian royal diplomas

Sound position	Initial	Medial	Examples
*/þ/	\<th>	\<d>	*Theudericus, Madalfrido*
*/χ/	\<ch>, \<h>	\<ch>, \<cth>[45]	*Childericus, Chrodochilde, Dagobercthus*
*/w/	\<uu>	\<o>	*Uuandeberctus, Ansoaldus*

Another important source for Merovingian orthography comes from names on coins, which mainly date from a period between 570 and 670 and attest a total of 645 Germanic names (or fragments thereof). The material has been investigated by Felder; details are provided from his study.[47] The spellings of Frankish personal names transmitted in the royal diplomas are remarkably uniform. Wells asserts that there was an 'established orthographical convention for the rendering of Germanic names in the royal Merovingian chancelleries' (141). Apparently, inscriptions and private charters from the period are less consistent. In general, there is a tendency to avoid digraphs in coin legends.

In the diplomas, the digraph \<th> is consistently used for Gmc. */þ/ in initial position; it needs to be pointed out, however, that it is exclusively attested in the name of *Theuderic*. On coins, initial \<th> alternates with \<t>.[48] Medially, \<d> is the principal graph both in charters and coins, unless /þ/ is directly followed by */h/, in which case the entire cluster is represented by \<th>, as in *Chlotharius*. This name is frequently attested

[45] *Die Urkunden der Merowinger I*, ed. by Theo Kölzer and Carlrichard Brühl, Monumenta Germaniae Historica (Hannover: Hahn, 2001). The original royal diplomas are numbers 22, 28, 32, 41, 72, 74, 75, 85, 88, 89, 93–95, 121–23, 126, 131, 135–38, 141–44, 147, 149, 150, 153, 155–57, 166–68, 170, 173 (see Kölzer and Brühl, p. xix).

[46] The trigraph \<cth> represents the cluster /χt/ (see below); it is also attested in an acrostic by Venantius Fortunatus which spells the name *Dagobercthus* (*Carmina* IX, 5, see also Reichert, p. xxi).

[47] Egon Felder, *Die Personennamen auf den merowingischen Münzen der Bibliothèque nationale de France* (Munich: Verlag der Bayerischen Akademie der Wissenschaften, 2003).

[48] Felder, pp. 319–24.

as *Chlothacharius*; however, such forms are considered 'learned constructions' by Felder rather than actual name forms (210). Since the same name element is consistently spelled with <d> in *Chlodovechus* (there are only very few exceptions with <th>), this seems likely. The <th> spelling of *Chlothacharius* may be some kind of dittography, deriving from the form without *Fugenvokal*. In any case since the first element of the name probably goes back to **hluda-* (< pre-Gmc. **klutós*), it even seems doubtful that the name actually contains Gmc.**þ*.[49] The use of <d> for the dental fricative in medial position is most likely due to two factors: on the one hand, lenition of Latin /d/ to [ð] in the post-Classical period and, on the other hand, voicing of Gmc. */þ/ to [ð] in medial position. As a consequence of both sound changes, the Latin character <d> had turned into an ideal representation of the Germanic sound.[50] Old High German sources – and, as I have pointed out above, some early Old English also – display the same distribution of graphs: <th> is used initially and <d> medially, for example, in the Old High German translation of Tatian's gospel harmony or in the Northumbrian Bede manuscripts. The practice may be due to the direct influence of Merovingian spellings but it is also possible to think of independent parallel developments based on the same preconditions.

The digraph <ch> is the most common representation of Gmc. */h/. It is particularly frequent in initial position before both vowels and consonants, occurring in first and second elements of dithematic names. The name element Gmc. **berhta-* 'bright', however, is regularly rendered as *bercth*, with *berth* or *bert* as minority variants – the last being most common on coins;[51] <cth> appears to be a trigraph that renders the entire cluster /χt/ (cf. above). Only one of the royal diplomas from the end of the seventh century uses <h> in a significant number of instances (Kölzer no. 143; Paris, Archives Nationales K 3, No. 9; by Childebert III, dated to 694). In this diploma, the name of the abbot of Saint-Denis is rendered

---

[49] Alternative explanations have been proposed, for example, interference with Gmc. **hlōþō-* f. 'crowd' or the existence of non-Vernerised variants. The etymological basis of the name element has been a matter of considerable debate; for a discussion and references, see Felder, pp. 208–10.

[50] I am indebted to the anonymous reader for this suggestion. The Latin sound change is difficult to trace in writing since Latin spelling remained virtually unchanged. Stotz, *Lautlehre*, §194.1, cites *aorer* < Lat. *adorare* and *obeir* < Lat. *oboedire*, two learned Latin borrowings into Old French, as examples where medial *d* had been lost after having undergone lenition.

[51] Wells, pp. 120–34; Felder, p. 92.

six times as *Haino* rather than *Chaino/Chaeno/Chagno* as elsewhere.[52] Since later diplomas again use <ch>, but <h> appears also in other parts of Gallia (on some coins, for example), Wells concludes on the 'presence of several orthographical systems in Gallia' (132) and argues that 'it might be construed as influence of orthographical conventions from other – possibly eastern – regions' (142). However, as in those areas literacy only caught on with the foundations of monasteries such as Echternach and Fulda in the course of the eighth century, the last point seems unlikely; the earliest charter from east of the Rhine dates to 704.[53]

If a transfer of graphemes has taken place between Eastern and Western Frankish orthography, it must have gone in the opposite direction. Kauff-mann, in his study on early Old High German orthography, reached the same conclusion. In Old High German, the digraph <ch> is used for /χ(χ)/ from Gmc. */k/ by the Second Consonant Shift, but rarely for Gmc. */h/. According to Kauffmann, the reason for this lies in the fact that 'in the West <ch> was replaced by <h> already before the begin-ning of the eighth century'.[54] The orthographic change in West Frankish territory may well have been triggered by a sound change that affected the developing Romance vernacular and hence also the pronunciation of Latin. In Gallo Romance, /k/ was palatalised first of all before the palatal vowels /e/ and /i/, but by the eighth century also before /a/. When this change took hold, <c> ceased to be an appropriate rendering of the Germanic palatal/velar stop /k/ as it represented palatalised /ts/ in many positions. Since <ch> had become an alternative of <c> mainly in Greek loanwords in Latin, this graph was substituted for <c>. Subsequently, in a kind of pull-chain change, <h> became the graph used for Gmc. */h/. In the Merovingian charters, assibilated pronunciation of Latin <c> before palatal vowels is attested indirectly by numerous examples in which <c> replaces <t> as in *eciam* for *etiam*, *gracia* for *gratia* (Kölzer nos. 22, 28); on the other hand, the digraph <ch> represents /k/ in the Greek loanwords

---

[52] As Wells has pointed out, <h> also occurs in a second charter (Kölzer no. 149, Paris, Archives Nationales K 3, No. 12¹; by Childebert III, 697) in the form *Hociobercthus, -o.* This charter, though, also uses <ch> in various other names.

[53] Kölzer, p. xiv.

[54] Friedrich Kauffmann, 'Über Althochdeutsche Orthographie', *Germania*, 37 (n.s. 25) (1892), 243–64 (p. 246): 'Die altfränkische Weise *h-* im Anlaut der Wörter mit *ch* zu bezeichnen, hat außer den bereits genannten Resten vor *chr-* keine Spuren hinterlassen [...], offenbar deswegen nicht, weil im Westen selbst schon vor Anfang des 8. Jh. *h-* an die Stelle des *ch-* getreten ist.'

monachis, archicapellanus, or the name *Christo* (Kölzer nos. 28, 34, 76).[55]
Looking across the Channel, it may be significant that the short phase of
<ch> spellings and their subsequent replacement by <h> also happened in
the course of the eighth century. The graphemic change in Old English
may well have been influenced by that on the Continent.

Gmc. */w/ in initial position is almost universally represented by <uu>.
There are only two exceptions, namely when /w/ occurs at the beginning
of second elements of dithematic names, in which case it is rendered by
<o>, e.g. *Uuandeberctus* vs. *Ansoaldus*. Single <u> is rare, even on coins,
except before the vowel /u/, e.g. *Uulfolaecus*.[56] That the digraph <uu> is
firmly established in Merovingian orthography is further attested by its
presence in the spelling of Germanic loanwords in Medieval Latin, for
example, in *uuaddium* 'pledge', which occurs several times in the thirty-
eight Merovingian royal diplomas. In Old High German <uu> is also the
normal rendering of /w/ throughout (except before /u/ and in consonant
clusters). The digraph <uu> is clearly the youngest of the three as it can
only be traced back as far as the fifth century, whereas <th> and <ch> are
already attested in Classical sources for Germanic names alongside <t>
and <c> or <h>.[57] The Merovingian chancery scribes are most likely the
inventors of the digraph <uu> and they appear to have generalised the
use of <th> and <ch> to create a consistent representation of Frankish
phonology.

To sum up, all three digraphs are a fixture of Merovingian orthography
and their use was undoubtedly taken over into Old High German spelling.
As connections between Anglo-Saxon England – in particular East Anglia
and Kent – and Merovingian Gaul were strong,[58] it is very plausible that
the southern Anglo-Saxons also adopted them, keeping in mind that the
digraphs were most extensively used in Southumbrian texts. In contrast
to the Irish hypothesis, Merovingian orthography provides a model for all

---

55 Wells, p. 133 and Seiler, *The Scripting*, p. 165. On <c> for [ts] and <ch> for
[k] in Old French, see Roger Wright, *Late Latin and Early Romance in Spain and
Carolingian France* (Liverpool: Francis Cairns, 1982), p. 129.

56 On *-uius/-ueus*, see Felder, pp. 331–33.

57 For example *Theudatus, Tingsus, Cimberius, Tencteri, Cherusci, Harudes*; Gmc.
*/w/ is rendered by <u> in Classical sources, Moriz Schönfeld, *Wörterbuch der
altgermanischen Personen- und Völkernamen* (Heidelberg: Winter, 1911), p. xxii. See
also Reichert, p. xxviii.

58 See, for example, Paul Fouracre, 'Franks', in *The Wiley Blackwell Encyclopedia
of Anglo-Saxon England*, ed. by Michael Lapidge and others (Chichester: Wiley
Blackwell, 2014), pp. 198–99; Joanna Story, *Carolingian Connections: Anglo-Saxon
England and Carolingian Francia, c. 750–870* (Burlington: Ashgate, 2003).

three digraphs. Apart from that, it is not necessary to imagine bilingual writers in this scenario: West Frankish and Old English were certainly in part mutually intelligible, especially when it came to the onomastic part of the lexicon in which the digraphs were employed.

Moreover, it seems likely that the digraphs were considered 'Latin' rather than 'vernacular' spellings and were transmitted as part of Latin orthography. In the same way the digraphs had been used for Greek loan-words in Latin, they were now employed for Germanic names and words. This interpretation is supported by the fact that in all the early texts that make use of the digraphs Old English is embedded in a Latin context. Also, when the runes *wyn* and *thorn* were adopted for Old English writing, the digraphs <th> and <uu> survived in Anglo-Latin orthography. The digraph system replaces an older – Classical – way of representing Germanic phonology in Latin, which makes use of the single graphs <d> (alongside <th>), <c>, and <u> for the same sounds – in Old English as well as in Continental sources. Most of the vernacular writing systems in the Early Middle Ages represent individual attempts at transferring the letter-sound correlations of Latin to the scribe's first language.[59] Therefore, it is more plausible to assume that the digraph spellings spread from Merovingian Latin orthography to the vernaculars than to imagine that they were carried over from one vernacular to another. After all, Latin, the 'father tongue' of the Middle Ages, provided the basis for all Roman-alphabet writing.

Having said that, I believe that Irish influence should not be completely discounted, especially as a model for the more limited use of <th> and <ch> in Northumbrian sources. Clearly, the question of the origin of the digraphs in Old English need not have a single answer – nor even only two. In fact, spelling change often appears to proceed along the lines of an 'invisible hand' process with different factors contributing to the same result and this may well be the case here.[60] Harvey places the responsi-bility for using <th> and <ch> for fricatives with a single Old Irish scribe. However, orthographic history has shown that spelling reforms under-

---

[59] On the importance of Merovingian Latin orthography for the spelling of the Germanic languages, see Horst Haider Munske, 'Die Rolle des Lateins als Superstratum im Deutschen und in anderen germanischen Sprachen', in *Die Leistung der Strataforschung und der Kreolistik: Typologische Aspekte der Sprachkontakte*, Akten des 5. Symposions über Sprachkontakt in Europa, Mannheim 1982, ed. by Per Sture Ureland (Tübingen: Niemeyer, 1982), pp. 237–63 (p. 245).

[60] On 'invisible hand' processes in language change, see Rudi Keller, *Sprachwandel: Von der unsichtbaren Hand in der Sprache* (Tübingen: Francke, 2003).

taken by individuals are rarely successful. Yet it is possible that not only one scribe but several people writing various vernacular languages, all in need of characters for sounds that did not exist in Latin, came up with the same solution. After all the use of <h> as a diacritic to differentiate phonetically similar sounds in writing has many typological parallels. To end with a third potential explanation: we should not forget that Archbishop Theodore and Abbot Hadrian, who established a school in Canterbury at the end of the seventh century, were native speakers of Greek, who, at that time, would have pronounced <th> and <ch> as fricatives (as the equivalents of Greek theta and chi) and taught this pronunciation to their students. The fact that there are so many possible and plausible explanations for the use of the digraphs for fricatives must have facilitated the establishment of the new graphemes – graphemes that are now considered an intrinsic part of the writing systems of many modern European languages. The creation of the digraph <uu>, on the other hand, can only be attributed to the Merovingian Franks. Since they were also the first to exploit the potential of the digraphs <th> and <ch>, they have made a significant contribution towards shaping the written word to this day.

The New Heathens: Anti-Jewish Hostility in Early English Literature

GEORGE YOUNGE

THE ELEVENTH AND twelfth centuries were a transformative period for English literary culture.[1] Consecutive waves of immigration after the Danish and Norman conquests created new audiences for writing in Old Norse, French and Latin, diverting patronage away from Old English. After the death of Archbishop Wulfstan of York in 1023, English works were no longer composed in significant quantities by a single author. Instead, Benedictine monks, based principally in cathedral priories, edited and updated the existing homiletic corpus for a new generation, supplementing it with a thin stream of original translations.[2] The last texts copied in Old English overlap with the earliest works in Middle English, which were composed in the second half of the twelfth century and anthologised at the beginning of the thirteenth. Between the two invasions (1016 and 1066), England began to integrate more tightly into a common northwestern European cultural zone and experienced the first stirrings of the so-called 'twelfth-century renaissance'.[3] One of the many changes associated with this accelerated period of renewal was a sharp increase in hostility towards the Jews.

The following discussion focuses on references to the Jews as the 'heathen' in English pastoral and historical texts from the twelfth century.

[1] This article was written with financial support from the Danish National Research Foundation (DNRF102ID). My thanks to Richard Dance, Sara Harris, Jane Gilbert, John Munns, Miri Rubin, Andrew Scheil, Linda Stone and Elizabeth Tyler for commenting on drafts of the text.

[2] *The Production and Use of English Manuscripts 1060 to 1220*, ed. by Orietta da Rold and others (Leicester: University of Leicester, 2013) <http://www.le.ac.uk/ee/em1060to1220/> [accessed 15 September 2014]; *Rewriting Old English in the Twelfth Century*, ed. by Elaine Treharne and Mary Swan (Cambridge: Cambridge University Press, 2000); Elaine Treharne, *Living Through Conquest: The Politics of Early English, 1020–1220* (Oxford: Oxford University Press, 2012).

[3] For a recent overview of the period, emphasising the pace of change, see John Gillingham, 'A Historian of the Twelfth-Century Renaissance and the Transformation of English Society, 1066–*ca.* 1200', in *European Transformations: The Long Twelfth Century*, ed. by Thomas F. X. Noble and John Van Engen (Notre Dame, IN: University of Notre Dame Press, 2012), pp. 45–74.

This usage (and concept) was not current in the Anglo-Saxon period and first appears after the Norman Conquest.[4] There is no reliable evidence that the Jews settled in England or had any sustained form of contact with the English before 1066.[5] When the Anglo-Saxons wrote about the Jews or represented them in art, they were piecing together an image of the Jew from their reading of the Bible, Late Antique historical works, and patristic commentaries.[6] The first Jewish settlers migrated to England from Rouen with William the Conqueror, who employed them as money changers and exploited their trade links with the Rhineland.[7] As the twelfth century progressed, the Jews established communities in many provincial cities under the special protection of the Crown.[8] The settlement of the Jews in England coincides with a rise in anti-Jewish hostility across western Europe; the onset of the crusades in 1095, the foundation of secular schools, the growth of a credit-based economy, and the increasing popularity of affective modes of devotion coalesced to create new and more aggressive forms of anti-Jewish resentment.[9] In England,

[4]   *MED*, s.v. *hethen* (adj. and n.), sense 1d, 'applied to Jews'.
[5]   Robert C. Stacey, 'Jews and Christians in Twelfth-Century England: Some Dynamics of a Changing Relationship', in *Christians and Jews in Twelfth-Century Europe*, ed. by Michael A. Singer and John Van Engen (Notre Dame, IN: University of Notre Dame Press, 2001), pp. 340–54 (pp. 340–41); Anna Sapir Abulafia, *Christian-Jewish Relations, 1000–1300: Jews in the Service of Medieval Christendom* (Harlow: Longman, 2011), pp. 88–108. For a review of the largely unconvincing evidence that some Jews settled in England before 1066, see Norman Golb, *The Jews in Medieval Normandy: A Social and Intellectual History* (Cambridge: Cambridge University Press, 1998), pp. 112–14; Robin R. Mundill, *The King's Jews: Money, Massacre and Exodus in Medieval England* (London: Continuum, 2010), pp. 1–4.
[6]   Andrew P. Scheil, *The Footsteps of Israel: Understanding Jews in Anglo-Saxon England* (Ann Arbor MI: University of Michigan Press, 2004). Anglo-Saxon attitudes towards the Jews are discussed in greater detail below.
[7]   Robert C. Stacey, 'Jewish Lending and the Medieval English Economy', in *A Commercializing Economy: England 1086 to c. 1300*, ed. by Richard H. Britnell and Bruce M. S. Campbell (Manchester: Manchester University Press, 1995), pp. 78–101 (pp. 78–82).
[8]   Joe Hillaby, 'Jewish Colonization in the Twelfth Century', in *The Jews in Medieval Britain: Historical, Literary and Archaeological Perspectives*, ed. by Patricia Skinner (Woodbridge: Boydell and Brewer, 2003), pp. 14–40.
[9]   For an introduction to these issues, see Anna Sapir Abulafia, *Christians and Jews in the Twelfth-Century Renaissance* (London: Routledge, 1995); Robert Chazan, *The Jews of Medieval Western Christendom, 1000–1500* (Cambridge: Cambridge University Press, 2006); Jeremy Cohen, *Living Letters of the Law: Ideas of the Jew in Medieval Christianity* (Berkeley: University of California Press, 1999).

the earliest textual evidence that tensions between Christians and Jews were mounting comes from the 1150s, when Thomas of Monmouth, a monk of Norwich cathedral priory, accused the local Jewish population of killing a young boy called William.[10] This incident is often regarded as an isolated precursor to the bloody spate of massacres that took place after the coronation of Richard I in 1189/90.[11] The presentation of the Jews as the heathen in vernacular literature that antedates the pogroms of 1189/90 directly implicates English scribes and translators in the rise of popular antipathy towards the Jews.

In vernacular texts written before the Norman Conquest, the Old English noun *hæðen* (equivalent to Latin *paganus*) and its derivatives primarily refer to people who are not Jewish or Christian.[12] These include Vikings, Muslims, classical pagans, the enemies of the Israelites in the Old Testament, and gentiles in the New Testament. From the beginning of the eleventh century, and particularly in the works of Archbishop Wulfstan of York, the concept of heathenism was expanded to include unbaptised babies and degenerate Christians.[13] This shift is exemplified by a short treatise appended to the York Gospels (York, Minster Library, MS Additional 1), in which Wulfstan brings together a range of sinners under the

[10] *The Life and Miracles of St William of Norwich*, ed. by Augustus Jessopp and M. R. James (Cambridge: Cambridge University Press, 1896); *The Life and Passion of William of Norwich*, trans. by Miri Rubin (London: Penguin, 2014). Important studies of the text include Jeffrey J. Cohen, 'The Flow of Blood in Medieval Norwich', *Speculum*, 62 (2004), 26–65; Gavin Langmuir, 'Thomas of Monmouth: Detector of Ritual Murder', *Speculum*, 59 (1984), 820–46; John M. McCulloh, 'Jewish Ritual Murder: William of Norwich, Thomas of Monmouth, and the Early Dissemination of the Myth', *Speculum*, 72 (1997), 698–740.

[11] Chazan, pp. 157–60; McCulloh, pp. 698–740. For an overview of the massacres, see *Christians and Jews in Angevin England: The York Massacre of 1190, Narratives and Contexts*, ed. by Sarah Rees Jones and Sethina Watson (York: York Medieval Press, 2013), esp. Sethina Watson, 'Introduction: The Moment and Memory of the York Massacre of 1190' (pp. 1–14), and Joe Hillaby, 'Prelude and Postscript to the York Massacre: Attacks in East Anglia and Lincolnshire, 1190' (pp. 43–56).

[12] *An Anglo-Saxon Dictionary: Based on the Manuscript Collections of the Late Joseph Bosworth*, ed. by T. Northcote Toller (Oxford: Oxford University Press, 1898), with T. Northcote Toller, *Supplement* (Oxford: Clarendon Press, 1921), and Alistair Campbell, *Enlarged Addenda and Corrigenda* (London: Oxford University Press, 1972), s.v. *hæðen, hæðencynn, hæðendom, hæðenfolc*, etc.

[13] Audrey L. Meaney, '"And we forbeodað eornostlice ælcne hæðenscipe": Wulfstan and Late Anglo-Saxon and Norse "Heathenism"', in *Wulfstan, Archbishop of York: The Proceedings of the Second Alcuin Conference*, ed. by Matthew Townend (Turnhout: Brepols, 2004), pp. 461–500.

collective heading *Be Hæðendome* (1020 x 1023).[14] Opening with references to pagans and idolaters, Wulfstan goes on to list less conventional examples of the heathen, including prostitutes, priest murderers, slave traders, and oath breakers. This looser application of *hæðen* in contexts that do not have pagan connotations can be linked to the English experience of attacks by christianised Vikings in the early eleventh century. The interpretative anxiety that the newly converted Vikings occasioned is felt in a range of texts from the period. The author of the *Battle of Maldon*, for instance, anachronistically insists on the heathenism of the Viking army, though he must have known that many of the invaders were in fact Christian.[15] In the *Sermo Lupi ad Anglos* (*c.* 1014), Wulfstan clearly presents the Vikings as the heathen yet frets that God has chosen them to replace the faithless English, no doubt because he too was aware that the Vikings were no longer exclusively pagan.[16] This broadening of *hæðen* to include the 'cultural paganism' of newly christianised Scandinavian raiders established a precedent for portraying the Jews as the heathen after the Norman Conquest.[17]

As Andrew Scheil has shown, the Anglo-Saxons engaged imaginatively with the standard tropes of early medieval anti-Judaism.[18] Authoritative writers such as Bede and Ælfric of Eynsham frequently allude to the ignorance, unbelief, blindness and treachery of the Jews, especially those of the New Testament. In Scheil's opinion, a few texts that predate the tenth-century Benedictine reformation move beyond the standard stereotypes of the period, foreshadowing the 'somatic' anti-Judaism of the twelfth

---

[14] *Wulfstan: Sammlung der ihm zugeschriebenen Homilien nebst Untersuchungen über ihre Echtheit*, ed. by Arthur Napier (Berlin: Weidmann, 1883), Homily 60 (pp. 309–10). Wulfstan personally corrected the text in the York Gospels and the title, which implies that the entire list of sinners are heathens, should therefore be regarded as authorially sanctioned.

[15] *The Battle of Maldon*, ed. by D. G. Scragg (Manchester: Manchester University Press, 1981), ll. 55, 181. The invading force probably included Óláf Tryggvason (*d.* 999) and Swein Forkbeard (*d.* 1014). Óláf was baptised in Norway, confirmed at Andover in 994, and remembered in the sagas for spreading Christianity in Scandinavia, while Swein was the son of Harald Bluetooth, Denmark's first Christian king.

[16] *The Homilies of Wulfstan*, ed. by Dorothy Bethurum (Oxford: Oxford University Press, 1957, repr. with corrections, 1971), Homily 20, ll. 27, 31.

[17] Judith Jesch, 'Scandinavians and "Cultural Paganism" in Late Anglo-Saxon England', in *The Christian Tradition in Anglo-Saxon England: Approaches to Current Scholarship and Teaching*, ed. by Paul Cavill (Cambridge: D. S. Brewer, 2004), pp. 55–68 (p. 63).

[18] Scheil, pp. 1–22.

century.[19] Vercelli Homily 7, for example, and (in a more understated mode) the biblical poem *Andreas* both imply that the New Testament Jews were ruled by carnal desire and the demands of the body. Nonetheless, the irrational animosity towards the Jews in these pre-Conquest works remains significantly less pronounced than in their twelfth-century counterparts.

Despite the broad semantic range of Old English *hæðen* and its derivatives, Anglo-Saxon writers stopped short of applying this term to the Jews.[20] On the contrary, the Jews are often clearly differentiated from their pagan adversaries in Old English poetry and prose. In *Genesis A*, it is the Sodomites who are branded as the *hæðen* and in *Daniel* the Chaldeans.[21] The opening lines of the *Song of Azarias* lament the dispersal of the Jews and their suffering under *hæðen* rulers, whom the poet calls the 'wyrrestan eorðcyninga' [worst of Earth's kings].[22] The author of the Old English *Judith* repeatedly maligns the Assyrian general Holofernes with the epithet *hæðen*.[23] This juxtaposition of Jew and heathen in scriptural verse is mirrored in the pastoral tradition. Ælfric's homily on the Chair of Saint Peter, for instance, explicitly distinguishes between Jews and heathens:

> On ealdum dagum under moyses æ, noldon þa iudesican genealecan þam hæþenum ne mid him gereordian, and swyþe rihtlice þa forþan þe hi gelyfdon on þane lifigendan god and þa hæðenan gelyfdon on þa leasan godas.

> [In the old days under the Law of Moses, the Jews would not come near the heathens or feast with them, and rightly so because at that

---

[19] Scheil, pp. 240–82.

[20] This also appears to be true of Anglo-Norman writers of the twelfth century. While French texts routinely refer to the Jews using pejorative terms (*felun, vilain, tirant* etc.), I am not aware of any instance in which they are called pagans (*paen*), though the subject requires closer investigation. See Gerald Herman, 'A Note on Medieval Anti-Judaism as Reflected in the *Chansons de Geste*', *Annuale Mediaevale*, 14 (1973), 63–73.

[21] 'Genesis A' in *Old Testament Narratives*, ed. and trans. by Daniel Anlezark, Dumbarton Oaks Medieval Library, 7 (Cambridge, MA: Harvard University Press, 2011), ll. 2418, 2485, 2548; 'Daniel' in *Old Testament*, ed. and trans. by Anlezark, ll. 71, 54, 94, 221.

[22] 'Daniel' in *Old Testament*, ed. and trans. by Anlezark, ll. 304–5 (see also, 'Azarias', ll. 25–7). All translations are my own unless otherwise stated.

[23] 'Judith', in *The Beowulf Manuscript: Complete Texts and the Fight at Finnsburg*, ed. by R. D. Fulk, Dumbarton Oaks Medieval Library, 3 (Cambridge, MA: Harvard University Press, 2010), ll. 98, 110, 179.

time they themselves believed in the living God and the heathens believed in false gods.][24]

When Anglo-Saxon writers contemplated the heathen, they were responding to the insular world in which they lived. In the seventh and eighth centuries, the remnants of pre-Christian cultic practices were still being stamped out in some parts of England.[25] From the Alfredian period onwards, Viking raiders and settlers in the Danelaw constituted a new and more immediate heathen presence in the British Isles. As a migratory people living in the shadow of the heathen, the Anglo-Saxons perceived an echo of their own collective experience in the struggle between the Old Testament Jews and their pagan adversaries. The author of the Old English *Exodus* depicts the flight of the Israelites from the Egyptians as a prefiguration of the Saxon *adventus*.[26] For Ælfric, the spirited resistance of the Maccabees against the heathen Seleucids offered a model for English fortitude in the face of Viking raiders.[27] In contrast to the immediacy of paganism in pre-Conquest society, the Anglo-Saxon idea of the Jew was remote and theoretical, mediated entirely through textual traditions. After the Norman Conquest, and with the closer integration of England into northwestern Europe, this dynamic began to shift; around the same time as Viking Age heathenism receded from view, the Jews became a conspicuous feature of urban society and new ideas about the status of the Jew, both in the Gospels and the present day, began to emerge.

This tangled interplay of local and transnational historical forces forms the backdrop for the innovative portrayal of the Jews as the heathen in twelfth-century English literature. The earliest allusion to Jewish heathenism appears in the charged context of a debate between Saint James the Greater and the Jewish priesthood of Jerusalem. The sole copy of this little-known work is included under the heading *Of Jacobe, Johannes Broðer* in London, British Library, MS Cotton Vespasian D XIV, an Old English anthology compiled *c.* 1150 at Christ Church cathedral priory in

---

[24] *Ælfric's Lives of Saints: Being a Set of Sermons on Saints' Days Formerly Observed by the English Church*, EETS, o.s. 76, 82, 94, 114, 4 vols (London: Trübner & Co., 1881–1890), no. 10, ll. 178–82.

[25] Lesley Abrams, 'The Conversion of the Danelaw', in *Vikings and the Danelaw: Selected Papers from the Proceedings of the Thirteenth Viking Congress*, ed. by James Graham-Campbell (Oxford: Oxbow, 2001), pp. 31–44.

[26] Nicholas Howe, *Migration and Mythmaking in Anglo-Saxon England* (New Haven, CT: Yale University Press, 1989), pp. 72–107. While the author of *Exodus* does not use the word 'heathen', he clearly regarded the Egyptians as pagans.

[27] Scheil, pp. 313–30.

Canterbury.[28] The text is a difficult work to date on the basis of its sources and language alone; the *Passio sancti Iacobi apostoli* was known in late Anglo-Saxon England and theoretically the Old English translation could have been made at any point between the beginning of the ninth century and the compilation of MS Cotton Vespasian D XIV in the middle of the twelfth.[29] On balance, however, the growth of James' cult after Henry I donated the apostle's arm relic to Reading abbey in 1126 and the translator's evident interest in Christian-Jewish debate points to an origin in the second quarter of the twelfth century.[30]

Of Jacobe, Johannes Broðer is a relatively faithful translation of the central sections of the *Passio sancti Iacobi apostoli*, a full-length hagiography of James attributed to the Babylonian bishop Abdias.[31] The Old English translator passes over the opening sections of the pseudo-Abdian *Passio*, describing James' mission to Palestine and his conversion of the sorcerer Hermogenes, and begins his narrative at the point in the story when the Jews bribe a group of Roman centurions to arrest the apostle. As the soldiers escort James to prison, he engages the Jews in an impromptu debate before a large crowd and proceeds to discredit them by citing a string of messianic prophecies from the Old Testament. Fearful that the mob is warming to James' address, Abiathar, the high priest of Jerusalem, stirs up a riot and blames it on the apostle, who is brought before Herod Agrippa and beheaded. Throughout the Latin *Passio*, James' interlocutors are referred to either as Jews (*Iudeas*) or by their proper names, and at no point are they described as *pagani*. The Old English translator carries over most of the references to *Iudeas*, but deviates from his source at two key moments in the narrative by describing the Jews as 'heathens'. In a phrase that occurs uniquely in the English translation, the debate is introduced as a 'mycel geflit betwux þan crestenan *and* þan hæðenan' [great dispute

---

[28] 'Of Jacobe, Johannes Broðer' in *Early English Homilies from the Twelfth-Century MS Vesp. D.XIV*, ed. by Rubie D.-N. Warner, EETS, o.s. 152 (London: Kegan Paul, 1917), pp. 21–25. For further discussion of the anthology, see George Younge, 'An Old English Compiler and his Audience: London, British Library, Cotton Vespasian D.xiv', *English Manuscript Studies*, 17 (2012), pp. 1–26.

[29] An early copy of the *Passio* is included in Paris, Bibliothèque Nationale de France, MS Latin 10861, fols 3–7 (Christ Church, Canterbury, s. ix¹).

[30] Simon Yarrow, *Saints and their Communities: Miracle Stories in Twelfth-Century England* (Oxford: Oxford University Press, 2006), pp. 190–95.

[31] *Sanctuarium seu vitae sanctorum*, ed. by Boninus Mombritius, 2nd edn, 2 vols (Paris: Albert Fontemoing, 1910), ii, 27–40. See also Joanna Proud, 'St James the Greater (Cameron C.B.3.3.11)', in *Fontes Anglo-Saxonici: World Wide Web Register* <http://fontes.english.ox.ac.uk> [accessed 15 September 2014].

between the Christians and the heathens], and in the climactic lines that
lead up to James' death sentence 'Abiathar pontifex' is rendered 'Abiathar
se hæðene biscop' [Abiathar the heathen bishop].[32]

A second reference to Jewish heathenism in MS Cotton Vespasian D
XIV occurs in a brief eschatological text known as the *Coming of the
Antichrist*. Like *Of Jacobe*, *Johannes Broðer*, the *Coming of the Antichrist*
was probably composed after the Norman Conquest. As Stephen Pelle has
shown, the homily's principal source is a first recension copy of the *Revelationes* of Pseudo-Methodius, a Syriac treatise composed in the seventh
century and translated into Greek and Latin in the eighth.[33] There is
no firm evidence that the Anglo-Saxons were aware of the first recension of the *Revelationes* and the treatise was probably brought to England
by continental clerics after the Conquest. The earliest English copy of a
Recension 1 version of the *Revelationes* appears in a manuscript produced
at Salisbury cathedral between 1075 and 1100, a post-Conquest foundation responsible for importing many previously unknown works from
mainland Europe.[34] On this basis, the *Coming of the Antichrist* can be
tentatively assigned to the period 1075 x 1150.

In the preface to the *Coming of the Antichrist*, the author implies that
the heathen are living in the midst of present-day society. This section
of the text has no parallel in the *Revelationes* and seems instead to be an
original contribution by the post-Conquest translator, alerting his audience to the contemporary relevance of the Antichrist legend:

Hit sæigð on halgen bocan, þæt æfter gearan ymbyrne swa gewurðen
scule, þæt eall middeneard mid hæðenra þeode geðrynge (by), *and*
mid heor(d)an hæftnysse swa swyðe gedrecced *and* gedrefod wurðeð,
þæt hine uneaðe ænig riht gelefed mann mid þan heofonlicen kinges
tacne gebletsigen mote, oððe gesenigen durre. Þas geswæncennysse we
mugen nu mycele mare on us sylfen ongyten, þonne we hit on bocan
leornigen.

[It says in holy books that after a course of years it will come to pass
that the whole world will be so afflicted and troubled by a throng of

32 Warner, p. 21, l. 5 and p. 23 l. 33.
33 Stephen Pelle, 'The *Revelationes* of Pseudo-Methodius and "Concerning the
Coming of the Antichrist" in British Library MS Cotton Vespasian D. XIV',
N&Q, n.s., 56 (2009), 324–30.
34 The earliest Recension 1 copy of the *Revelationes* is in Salisbury, Cathedral
Library, MS 165, fols 11r–22v. The manuscript is dated in Teresa Webber, *Scribes
and Scholars at Salisbury Cathedral, c. 1075–c. 1125* (Oxford: Oxford University
Press, 1992), pp. 15, 153.

heathen peoples and by hard captivity that any man of correct belief will not easily be able to bless himself or dare to sign himself with the heavenly king's token [i.e. the sign of the cross]. We are now able to perceive these afflictions much more in ourselves than by learning about them in books.][35]

Some of the ideas expressed in the preface derive from Gregory the Great's homily for the Second Sunday in Advent, which expounds upon the signs of the apocalypse in Luke 21.25–32.[36] Gregory states, for example, that the end of days will commence when nation rises against nation, a phenomenon that he suggests can be observed in contemporary society more readily than in books. Gregory's experience of the barbarian invasions of the sixth century appears to have resonated with the author of the *Coming of the Antichrist*, who claims that the heathen are living among the English in his own time. Pelle proposes that the most likely referents of the phrase 'hæðenra þeode' are the Vikings or the Normans, but both of these suggestions are problematic.[37] The Viking settlers had integrated beyond recognition into English society by the late eleventh century and it is highly unlikely that a monastic author would describe his Norman co-religionists as the heathen. A more plausible interpretation of the preface is that it alludes to the Jews, whose conversion at the end of days forms a conventional element of the Antichrist legend. During the course of the twelfth century, commentators adopted an increasingly hostile attitude to the role of the Jews in the final scenario, aligning the Antichrist with the Jewish Messiah and presenting ordinary Jews as his willing servants.[38] This interpretation of the preface would also make sense of the translator's remark that the heathens were known up to 'now' only from books, as was the case with the Jews until the Norman Conquest.

These allusions to Jewish heathenism in MS Cotton Vespasian D XIV are paralleled in a manuscript produced slightly later in the twelfth century at Rochester cathedral priory, an institution with close ties to

---

[35] Warner, p. 66, l. 27, p. 67, l. 1. A later corrector, probably the manuscript's main scribe, added 'by' (= OE *beo*) after 'geðrynge' [throng] and emended 'heoran' [their] to 'heordan' [hard].

[36] *Gregorius Magnus: homiliae in evangelia*, ed. by Raymond Étaix, CCSL, 141 (Turnhout: Brepols, 1999), Homily 1 (pp. 5–11). See Matthew 24.1–21.

[37] Pelle, 'Antichrist', p. 329.

[38] Andrew Gow, 'The Jewish Antichrist in Medieval and Early Modern Germany', *Medieval Encounters*, 2 (1996), 249–85 (pp. 249–66); Debra Strickland, *Saracens, Demons, and Jews: Making Monsters in Medieval Art* (Princeton, NJ: Princeton University Press, 2003), pp. 212–21.

Christ Church, Canterbury. London, British Library, MS Cotton Vespasian A XXII contains a miscellaneous collection of chronicles, lists and charters compiled by a group of Rochester scribes in the first half of the thirteenth century.[39] Bound up with these official house documents is a freestanding quire (fols 54–58) containing four Old English texts in a hand dated to the last decades of the twelfth century.[40] This modest booklet was probably compiled by a Rochester monk for personal use before being swept up into a larger compilation. Two of the items in the quire draw on post-Conquest sources, including works of monastic spirituality by Saint Anselm of Canterbury, an early exponent of Christian-Jewish polemic.[41] The remaining items are a heavily rewritten version of Ælfric's *De initio creaturae* (*CH* I.1) and the pericope from his homily for the Fourth Sunday before Pentecost (*CH* I.24).[42]

The excerpt from the Fourth Sunday homily consists of Christ's parable of the lost sheep, the story of a shepherd who leaves his flock untended while he searches for a stray lamb.[43] Christ's decision to address the parable to a gathering of tax collectors and sinners angers the Pharisees and scribes. Whereas Ælfric refers to these men as 'ða sunderhalgan *and* ða boceras Iudeiscre ðeode' [the Pharisees and the scribes of the Jewish people], the Vespasian A XXII redactor alters the wording of his source to 'þa sunder halȝan *and* þa boceras þer heðen þeode' [the Pharisees and the scribes of the heathen people].[44] Once again, this is a freighted context in which to describe the Jews as the heathen; Christ's appeal to tax collectors and sinners challenges Mosaic law and triggers a direct confrontation

[39] Colin Flight, *The Bishops and Monks of Rochester, 1076–1214* (Maidstone: Kent Archaeological Society, 1997), pp. 71–83.

[40] *Old English Homilies and Homiletic Treatises of the Twelfth and Thirteenth Centuries*, ed. by Richard Morris, EETS, o.s. 29, 34 (London: Trübner & Co., 1868), Homilies 24–27 (pp. 216–45). The date of the manuscript is given on the authority of Elaine Treharne in Mary Swan, 'Preaching Past the Conquest: Lambeth Palace 487 and Cotton Vespasian A.XXII', in *The Old English Homily: Precedent, Practice, and Appropriation*, ed. by Aaron J. Kleist (Turnhout: Brepols, 2007), pp. 403–23 (p. 414). See also Mary Richards, 'MS Cotton Vespasian A.XXII: The Vespasian Homilies', *Manuscripta*, 22 (1978), 97–103.

[41] Bella Millett, 'Change and Continuity: The English Sermon before 1250', in *The Oxford Handbook of Medieval Literature in English*, ed. by Elaine Treharne and Greg Walker (Oxford: Oxford University Press, 2010), pp. 221–39 (p. 229).

[42] *Ælfric's Catholic Homilies: The First Series: Text*, ed. by Peter Clemoes, EETS, s.s. 17 (Oxford: Oxford University Press, 1997) (*CH* I).

[43] Ælfric's version of the parable combines Matthew 18.12–14 and Luke 15.3–7.

[44] Compare Clemoes, p. 371, ll. 3–4 with Morris, pp. 243, l. 29–245, l. 1.

with the Jews. In their study of the revisions made to *De initio creaturae*, Robert McColl Millar and Alex Nicholls argue that the four pieces in MS Cotton Vespasian A XXII are the 'work of one man, acting as writer and adapter'.[45] The replacement of *iudeisc* with *hæðen* can probably be attributed to this individual, and the change in emphasis dated along with the booklet as a whole to the final decades of the twelfth century.

Comparable examples of an author updating an Anglo-Saxon homily to reflect post-Conquest perceptions of Jewish heathenism appear in London, Lambeth Palace Library, MS 487, a collection of early Middle English homilies copied in the vicinity of Worcester around the year 1200.[46] Most of the seventeen Lambeth Homilies have no parallel in Old English literature and were probably composed in the decades leading up to or immediately following the Third Lateran Council (1179). An increasing concern for the spiritual wellbeing of the laity in this period has been credited with stimulating a 'revival of vernacular religious prose'.[47] Four of the sermons in the collection, however, consist partly or entirely of recycled material by the pre-Conquest writers Ælfric and Wulfstan (Lambeth 2 and 9–11). It is not possible to ascertain with certainty when the Anglo-Saxon homilies were reworked, though a date between the first and the third quarters of the twelfth century seems likely.[48] One of these homilies,

[45] 'Ælfric's *De Initio Creaturae* and London, BL Cotton Vespasian A.XXII: Omission, Addition, Retention, and Innovation', in *The Preservation and Transmission of Anglo-Saxon Culture*, ed. by Paul Szarmach and Joel T. Rosenthal (Kalamazoo, MI: Medieval Institute Publications, 1997), pp. 431–63 (p. 432).

[46] The contents of London, Lambeth Palace Library, MS 487 are printed in Morris, pp. 1–191.

[47] Bella Millett, 'The Pastoral Context of the Trinity and Lambeth Homilies', in *Essays in Manuscript Geography: Vernacular Manuscripts of the English West Midlands from the Conquest to the Sixteenth Century*, ed. by Wendy Scase (Turnhout: Brepols, 2007), pp. 43–64 (p. 61).

[48] According to Celia Sisam, 'The Scribal Tradition of the *Lambeth Homilies*', *Review of English Studies,* 2 (1951), 105–13, Homilies 9 and 11 descend from a common source (X). Other sermons that derive from the same exemplar show signs of a twelfth-century origin: Lambeth 3 borrows from the *Elucidarius* of Honorius Augustodunensis (*c.* 1100) and Lambeth 13 is structured using *divisiones*, a technique which anticipates thematic sermons of the early thirteenth century. While these features suggest the pre-Conquest material was revised in the twelfth century (i.e. when the exemplar was compiled), there is no evidence that the material in (X) post-dates 1189/90. See Stephen Pelle, 'Source Studies in the Lambeth Homilies', *Journal of English and Germanic Philology*, 113 (2014), 34–72 (pp. 49–55) [Lambeth 3]; Bella Millett, 'The Discontinuity of English Prose: Structural Innovation in the Trinity and Lambeth Homilies', in *Text and Language in Medieval English Prose: A Festschrift for Tadao Kubouchi*, ed. by Akio Oizumi,

Lambeth 9, is a lightly revised copy of Ælfric's sermon for Pentecost (*CH* I.22), in which he elaborates upon God's gift of the ten commandments to Moses, the descent of the Holy Spirit, and the apostles' foundation of the first Christian community. As throughout the *Catholic Homilies*, Ælfric is at pains to clarify the relationship between Christians and Jews in this sermon, delineating the three ages of the world (before the Law, under the Old Law, and after the coming of Christ), and citing various proof texts that attest to the succession of the Christian Church. While the sections of the homily that concern the Old Testament are broadly neutral in their attitude to the Jews, Ælfric follows his biblical source (Acts 2.1–47) in reporting the antagonistic stance of the New Testament Jews towards the apostles: 'ða apostoli ne dorston bodian ðone soðan geleafan for ogan iudeisces folces' [the apostles did not dare preach the true faith for fear of the Jewish people].[49] In the equivalent section of Lambeth 9, the compiler alters the wording of Ælfric's homily to state that the apostles were intimidated by 'þon heðene'.[50] Elsewhere in Lambeth 9, references to the Jews (*Iudeas*) are carried over from the Ælfrician source, suggesting that on this occasion, as in the preceding examples, the lexical substitution is a response to Christian-Jewish tensions depicted in the source narrative.

A comparable series of changes appear in Lambeth 11, a composite sermon on the Passion consisting of excerpts from Ælfric's homily for Palm Sunday (*CH* I.14) embedded in a freshly composed frame.[51] Ælfric commences his Palm Sunday homily with a precise definition of what he means by the word *hæðen*, presumably to forestall confusion later in the sermon: 'Ic cweðe hæðen. for ðy ðe eall mennisc wæs þa gyt wuniende on hæþenscipe. buton þam anum iudeiscan folce. þe heold þa ealdan æ on þam timan' [I say 'heathen' because all mankind was still living in heathenism then, except the Jewish people alone who followed the Old Law at that time].[52] In contrast, the compiler of Lambeth 11 deliberately conflates the Jews with the heathen, systematically revising sections of Ælfric's homily that contradict this position. In a passage that exemplifies the close ties between affective devotion and the perception of Jewish

Jacek Fisiak and John Scahill (Frankfurt: Peter Lang, 2005), pp. 129–50 (pp. 136–37) [Lambeth 13].

49 Clemoes, p. 361, ll. 192–93.

50 Morris, p. 97, ll. 31–32.

51 The use of *CH* I.14 in Lambeth 11 is discussed in Mary Swan, 'Old English Made New: One Catholic Homily and its Resuses', *Leeds Studies in English*, 28 (1997), 1–13 (pp. 8–11).

52 Clemoes, p. 361, ll. 43–45.

guilt, the compiler lingers on Christ's wounds and the flow of blood from his side before denouncing the 'heathen' as his killers: 'Ðas pine and monie oðre ure drihten þolede of ðan heðene folke in þisse timan' [This torture and many others our Lord suffered from the heathen people at this time].[53] Immediately thereafter, the compiler turns to Ælfric's Palm Sunday sermon, borrowing a passage in which the Anglo-Saxon homilist argues that Christ did not force the Jews to kill him, rather they were misled by the devil: 'ne nydde he na þæt iudeisce folc to his cweale' [he did not compel the Jewish people to put him to his death].[54] Instead of referring to the 'Iudeisce folc', Lambeth 9 states that Christ did not compel the 'heðene folc' [heathen people] to put him to death.[55] Viewed in isolation, the first of these two references to the *hæðen* might be interpreted as an allusion to the Roman centurions who arrested Christ and nailed him to the cross. The Lambeth homilist's subsequent revision of the Ælfrician passage on compulsion, however, confirms that he has the Jews in mind.

The description of Christ's killers as Jewish heathens in Lambeth 9 has a direct parallel in the *Vices and Virtues*, an early Middle English dialogue between a penitent soul and Reason.[56] This text survives uniquely in London, British Library, MS Stowe 34, a codex copied in southeastern England during the first quarter of the thirteenth century.[57] The *Vices and Virtues* was itself composed considerably earlier than the copy in MS Stowe 34 and is usually dated to the second half of the twelfth century.[58] As such, it belongs to the same phase of pastoral renewal as the Lambeth Homilies. Although the author of the *Vices and Virtues* addresses an unlearned audience, he has been characterised as 'intelligent, well-educated, and fully versed in contemporary theology', probably as a

---

[53] Morris, p. 121, ll. 17–18.

[54] Clemoes, pp. 295–6, ll. 164–65.

[55] Morris, p. 121, l. 32.

[56] *Vices and Virtues: Being a Soul's Confession of its Sins with Reason's Description of the Virtues*, ed. by F. Holthausen, EETS, o.s. 89, 159 (London: Trübner & Co, 1888–1921).

[57] Margaret Laing, *Catalogue of Sources for a Linguistic Atlas of Early Medieval England* (Cambridge: D. S. Brewer, 1993), p. 106.

[58] Cate Gunn, '*Vices and Virtues*: A Reassessment of Manuscript Stowe 34', in *Sin in Medieval and Early Modern Culture: The Tradition of the Seven Deadly Sins*, ed. by Richard Newhauser and Susan Ridyard (York: York Medieval Press, 2012), pp. 65–84 (pp. 68–69); Stephen Pelle, 'The Date and Intellectual Milieu of the Early Middle English *Vices and Virtues*', *Neophilologus* <http://dx.doi.org/10.1007/s11061-014-9397-1> [advanced access 13 September 2014].

result of spending time in the Parisian schools.[59] Northern France was an innovative centre of biblical scholarship in the second half of the twelfth century and the author of the *Vices and Virtues* may well have attended lectures on the Passion that emphasised the guilt of the Jews.[60]

In the section of the dialogue entitled 'Of Edmodnesse', Reason points to Christ as the ultimate embodiment of humility and observes that his perfection undermined the authority of the devil. On account of Christ's incomparable humility, Reason continues, the devil was deceived and,

> beuall þo haðene mid his leðre meneȝinges al hwat hie hine fordemden to deaðe mid muchele unrihte, *and* ec ðane forcuþeste deað, *and* ðane laðlicheste ðe hie beðenchen mihten, þat was on rode, *and* iec betwenen twa þieues

> [incited the heathen with his wicked exhortations until they condemned him to death with great injustice, the most miserable and fearsome death they were able to devise, that is on the cross and also between two thieves.][61]

Taken in conjunction with a reference earlier in the same passage to the blindness of Christ's accusers, there can be little doubt that the word heathen is again being used to refer to the Jews, in this instance specifically to the high priests of the Sanhedrin.[62]

A subsequent passage in the *Vices and Virtues* verifies that the author regarded the Jews as heathens. This occurs in the context of a long denunciation of usury, in which Reason refers directly to the presence of Jewish moneylenders in contemporary society:

> *Qui iurat proximo suo, et cetera.* 'Se ðe swereð soð his nexte, þat is, his emcristenn, *and* him naht ne beswikð mid none chiepinge ne mid nan oðre ðinge; *and* se ðe ne ȝifð naht his eihte te goule, *and* se ðe ne nimð none mede of ða innocentes, ðat bien uneilinde menn ðe none

[59] Pelle, 'Intellectual Milieu'.

[60] Abulafia, *Christians and Jews*, pp. 11–22.

[61] Holthausen, p. 51, ll. 11–14. This passage is cited in the *MED* under s.v. *hethen* (adj. and noun) (sense 1d, 'applied to Jews'). The other three quotations for sense 1d are from the fifteenth century.

[62] Holthausen, p. 51, ll. 5–7: 'Ðies ilke hlauerd Iesus Crist, he was her on ðese liue wuniȝende þrie and þrihti wintre *and* an half mang senfulle mannen, soð godd (ðe hie ne mihten isien), *and* soð mann, ðe hie isien mihten' [The same Lord Jesus Christ lived here in this world for thirty-three and a half years among sinful men, truly God (which they could not see), and truly man, which they could see].

ma*n*ne euel ne wille∂: ∂ese mu3en wuni3e*n* on godes telde, *and* uppen
his munte he*m* reste*n*' (Psalm 14.1–5). *And* ∂a ∂e mede neme∂, hie ne
scule*n* ∂ar neure cume*n*, 3if hie bie*n* ∂ar mide 3enomene. Nu bie*n*
sume o∂re ∂at healden he*m* selue*n* wise *and* 3eape, and befaste∂ here
pane3es ∂e ha∂ene men*n*, for to habbe*n* of hi*m* bi3eate; *and* sume, hi
læne∂ here emcr*i*sten to halue bi3eate, ∂e fare∂ ∂ar mide be londe *and*
be watere on michele hahte on liue *and* on saule, and mid michele
swinke: and hie sitte∂ at ham *and* ne haue*n* ∂arof no*n* 3eswink, but on
here ∂ohtes *and* on here spaches.

[*He who swears to his neighbour, etc.* 'He who swears truth to the next
man, that is his fellow Christian, and does not deceive him with any
bargaining or with any other such activity; and he who does not lend
money at interest, nor charges the prevailing fee from the *innocentes*
– that is, harmless men who intend evil to no one – these people will
dwell in God's tent and rest themselves upon his hill' (Psalm 14.1–5).
And those who charge the prevailing fee shall never come there, if
they are caught out by it. In the present time, there are some people
who consider themselves wise and crafty, and entrust their money to
heathen men in order to have interest from it; and others lend at half
interest to their fellow Christians, who use it to travel by land and
water in great danger to life and soul, and with great toil, while they
(the creditors) sit at home and have no trouble for it, except in their
thoughts and in their speeches.][63]

Paraphrasing Psalm 14.1–5, the opening lines of this passage unambigu-
ously condemn the practice of usury (*gavel*).[64] Only those who refrain
absolutely from lending at interest (*niman mede*) will be permitted entry
into the kingdom of heaven. Reason's commentary on the biblical quotation, however, suggests that Christians were coming up with creative strategies for bypassing the ecclesiastical prohibition against usury, firstly by
'loaning' or 'entrusting' (*bifasten*) their money to the heathen (*hæ∂en*) in
return for a share of the profits, and secondly by financing the speculative
ventures of 'fellow Christians' (*emcristen*). The juxtaposition of 'ha∂ene
menn' and 'emcristen' once again confirms that *hæ∂en* is being used to
refer to the Jews, the most prominent group of moneylenders and bankers
in twelfth-century society.[65]

63 Holthausen, p. 79, ll. 3–16.
64 For the translation of key terms in this passage, see *MED*, s.v. *bifasten* (v.); s.v.
biyete (n.) (sense 1b); s.v. *gavel* (n.(1)) (sense 2a); s.v. *mede* (n.(4)) (sense 1b).
65 Mundill, pp. 21–42; Stacey, 'Jewish Lending', pp. 78–101.

The foregoing examples establish that the perception of Jewish heathenism was widespread in twelfth-century English pastoral literature. These explicit references to the Jews as heathens are supplemented by the less direct but no less psychologically revealing alignment of Jews and heathens in the second continuation of the Peterborough Chronicle (Oxford, Bodleian Library, MS Laud Misc. 636).[66] Often regarded as the first work in Middle English, the second continuation was composed by a monk of Peterborough abbey around the year 1155.[67] In an entry dated anachronistically to 1137, the chronicler looks back at the suffering of noncombatants during the Anarchy of King Stephen's reign (1135–1154). Cecily Clark has remarked on the emotive quality of this annal, which 'eloquently expresses a contemporary civilian's feelings when faced with the brutality of robber barons'.[68] The spontaneous tone of the entry, however, belies its underlying intertextuality and literary sophistication. Weaving together an array of textual sources, the first half of the annal for 1137 describes the tortures endured by the civilian populace under the barons, culminating in the memorable statement that people 'sæden openlice ðat Crist slep, and his halechen' [said openly that Christ and his saints were asleep].[69]

The sensational account of civilian suffering in the first part of the annal has inevitably attracted more critical attention than its concluding section, which describes the process of recovery after the fighting ends. The postwar regeneration begins locally at Peterborough under Abbot Martin before extending to the national level with the metaphorical awakening of the saints in the form of William of Norwich:

> Nu we willen sægen su*m* del wat belamp on Stephn*es* kinges time. On his time þe Iudeus of Noruuic bohton an Cristen cild beforen Estren, *and* pineden hi*m* alle þe ilce pining ðat ure Drihten was pined, *and* on Lang Fridæi hi*m* on roden hengen for ure Drihtines luue *and* sythen byrieden hi*m*; wenden ðat it sculde ben forholen. Oc ure Dryhtin atywede ðat he was hali m*art*yr. a t(e) munekes hi*m* namen *and* beby-

[66] *The Peterborough Chronicle, 1070–1154*, ed. by Cecily Clark, 2nd edn (Oxford: Clarendon Press, 1970), s.a. 1132–1154.

[67] Clark, pp. xxiv–xxviii.

[68] Clark, p. xxxvi.

[69] Clark, s.a. 1137, ll. 55–6. The textual analogues of the annal are listed in *The Anglo-Saxon Chronicle: A Revised Translation*, trans. by Dorothy Whitelock, with the assistance of David Douglas and Susie Tucker (New Brunswick, NJ: Rutgers University Press, 1961), p. 199, n. 2.

ried hi*m* heglice in þe minst*re*. *and* He maket þur(h) ure Drihtin wulderlice *and* manifældlice miracles; *and* hatte he *Sanct* Willelm.

[Now we wish to describe to some extent what happened in King Stephen's time. In his time, the Jews of Norwich bought a Christian child before Easter, and tortured him with all the torture that our Lord was tortured with; and on Good Friday they hanged him on a cross on account of our Lord, and then they buried him. They expected it would be concealed, but our Lord made it plain that he was a holy martyr, and the monks took him and buried him with ceremony in the monastery, and through our Lord he works wonderful and varied miracles, and he is called Saint William.][70]

This passage derives ultimately from Book 1 of Thomas of Monmouth's *Life and Passion of William of Norwich*, a work begun around 1150 and completed in 1155.[71] Thomas' paranoid text records his personal quest to expose an international Jewish conspiracy to kill a Christian child every Easter, fulfilled in 1144 by the Jews of Norwich. The author of the Peterborough annal for 1137 clearly sympathised with the underlying aim of Thomas' work, which attempts to heal the fractures of postwar society by presenting the assimilation of 'Norwich's diverse population into a single *Christianitas* at the expense of the Jews'.[72] In situating the story of William's 'martyrdom' at the end of the entry for 1137 (anachronistically), the chronicler follows Thomas' example, positing William's cult as a focal point for postwar renewal.

The interest of the annal for 1137 from the perspective of the present discussion lies in its appropriation of the Vikings and the Jews as twin precedents for the savagery of the barons. In the context of an account of the desecration of churches and graveyards, the chronicler compares the warring magnates of the Anarchy to the Viking raiders who plundered the fenland abbeys in the Anglo-Saxon period: 'Wes næure gæt mare wrec-cehed on land ne næure hethen men werse ne diden þan hi diden' [There had never been until then greater misery in the country, nor had heathen men ever done worse than they did].[73] The alignment of the barons with the Jews, on the other hand, occurs at the subtler level of allusion, with the tortures inflicted on civilians echoing Thomas' description of William's death. The connection between William's murder and the war crimes

[70] Clark, s.a. 1137, ll. 76–84 (trans. Whitelock, p. 200).
[71] Langmuir, pp. 838–40.
[72] Cohen, 'Flow of Blood', p. 62.
[73] Clark, s.a. 1137, ll. 44–46.

perpetrated by the barons is signalled by the ironic remark that 'ne uuæren
næure nan martyrs swa pined' [no martyrs were ever so tortured] as the
English.[74] Thereafter, the chronicler incorporates a sequence of details that
link the brutality of the barons to that of the Jews. The 'beam' (*bem*) that
the magnates use to torture their prisoners, for example, is reminiscent
of the beam from which the Jews hang William in Thomas' narrative.[75]
More precisely, the chronicler's claim that the barons fastened a device
of 'cnotted strenges' [knotted strings] around their victims' heads and
'uurythen it *ðat* gæde to þe hærnes' [twisted it until they penetrated to
the brains] draws directly on Thomas' description of William's murder:

> Postmodum uero breui funiculo auricularis fere digiti habente grossi-
> tudinem arrepto, trinumque in eo certis locis assignantes nodum, caput
> illud innocens a fronte in occiput circumcingunt: medium quippe
> fronti nodum extremosque alios hinc et inde timporibus imprimentes,
> utrarumque partium capitibus ad occiput strictissime contractis, et
> strictissimo confecto ibi nodo, quod funiculi supererat circa collum
> itidem hinc et inde ad anteriora colli sub mento contrahendo reducunt,
> ibique illud insolitum tormenti genus in quinto nodo consummant.

> [the Jews took a short rope, about as thick as a little finger, and made
> three knots in places marked on it, and encircled that innocent head
> from forehead to back; in the centre of the forehead they pressed a
> knot, as they did at each temple. Both sides of the head were tied to
> the back, extremely tightly, and there a firm knot was made. The ends
> of the rope were tied round the neck and around under the chin, and
> there this unheard of type of torture was completed in a fifth knot.][76]

Most scholars consider the second continuator's account of William's
murder to be based on oral report or rumour, as opposed to consultation
of a written version of Thomas' work.[77] While the passage on William's
death contains some notable parallels with the *Life and Passion*, such as
the claim that the Jews 'bought' William with bribes, a number of details
differ from the Latin text. William's murder, for instance, is placed on
Good Friday in the chronicle but on the preceding Wednesday in Thomas'
narrative. The theory that the story was spread through rumour, however,

---

[74] Clark, ll. 20–21.
[75] Clark, l. 31.
[76] Clark, ll. 23–24; Jessopp and James, i.5 (trans. Rubin, pp. 16–17). See Rubin,
pp. xxi–xxii.
[77] Langmuir, p. 821; McCulloh, pp. 712–17.

overlooks the correspondences between Thomas' work and the section of the Peterborough Chronicle covering the Anarchy. These shared details indicate that the chronicler had direct access to Book 1 of the *Life and Passion*, or at least received an oral report that adhered closely to the Latin narrative. This probable use of a written source is significant, since it implies that the spread of the ritual murder allegation was a 'textually generated event', actively promoted within Benedictine circles rather than casually disseminated by word of mouth.[78]

Regardless of how the story of William's death reached the monks of Peterborough, the chronicler's alignment of Vikings and Jews as prototypes for the cruelty of the barons suggests the common space that these two groups occupied in the imagination of a twelfth-century Englishman. In searching for a way to represent the near inexpressible trauma of the Anarchy, the chronicler looked back at the atrocities of the Viking Age and forward to the alleged savagery of the Jews in his own time. These two groups stand in typological relation to each other, embodying a displaced anxiety about heathen acts perpetrated by Christians during the Anarchy. A strikingly similar connection is made in the *Life and Passion*, where Thomas compares William's murder to Saint Edmund's martyrdom at the hands of the Vikings: 'Sustinuit ille paganos in legem Christi deseuientes, pertulit iste iudeos in se quasi mortem Christi reiterantes' [One sustained the law of Christ, which was being savaged by the pagans; the other endured the Jews, who were repeating, as it were, the death of Christ].[79] Vikings and Jews, in other words, are intimately linked in the minds of the Peterborough chronicler and Thomas of Monmouth, who regard these two groups as archetypal enemies of a stable Christian society.

The literary and historical texts discussed above trace the changing perception of the Jews across the Norman Conquest. Before 1066, Anglo-Saxon writers maintained a clear, if occasionally uneasy, distinction between Jews and heathens. The post-Conquest works under consideration do not indicate that English writers came to regard the Jews as pagans in a literal sense; rather, they testify to the further extension of Wulfstan's loose definition of *hæðen* as 'degenerate' or 'immoral' to include the Jews, a group previously exempt from the charge of 'cultural paganism'. In the context of reworked homilies by Ælfric, the replacement of *Iudeas* or *Iudeisc* with *hæðen* stands apart from comparable instances of lexical

---

[78] Anthony Bale, 'Fictions of Judaism in England before 1290', in *The Jews of Medieval Britain: Historical, Literary and Archaeological Perspectives*, ed. by P. Skinner (Woodbridge: Boydell, 2003), pp. 129–44 (p. 131).

[79] Jessopp and James, vi.10 (trans. Rubin, p. 159).

updating, such as the gradual phasing out of *æ* (OE 'law') in favour of
the Norse loanword *lagu*.[80] In contrast to this type of modernisation, the
substitutions considered above are indicative of a deeper reconfiguration
of the way the Jews were categorised in relation to other types of outsider.
The tripartite division of the Anglo-Saxon worldview into Christians, Jews
and heathens gives way in these texts to a polarised schema in which
human society is carved up bluntly into Christians and non-Christians,
those inside the Church and those outside it.

How are we to account for this lexical and conceptual shift in the
meaning of *hæðen*? One explanation is that anti-Jewish ideas formulated
in scholarly circles began to percolate into the vernacular during the
twelfth century. It is significant in this regard that most of the manuscripts considered above were produced in monastic cathedrals, where
English writers coexisted with monastic elites who were actively involved
in composing, acquiring and propagating anti-Jewish texts. One of the
most influential vehicles for disseminating new ideas about the Jews was
the biblical commentary, which eroded the position of tolerance advo-
cated by patristic theologians.[81] Compilations such as the *Glossa ordinaria*,
a standard reference work in the twelfth-century cathedral schools, placed
a new emphasis on the guilt of the Jews and their culpability for the
death of Christ. Another strand of monastic scholarship sought to refute
Jewish disbelief with rational argument.[82] In the final chapter of the *Cur
deus homo*, Anselm of Canterbury states that his reasoning would satisfy
'non solum Iudaeis sed etiam paganis' [not only the Jews but also the
pagans].[83] This pairing recurs throughout Anselm's letters and dialogues,
to such an extent that we rarely find him mentioning pagans without also
referring to Jews.[84] Anselm's attack on Jewish disbelief spawned numerous

---

[80] Richard Dance, '*Ealde æ, niwæ laʒe*: Two Words for "Law" in the Twelfth
Century', *New Medieval Literatures*, 13 (2012), pp. 149–82. For an overview of
lexical modernisation in this period, see Andreas Fischer, 'The Vocabulary of Very
Late Old English', in *Studies in English Language and Literature: 'Doubt Wisely':
Papers in Honour of E. G. Stanley*, ed. by M. J. Toswell and E. M. Tyler (London:
Routledge, 1996), pp. 29–41.

[81] Jeremy Cohen, 'The Jews as the Killers of Christ in the Latin Tradition: From
Augustine to the Friars', *Traditio*, 39 (1983), 1–27.

[82] Abulafia, *Christians and Jews*, pp. 23–33; Cohen, *Living Letters*, pp. 167–218.

[83] *S. Anselmi Cantuariensis archiepiscopi opera omnia*, ed. by F. S. Schmitt, 6 vols
(Edinburgh: Thomas Nelson and Sons, 1946–1961), *Cur deus homo* i.22 (ii, 133).

[84] Anna S. Abulafia, 'St Anselm and Those Outside the Church', in *Faith and
Identity: Christian Political Experience*, ed. by David Loades and Katherine Walsh
(Oxford: Basil Blackwell, 1989), pp. 11–37 (p. 18).

imitators, including his close friend and correspondent Gilbert Crispin. In the *Disputatio Iudaei et Christiani*, Gilbert directed his proof of the necessity of the incarnation towards a Jewish detractor.[85] The sense of Christian identity and Jewish otherness formulated in these scholastic works trickled down to the lower strata of monastic communities. In a parable related to the monks of Christ Church, for instance, Anselm compared the monastery to a citadel, surrounded by a hostile world of 'Iudaeos atque paganos' [Jews and pagans].[86]

While these scholarly texts resist conflating Jews and pagans, they establish an equivalence between the two categories that is only a short step away from the perception of Jewish heathenism witnessed in vernacular works. As R. I. Moore argues, the Jews were virtually interchangeable in the eyes of twelfth-century scholars with other heretical groups, exemplifying an impurity that threatened the fabric of Christian society.[87] Anti-Jewish polemic formulated in scholarly circles has an obvious resonance with some of the works produced for English-speaking audiences. The presentation of the Jews as the heathen in *Of Jacobe, Johannes Broðer* occurs in the context of a heated debate that recalls disputational literature of the period. Moreover, the Old Testament proof texts that James uses to discredit the Jews are a standard component of twelfth-century polemical texts, featuring prominently in Gilbert Crispin's *Disputatio Iudei et Christiani*.[88] Likewise, the crucifixion scenes in Lambeth 11 and the *Vices and Virtues*, which portray Christ's killers as simultaneously Jewish and heathen, echo the terminology employed in the *Glossa ordinaria*. These correspondences suggest that English writers were receptive to anti-Jewish ideas that originated in scholarly circles.

In addition to the influence of scholasticism, the perception of Jewish heathenism in vernacular texts may also be a response to daily interaction with the Jews. By the end of the twelfth century, Jews were a promi-

---

[85] *The Works of Gilbert Crispin, Abbot of Westminster*, ed. by Anna Sapir Abulafia and G. R. Evans (London: Oxford University Press for the British Academy, 1987), pp. 1–87.

[86] 'Liber de humanis moribus', in *Memorials of Saint Anselm*, ed. by R. W. Southern and F. S. Schmitt (London: Oxford University Press for the British Academy), chs. 75–76 (pp. 66–67).

[87] R. I. Moore, *The Formation of a Persecuting Society: Power and Deviance in Western Europe, 950–1250*, 2nd edn (Oxford: Blackwell, 2007), pp. 26–42.

[88] Anna Sapir Abulafia, 'Christians Disputing Disbelief: St Anselm, Gilbert Crispin and Pseudo-Anselm', in *Religionsgespräche in Mittelalter*, ed. by Bernard Lewis and Friedrich Nimböhner (Wiesbaden: Harrassowitz, 1992), pp. 131–48 (pp. 136–37, 142).

nent and often wealthy component of many English cathedral cities. The place names associated with provincial Jewries in these towns resonate with vernacular pastoral literature. A Christ Church charter of *c.* 1180, for example, describes modern-day Stour Street, the heart of the medieval Jewry in Canterbury, as the 'vicum qui anglice appellatur hethenman-neslane' [street which in English is called Heathenman Lane].[89] Later references to Jewries on 'Hethenmannestrete' in Bury Saint Edmunds (*c.* 1250) and 'Heathen Lane' in Thetford (1779) show that the toponym was relatively widespread.[90] The English texts discussed above contain traces of the anxiety occasioned by the new Jewish presence in English cities. The *Coming of the Antichrist* encourages its audience to interpret the arrival of the Jews as a sign of the imminence of the apocalypse, while the *Vices and Virtues* betrays a similar concern about the contaminating effect of Jewish commercialism on the Christian populace. These fears approach dangerous levels in the Peterborough Chronicle, where the Jews are categorised along with the Vikings as exemplary unbelievers and enemies of the Church.

The early development of the vernacular as a language of the book in Anglo-Saxon England, successive waves of colonisation by Danish and French speakers, and the arrival of the Jews after the Norman Conquest are factors that distinguish the English experience of the twelfth-century renaissance from that of other regions in Europe. Benedictine scribes and translators working in English were highly responsive to these cultural transformations. During the eleventh century, a looser definition of heathenism emerged, perhaps as a result of the conversion of the Vikings. This in turn established a precedent for the portrayal of the Jews as the heathen after the Norman Conquest, a hostile stereotype that monastic writers actively promoted among English-speaking audiences. Closer investigation of other vernacular works from the period (both English and French), as well as visual sources such as stained glass windows and Psalter illustrations, is likely to confirm the pervasiveness of anti-Jewish sentiment

---

[89] Canterbury, Cathedral Archives, Chartae Antiquae C 770, transcribed in Michael Adler, *The Jews of Medieval England* (London: Edward Goldston for the Jewish Historical Society of England, 1939), Appendix V (p. 108).

[90] *Charters of the Medieval Hospitals of Bury St Edmunds*, ed. by Christopher Harper-Bill (Woodbridge: Boydell Press, 1994), pp. 36, 55; Alan Crosby, *A History of Thetford* (Chichester: Phillimore & Co., 1986), Plate 1, reproducing a plan drawn up by Thomas Martin for his *History of Thetford* (1779). See also *The Palgrave Dictionary of Medieval Anglo-Jewish History*, ed. by Joe Hillaby and Caroline Hillaby (Basingstoke: Palgrave Macmillan, 2013), p. 70.

in the twelfth century.[91] Scholars have yet to explain satisfactorily how the learned attack on the Jews mounted by Anselm and his contemporaries evolved into the more virulent strain of anti-Jewish hostility that led to the pogroms of 1189/90. Poised between the worlds of the cloister and the laity, English pastoral texts are one example of a medium in which clerical and popular attitudes towards the Jews converged and reached a wider audience.

[91] I discuss the representation of the Jews in the *Ormulum*, the *Gospel of Nichodemus*, and the *Avenging of the Saviour* in my forthcoming monograph, *The English Renaissance of the Twelfth Century*. For preliminary remarks on anti-Jewish themes in Old French texts, see Herman, '*Chansons de Geste*'; Jennifer Shea, 'Adgar's *Gracial* and Christian Images of Jews in Twelfth-Century Vernacular Literature', *Journal of Medieval History*, 33 (2007), 181–96. Visual representations of the Jews are touched upon in Madeline Harrison Caviness, *The Early Stained Glass of Canterbury Cathedral, circa 1175–1220* (Princeton, NJ: Princeton University Press), pp. 118–19; George Henderson, 'The Textual Basis of the Picture Leaves', in *The Eadwine Psalter: Text, Image, and Monastic Culture in Twelfth-Century Canterbury*, ed. by Margaret Gibson and Richard Pfaff (London: Modern Humanities Research Association, 1992), pp. 35–42.

Latin Composition in Medieval Norway

AIDAN CONTI

IN THE PAST DECADE, the study of Latin writing in Scandinavia has enjoyed a resurgence. Lavishly illustrated collections of papers have examined the Latin manuscript culture for both Sweden and Norway.[1] Based on the cataloguing of the fragments of the National Library of Finland, an account of Latin in Finland (then eastern Sweden) has been produced.[2] The dictionary of medieval Latin covering Sweden has been completed, and that for Denmark is nearly complete.[3] In the field of literary history, the late Karsten Friis-Jensen has surveyed the production of Latin works in Scandinavia;[4] Gottskálk Jensson has reclaimed the place of Latin learning within the literary landscape of Iceland in particular.[5] The entire region has an electronic handbook that covers known literary works from before the Reformation.[6] This body of work has had a salutary effect on rehabilitating an area of study often overlooked, the interna-

---

[1] *Medieval Book Fragments in Sweden: An International Seminar in Stockholm, November 2003*, ed. by Jan Brunius (Stockholm: Kungl. Vitterhets historie och antikvitets akademien, 2005); *Latin Manuscripts of Medieval Norway: Studies in Memory of Lilli Gjerløw*, ed. by Espen Karlsen (Oslo: Novus Press, 2013).

[2] Tuomas Heikkilä, 'The Arrival and Development of Latin Literacy on the Edge of Europe: The Case of Medieval Finland', in *The Performance of Christian and Pagan Storyworlds: Non-Canonical Chapters of the History of Nordic Medieval Literature*, ed. by Lars Boje Mortensen and Tuomas Lehtonen (Turnhout: Brepols, 2013), pp. 67–108. The catalogue can be accessed at: <http://fragmenta. kansalliskirjasto.fi/> [accessed 26 June 13].

[3] Ulla Westerbergh and Eva Odelman, *Glossarium till medeltidslatinet i Sverige / Glossarium mediae latinitatis Sueciae* (Stockholm: Almqvist & Wiksell, 1968–2002); Franz Blatt and others, *Ordbog over dansk middelalderlatin / Lexicon mediae latinitatis Danicae* (Aarhus: Aarhus Universitetsforlag, 1987).

[4] Karsten Friis-Jensen, 'Regional Variation: The Case of Scandinavian Latin', in *The Oxford Handbook of Medieval Latin Literature*, ed. by Ralph Hexter and David Townsend (Oxford: Oxford University Press, 2012), pp. 106–23.

[5] Gottskálk Jensson, 'The Lost Latin Literature of Medieval Iceland: The Fragments of the *Vita Sancti Thorlaci* and Other Evidence', *Symbolae Osloenses*, 79 (2004), 150–70.

[6] *Medieval Nordic Literature in Latin: A Website of Authors and Anonymous Works c. 1100–1530*, ed. by Stephan Borgehammar and others <https://wikihost.uib.no/ medieval/index.php/Medieval_Nordic_Literature_in_Latin> [accessed 28 June

tional dimensions of which have often been passed over in favour of more
narrowly defined national material from the Middle Ages.[7] As a result of
this perceived absence, in the popular imagination the culture of Latin
learning, and often relatedly the thoroughness of Christianisation, has
been seen as minimal and perhaps not as consequential as in other parts
of Europe.[8] The present piece will offer an overview of the corpus of Latin
composed in Norway in the Middle Ages and consider this production
as part of a larger landscape of Latin learning to suggest a holistic view
of Latin in Norway. Recent work on the manuscript culture of Norway
has been particularly instrumental in redressing our understanding of
Latin writing in Norway; the destruction of Latin material during the
Lutheran Reformation effectively erased from consideration the range of
Latin material that had been reproduced, transmitted and circulated in
the north during the medieval period.[9] Moreover, increasing evidence
from inscribed material promises to inform further our understanding
of popular Latin literacy. A consideration of the literary production of
Latin composed in the country offers something of a counter-balance to
the perspective.

The parameters of the corpus of medieval Latin from Norway – what
it comprises and its limits – is very much a story of efforts to assemble
a dictionary of Norwegian medieval Latin. In the 1940s material began
to be compiled and excerpted under the direction of Eirik Vandvik at
the University of Oslo. After Vandvik's early death in 1953, Vegard Skånland continued the preparation of a draft dictionary, but this work largely
came to a halt when Skånland became professor in Bergen in 1971. In
the 1990s under the direction of Lars Boje Mortensen, Vandvik and
Skånland's manuscript was typed and saved as an electronic file; at the
same time the work was expanded by adding headwords from a number

---

2014]. As stated on the title page, there are some notable absences such as Birgitta
of Sweden and Mattias of Linköping.

[7] See Lars Boje Mortensen, 'The Study of Medieval Latin Literature – an
Expanding Field of Little Impact?', in *Mediävistik in 21. Jahrhundert. Stand und
Perspektiven der internationalen und interdisziplinären Mittelalterforschung*, ed. by
Hans-Werner Goetz and Jörg Jarnut (Munich: Wilhem Fink Verlag, 2003), pp.
135–47.

[8] For a short overview, see Kurt Villads Jensen, Torstein Jørgensen and Kirsi
Salonen's 'Introduction' to *Medieval Christianity in the North*, ed. by K. Salonen,
K. Villads Jensen and T. Jørgensen (Turnhout: Brepols, 2013), pp. 1–6.

[9] Gunnar Pettersen, 'From Parchment Books to Fragments: Norwegian Medieval
Codices before and after the Reformation', in *Latin Manuscripts of Medieval
Norway*, ed. by Espen Karlsen, pp. 41–65.

of twelfth-century works that had not been incorporated. Due to this extended period of time (including a period of inactivity), the list of works compiled by Vandvik is in need of updating and expansion. Not only must new editions of previously edited material be added, but so must recent editions of material which had not been edited when Vandvik and Skånland were active.

Consequently, at present researchers have no access to a definitive, digital form of the corpus of Norwegian medieval Latin. Although this circumstance prohibits concrete numbers and statistics on the corpus, nonetheless the overall shape and character of the material can be considered. First, it should be noted that the corpus, as defined for the purpose of compiling a dictionary, comprises not only material composed in Norway and/or by Norwegians, but also material written abroad with a direct to link to medieval Norway; the most important of such works is the large body of correspondence from the papacy to the Norwegian church. With respect to this principle for inclusion, the Norwegian project is similar to those of Denmark and Sweden.

Indeed, the *Diplomatarium Norvegicum*, the ongoing multi-volume collection of Norwegian letters and documents written before 1590, comprises the overwhelming majority of Latin from and relating to Norway.[10] While there are no statistics that break down the documents of the *Diplomatarium* according to language and/or place of issue, a rough estimate of the Latin in the *Diplomatarium* published to date suggests a number of approximately 1,165,000 words, a large number of which represent material issued abroad but pertaining to Norway.[11] An additional body of material comprising material outside the *Diplomatarium* but part of the list of works detailed by Vandvik/Skånland was compiled in the 1990s comprising approximately 65,000 words. While this small

10 To date, twenty-three volumes have been published dating from 1847 to 2011 comprising 20,000 documents.

11 This preliminary accounting is based on a progress report for the Dictionary that estimates the Latin in the *Diplomatarium* as one-fifth of the twenty-two volumes that were completed in 2000. Preliminary electronic files for volumes 1–20 counted approximately 4,925,000 words, although this number is somewhat exaggerated; culling and editing will bring it down marginally. However, the number does not include more recent volumes. Latin documents for volumes 1–7 were isolated and totalled 425,000 words; the total number of words of all languages in the same volumes was approximately 1,854,000 words. The Latin then represents about 23% for those volumes. An estimate of 60,000 Latin words per volume seems to be reasonable for the remaining three volumes (21, 22, 23), bringing the total to approximately 1,165,000 Latin words in the entire set.

body does not include a number of recently edited works, the two groups taken together represent a fair idea of the number of words in the corpus of Norwegian medieval Latin, around or perhaps somewhat more than 1,250,000 words.

By contrast, the corpus of Shakespeare is just over 835,000 words.[12] The corpus of Old English is estimated to be almost five times that of Shakespeare.[13] *Heimskringla* alone is about 235,000 words (or tokens) and the collected family sagas (or *Íslendingasögur*) about 1,100,000 words.[14] Similarly, from another perspective, there are less than approximately 10,000 headwords that are listed in Vandvik and Skånland's draft dictionary. As a point of reference from more familiar, contemporary lexicographical tools, the *Oxford English Dictionary* is 300,000 headwords, *Deutsches Wörterbuch* is 330,000. Present estimates suggest that a dictionary of medieval Latin from Norwegian material will produce a single volume of about 350 pages. The dictionary of Swedish medieval Latin is about 1100 pages, Denmark is comparable thereto at 700 pages through the first third of 'R'. The *Dictionary of Medieval Latin from British Sources* runs to over 35,000 pages at completion.[15] The *index verborum* of Saxo's *Gesta Danorum* is 900 pages alone.[16] In short, the amount of material in Latin composed (as opposed to copied) in Norway is relatively small.

Understandably, literary surveys often acknowledge in passing the place of Latin in the early stages of Norwegian literary history. With this in mind, before turning more in depth to the corpus itself, it is worth considering two recent attempts to redress the role of Latin learning in Nordic literary history in order to understand better the rationale underlying these entreaties. In the first, Gottskálk Jensson, responding directly to the claim that Iceland was radically different from other nations of western and central Europe with respect to the use of Latin, produced a list of eight works composed in Iceland including a guide for pilgrims, two long royal biographies, a legendary saga and three full lives of Icelandic

---

[12] Ulrich Basse, *Linguistic Variation in the Shakespeare Corpus: Morpho-syntactic Variability of Second Person Pronouns* (Amsterdam: John Benjamins, 2002), p. 1.

[13] 'About the Dictionary of Old English' <http://www.doe.utoronto.ca/pages/about.html> [accessed 27 June 2014].

[14] Eiríkur Rögnvaldsson, *The Saga Corpus* <http://www.malfong.is/index.php?lang=en&pg=fornritin> [accessed 27 June 2014].

[15] R. E. Latham, David Howlett and Richard Ashdowne, *Dictionary of Medieval Latin from British Sources* (Oxford: Oxford University Press, 1975–2013).

[16] Franz Blatt, *Saxonis Gesta Danorum*. Vol. 2: *Index verborum* (Copenhagen: Levin & Munksgaard, 1957).

bishops, many of which can be attributed to specific Icelandic authors.[17] As Gottskálk notes, if these works were all extant today, Iceland would not appear as exceptional with respect to the use of Latin. Indeed, as these works are centred around royal histories and ecclesiastical biographies, it appears that the Church in Iceland used Latin as a 'proven medium of authority and power'.[18] Although this literature is largely lost, it is important to recognise that Latin compositions represent fundamental models for major genres of vernacular literature. However, Latin literary production is nonetheless more restricted than elsewhere.

A second recent assessment by Karsten Friis-Jensen surveys Latin throughout Scandinavia, emphasising the quality of some of the region's most famous authors and works. As is the case with Iceland, Norway and Denmark witness an initial 'very productive phase of Scandinavian medieval Latin of the late-twelfth and early thirteenth centuries'[19] comprising the early historical writings of Norway and similar products in Denmark such as Sven Aggeson's work and most famously Saxo Grammaticus' *Gesta Danorum*.[20] While this initial period marks the most productive era for Latin work in Norway and Iceland – thereafter Old Norse becomes the

[17] Gottskálk Jensson, pp. 153–54. The authors in question are: Sæmundr Sigfússon (1056–1133), who most likely wrote on Norwegian kings in Latin; Gizurr Hallsson (d. 1206), who composed a guidebook for pilgrims, *Flos peregrinationis*; Oddr Snorrason (fl. 1150–1200), responsible for *Vita Olaui Tryggvini* (Ólafs saga Tryggvasonar), and possibly *Historia Ingvari late peregrinantis* (Yngvars saga viðförla); Gunnlaugr Leifsson (d. 1218/19), who wrote *Historia Olaui regis Tryggvini* (Ólafs saga Tryggvasonar), and *Vita beati Johannis*; and Arngrímr Brandsson (fl. ca. 1345), *Vita Godemundi boni* (Guðmundar saga góða). Of the works named by Gottskálk, the *Vita Sancti Thorlaci* is anonymous.

[18] Gottskálk Jensson, p. 168.

[19] Friis-Jensen, 'Scandinavian Latin', p. 108.

[20] On these two figures, see the entries in *Medieval Nordic Literature in Latin*: Eric Christiansen, 'Sueno Aggonis', <https://wiki.uib.no/medieval/index.php/Sueno_Aggonis> [accessed 26 August 2014] and Karsten Friis-Jensen, 'Saxo Grammaticus' <https://wiki.uib.no/medieval/index.php/Saxo_Grammaticus> [accessed 26 June 2014]. Mia Münster-Swensen offers a major reassessment of Sven Aggesen, see Mia Münster-Swensen, 'The Making of Danish Court Nobility: The "Lex castrensis sive curiae" of Sven Aggesen reconsidered', in *Statsutvikling i Skandinavia*, ed. by S. Bagge and others (Oslo: Novus, 2012), pp. 257–79. Saxo's work enjoys a recent edition with Danish translation: *Saxo Grammaticus: Gesta Danorum, Danmarkshistorien*, ed. by Karsten Friis-Jensen and trans by Peter Zeeberg, vols 2 (Copenhagen: Gad, 2005); and a newly released edition with English translation, *Saxo Grammaticus, Gesta Danorum, The History of the Danes*, ed. by Karsten Friis-Jensen and trans by Peter Fisher, 2 vols, Oxford Medieval Texts (Oxford: Oxford University Press, 2015).

primary language for literary activity – Denmark and Sweden continue to produce a range of material in Latin.

To demonstrate the range of production and use of medieval Latin in Scandinavia, Friis-Jensen centres his survey on individual and prominent figures. These include: Andrew Suneson (Anders Sunesen, 1167–1228), fourth archbishop of Lund, who wrote a paraphrase/commentary of the *Lex Scaniae*, as well as a long didactic epic, the *Hexaëmeron* (8000 hexameters), in which he translates the language of scholastic theology (namely the works of Peter Comestor and Stephen Langton) into poetic hexameters;[21] the philosopher Boethius de Dacia (*c.* 1240–*c.* 1280) who wrote thirty works, including several commentaries on Aristotle;[22] Master Matthias of Linköping (*c.* 1300–1350) who composed a treatise on poetics (*Poetria*), a handbook for preachers, exempla to be used for preaching, and a commentary on the Apocalypse; and Birgitta of Sweden (*c.* 1303–1373), whose Swedish reports of her *Revelaciones* were edited and translated into Latin by her confessors (including Matthias). Based on these figures, whose literary Latin extends beyond the documentary and institutional monument building that we noted for the initial florescence of Latin in Norway and Iceland, Friis-Jensen concludes:[23]

> The few examples presented above of Latin texts written by Scandinavians in this period should suffice to show how quickly and how thoroughly this cultural assimilation took place (i.e. the north into central Europe). They also demonstrate that in some cases Scandinavians produced Latin works which bear comparison with those of their best-known European contemporaries; the historiographer Saxo Grammaticus, the philosopher Boethius de Dacia, and the mystic Birgitta of Sweden are such Scandinavians.

In other words, certain aspects of Latin literary production in Scandinavia conform to patterns witnessed elsewhere in Europe. But within the overall pattern local variations are evident that indicate divergent trajectories for Latin within the region. Norway, Denmark and Iceland demonstrate a burst of initial activity linked to institution building, ecclesiastical

[21] The compositional method can be seen in practice in Sten Ebbesen and Lars B. Mortensen, 'A Partial Edition of Stephen Langton's *Summa* and *Quaestiones* with Parallels from Andrew Sunesen's Hexaemeron', *Cahiers de l'institut du moyen-âge grec et latin*, 49 (1985), 25–224.

[22] Sten Ebbsen, 'Boethius de Dacia', *Medieval Nordic Latin Literature* <https://wiki.uib.no/medieval/index.php/Boethius_de_Dacia> [accessed 28 June 2014].

[23] Friis-Jensen, 'Scandinavian Latin', p. 117.

authority and the mythopoiesis of local figures who promote universal models.[24] While this level of activity is not sustained in Norway and Iceland, writers in Denmark continue to produce Latin works as Sweden, which adopted Christianity later, begins to conform to the pattern as well.

A survey of the Norwegian corpus might well then begin with the texts that comprise this initial stimulus of myth-making in Latin. In the second half of the twelfth century, two histories of the Norwegian people were produced: *Historia de antiquitate regum Norwagiensium* (between 1177 and 1188) by Theodoricus 'Monachus', about whom little is known but who likely studied at St Victor, Paris and was a leading cleric in Trondheim in the 1170s;[25] and the now fragmentary *Historia Norwegie* (between 1150 and 1200, perhaps *c.* 1150–1175).[26] Contemporary with these histories arises the initial composition of perhaps the most famous work of Norwegian medieval Latin literature, the *Passio Olavi*, the core of a larger dossier of material on the king.[27] It is likely that *legenda* for two other local saints,

---

[24] For a comparative perspective on this phenomenon (incorporating Scandinavia and Eastern Europe), see Lars Boje Mortensen, 'Sanctified Beginnings and Mythopoetic Moments: The First Wave of Writing on the Past in Norway, Denmark, and Hungary, c. 1000–1230', in *The Making of Christian Myths in the Periphery of Latin Christendom (c. 1000–1300)*, ed. by Lars Boje Mortensen (Copenhagen: Museum Tusculanum, 2006), pp. 247–73.

[25] See Lars Mortensen, 'Theodoricus Monachus' in *Medieval Nordic Literature in Latin* <https://wikihost.uib.no/medieval/index.php/Theodoricus_Monachus> [accessed 28 June 2014]. The attribution 'monachus' is post-medieval as is evidence for the title. A new edition by Egil Kraggerud of this work is forthcoming.

[26] On the date, see Lars Mortensen, 'Historia Norwegie' in *Medieval Nordic Literature in Latin* <https://wikihost.uib.no/medieval/index.php/Historia_Norwegie> [accessed 28 June 2014]. Again the title is post-medieval, but is often retained due to tradition and bibliography. The work was recently re-edited in *Historia Norwegie*, ed. by I. Ekrem and L. Mortensen, and trans. by Peter Fisher (Copenhagen: Museum Tusculanum, 2003).

[27] This is the traditional title, but the work is found as *Passio et miracula beati Olaui* in an early manuscript (Oxford, Corpus Christi College, MS 209), a title which reflects the division into a *legenda*, believed to be more or less composed in Trondheim in the second half of the twelfth century, and a series of miracles which were modified during the course of the transmission of the work. The entire dossier has presently been critically edited (in print) for the first time in Lenka Jiroušková, *Der heilige Wikingerkönig Olav Haraldsson und sein hagiographisches Dossier: Text und Context der Passio Olavi*, 2 vols. (Brill: Leiden and Boston, 2014). On the impetus behind this work, see Lars Boje Mortensen, 'Eysteinn and *Passio Olavi*: Author, Editor or Project Leader', in *Eystein Erlendsson-Erkebiskop, Politiker og Kirkebygger*, ed. by Kristin Bjørlykke and others (Trondheim: Nidaros Domkirkes Restaureringsarbeiders forlag, 2013), pp. 77–85.

Sunniva and Hallvard, were composed at this time as well.[28] In addition
to this specifically Norwegian material, a short anonymous account by a
Premonstratensian affiliated with both Tønsberg (in southern Norway)
and Børglum (northern Jutland) describes the expedition undertaken by
a group of Danes and Norwegians in 1191 to assist in the retaking of
Jerusalem.[29] The expedition, which arrived after a peace agreement had
been reached in 1192, was primarily led by magnates of the Danish king,
Knud, but also comprised possibly 200 Norwegians under the leadership
of Ulf of Lauvenes, who was closely linked to King Sverre (1177–1202).[30]
Apart from this crusading chronicle, the early historical mythopoetic
impulse centres around Trondheim and Archbishop Eystein Erlendsson of
Nidaros (1161–1188) (namely, the Olav material and Theodoricus' work),
Oslo (*Historia Norwegie* and the Hallvard legend), and Bergen (Sunniva).

Once the impetus for this initial wave expired, Latin continued as
a documentary medium especially for communication with ecclesiastical
authorities outside the land. In addition to the body of material in the
Diplomatarium are letters to and from the papal penitentiary comprising
petitions to the papacy on various matters of canon law, for example,
permission to marry within certain degrees of consanguinity.[31] Outside
of these rather cohesive groups of texts, we find a number of less easily
categorised works. For example, Mauritius de Dacia, a Franciscan based
in the convent in Bergen, wrote an itinerary (now fragmentary) of a party

---

[28] The dating of each has its difficulties, but the general consensus puts Sunniva's
legend around 1170, while Hallvard's is more difficult to ascertain. See Åslaug
Ommundsen, 'Sanctus Hallvardus' in *Medieval Nordic Literature in Latin* <https://
wikihost.uib.no/medieval/index.php/Sanctus_Hallvardus> [accessed 28 June
2014]; and Lars Mortensen and Åslaug Ommundsen, 'Sancta Sunniva' in *Medieval
Nordic Literature in Latin* <https://wikihost.uib.no/medieval/index.php/Sancta_
Sunniva> [accessed 28 June 2014]. The Sunniva legenda was recently edited by
Stephan Borghammer, 'Den Latinska Sunnivalegenden. En edition' in *Selja-Eilag
stad i 1000 år*, ed. by M. Rindal (Oslo: Universitetsforlaget, 1997), pp. 123–59.
An edition of the Hallvard material is in preparation by Åslaug Ommundsen.

[29] For a brief overview, see Lars B. Mortensen, 'Historia de Profectione Danorum
in Ierosolyma', in *Encyclopedia of the Medieval Chronicle* (Brill: Leiden, 2010).

[30] A new edition of this work is in preparation by Karen Skovgard-Petersen. On
its background, see Karen Skovgard-Petersen, *A Journey to the Promised Land:
Crusading Theology in the Historia de Profectione Danorum in Hierosolymam (c.
1200)* (Copenhagen: Museum Tusculanum, 2001).

[31] This material has been the focus of sustained study by Torstein Jørgensen. See
Letters to the Pope: Norwegian Relations to The Holy See in the Late Middle Ages,
with the assistance of Gastone Saletnich (Misjonshøgskolens Forlag: Stavanger,
1999).

of Norwegian pilgrims en route to the Holy Land in 1270.[32] He may also have written a ten-stanza *Carmen gratulorium*, *Ex te lux oritur*, to be performed at the wedding of Erik Magnusson to Margaret of Scotland in 1281.[33] Another work with somewhat loose links to the concept of Norwegian medieval Latin is the *Chronicle of the Kings of Mann*, the initial writing of which (1261–1262) occurred during Norwegian suzerainty (1237–1265).[34]

An additional two works come from non-indigenous archbishops of Nidaros. The German Henrik Kalteisen (archbishop 1452–58), kept a register (*kopibok*), which lists *questiones* and *responsiones* to queries encountered during his tenure.[35] A disputed papal appointment (made against the wishes of the cathedral chapter and the king), Kalteisen pleaded ignorance of the language, lamented his poor health, complained of the living conditions in Norway and asked to be removed from the position. It is perhaps not surprising that his copybook was written in Latin rather than the local vernacular. Likewise, Erik Walkendorf, a Dane and the penultimate Catholic archbishop of Nidaros (1510–1522), wrote a description of Finnmark, which was sent to Pope Leo X in 1520 (and printed in 1902).[36] Walkendorf was also responsible for the printing of the *Missale pro usu totius Noruegie* and the *Breuiarium ad usum ritumque sacrosancte Nidrosiensis ecclesiae* in Paris in 1519, important sources of Norwegian liturgical material.

Finally, there exist isolated Latin words and phrases within predominantly Norse texts. While there are a number of texts that contain Latin and a fair number of words scattered here and there, these are often quotations (or attributed as quotations) and titles. Examples include the *Oratio*

---

[32] See Lars Mortensen, 'Mauritius', in *Medieval Nordic Literature in Latin* <https://wiki.uib.no/medieval/index.php/Mauritius> [accessed 28 June 2014]. Based on the name, Storm, who edited the work in the nineteenth century, posited that the author was foreign, see *Monumenta Historica Norwegiae* [Christiania (Oslo): Brøgger, 1880], XXXXVII–XXXXIX & 165–68.

[33] See Åslaug Ommundsen, 'Carmen Gratulatorium' in *Medieval Nordic Literature in Latin* <https://wiki.uib.no/medieval/index.php/Carmen_gratulorium> [accessed 28 June 2014].

[34] *Cronica Regum Mannie & Insularum: Chronicles of the Kings of Man and the Isles*, ed. and trans. by George Broderick, 2nd edn (Douglas: Manx National Heritage, 1995).

[35] Alexander Bugge, *Erkebiskop Henrik Kaltisens Kopibog* (Christiania [Oslo]: Thronsen, 1899).

[36] K. H. Karlsen and G. Storm (eds.), 'Finmarkens Beskrivelse af Erkebiskop Erik Walkendorf', *Det Norske Geografiske Selskabs Aarbog*, 12 (1902), pp. 1–23.

contra clerum, written on behalf of King Sverre (1177–1202) during his struggle with the Church, short Latin phrases and titles in bishops' saga (particularly of Guðmundr) and Latin items in a number of property registers or cadastres (*jordebøker*).

This corpus represents an important body of material that testifies to the role that Latin played in the textual culture of the Norwegian Middle Ages. Nonetheless, comparison with other regions indicates the limits to the use of Latin in Norway. While arguments based on absence are dubious and a list of negative evidence could have no end, a consideration of comparable textual production, that is a consideration of the texts that were not produced in Norway, can be illustrative. The examples from Sweden and Denmark highlight the lack of philosophical (Boethius de Dacia), mystical (Birgitta and Mathias) and religious poetry (Anders Sunesen). Additional absences include genres popular and widespread throughout Europe: epic poetry, like the *Alexandreis* by Walter of Chatillon or the *Ilias* by Joseph of Exeter; debate literature, such as the *Visio Philiberti*, and satire, such as Nigel of Longchamp's *Speculum Stultorum* and Walter Map's *De nugis curialium*. While Scandinavia was able to produce literary figures who compare favourably with those active elsewhere, Norway in particular did not participate in the production of literary works on a sustained basis throughout the medieval period. In describing (rather disparagingly) the surge of epic poetry in Latin in the late twelfth century, Erich Auerbach characterised such literary production as 'little more than proficient technical exercises' arguing that outside the schools there was no public for them.[37] The Norwegian corpus of medieval Latin lacks what one might broadly call 'technical exercises' (the *Carmen gratulorium* representing a possible exception). We must assume that Norwegians were perfectly capable of composing Latin works, yet if so it appears that there was little support or incentive to do so.

If the corpus of Latin composed in and relating to Norway in the Middle Ages is limited, it need not follow that Latin textual culture and learning was superficial, backwards or lacking in any meaningful sense. Indeed, in spite of the absence of sustained literary activity, Latin may have enjoyed a wider circulation than is usually thought. As has been noted earlier, recent assessments of Latin book culture (largely lost due to Reformation) have established a fair number of books in the land and

[37] Erich Auerbach, *Literary Language and its Public in Late Latin Antiquity and the Middle Ages*, trans. by Ralph Mannheim (Princeton, NJ: Princeton University Press, 1993), p. 200. (This book was originally published posthumously in German in 1958, and translated into English in 1965.)

that Norwegian writing centres were connected into networks of Western Europe.[38] An important, additional part of the picture of Latin in Norway is the number of inscriptions (primarily in runes) in Latin. Typical are the prayers *Ave Maria*, numbering about thirty, and *Pater Noster*, numbering perhaps seventeen, as well as quotations from scripture or liturgical material.[39] Whereas vernacular formulations dominate rune-stones, monuments and church buildings, Latin inscriptions are more common on loose objects, such as runic sticks, lead plates and bands, and pieces of bone. Tentatively, the placing of vernacular inscriptions suggest that Norse was favoured to communicate publicly, while Latin, especially in set names and set phrases, appears on objects that were more personal and may reflect private concerns. Zilmer suggests the protection of contents, but one might also imagine devotional reasons.[40]

These three aspects of Latin writing in Norway – manuscript production, inscriptions and composition – offer a way of understanding Latin writing in the land as a multifaceted system. While excessive focus on one aspect skews perception, as a whole, we see aspects that thrive and those that appear less active. If the written Latin culture of medieval Scandinavia has only recently begun to enjoy the comprehensive attention that it deserves, there remains much to do.[41] For example, a socio-cultural perspective that considers how and why resources were allocated to certain aspects of production and the mechanisms of production might help to explain the uneven regional picture and augment the attention paid hitherto to exemplary authors and texts. Explanations for the lack of texts or

[38] Karlsen estimates 13,000–14,000 books owned by churches in Norway, but defers from conjecture on the overall total of books in the country. See Espen Karlsen, 'Latin Manuscripts of Medieval Norway: Survival and Losses', in *Latin Manuscripts of Medieval Norway*, ed. by Espen Karlsen, pp. 26–36 (p. 36). Further details on the estimates can be found in Espen Karlsen, 'Katalogisering av Latinske Membranfragmenter som Forskningsprosjektet: Del 2', in *Arkivverkets Forskningsseminar Gardermoen 2003*, rapporter og retningslinjer 16 (Oslo: Riksarkiven, 2003), pp. 58–88. Attinger and Haug, however, suggest a mere 2500–5000 liturgical books in churches, see Gisela Attinger and Andreas Haug, *The Nidaros Office of the Holy Blood, Liturgical Music in Medieval Norway* (Trondheim: Senter for middelalderstudier, 2003), p. 10.

[39] Kristel Zilmer, 'Christian Prayers and Invocations in Scandinavian Runic Inscriptions from the Viking Age and the Middle Ages', *Futhark* 4 (2013), 129–71 (p. 151). Zilmer cites statistics from an unpublished M.A. thesis (51 *Ave Maria*, 21 *Pater Noster*), but notes some problems with the classification and consequently prefers less precise numbers.

[40] Zilmer, p. 167.

[41] Friis-Jensen, 'Scandinavian Latin', pp. 120–21.

famous figures that appeal to the remoteness of Norway, its small and far-flung populace and the inevitable shift to the vernacular offer partial reasons, but are not wholly satisfactory. After the Reformation in 1537 (and the incorporation of the Norwegian church under the Danish king and the dissolution of the *riksråd*, or state council) Norway witnessed an increase in Latin composition.[42] There are an estimated 1400 titles of neo-Latin Norwegian works (again small compared to Denmark and Sweden, but numerous compared to medieval output). While many of these are short occasional verse (for weddings and burials, for example), they illustrate 'technical exercises' of the sort for which there was not much of an audience seemingly in the Middle Ages. Of course, during this period of Dano-Norwegian rule, attributing a particularly Norwegian element to literary production is difficult. Nevertheless, Oslo acted as a hub for a group of Latinists known as the Oslo humanists in the second half of the sixteenth century. A number of other figures, perhaps most notably Ludvig Holberg (1684–1754), born in Bergen but resident most of his adult life in Copenhagen, illustrate Norwegian contributions to a network of Latin activity in Western Europe. In short, with the advent of the Reformation we see the networks and groups inclined to support and encourage the production of Latin in Norway that we see for a short period but not in a sustained fashion throughout the Middle Ages. As the regional variety of Scandinavian medieval Latin becomes more accessible and studied, further consideration of the cultural, social and political motivations for its use, study or absence promise a better understanding of the intra-regional variation within Scandinavia.

---

[42] A brief overview of this period can be found in Vibeke Roggen Roggen and Hilde Sejersted, 'Latin i Norge', in Tore Jonson, *Latin: Kulturen, Historien, Språket*, trans. by Hilde Sejerstad (Oslo: Pax Forlag, 2004), pp. 146–53. A more in depth account can be found in Inger Ekrem, 'Norway', in *A History of Nordic Neo-Latin Literature*, ed. by Minna Skafte Jensen (Odense: Odense University Press, 1995), pp. 66–95. See also the database of Nordic Neo-Latin Literature, *Database of Nordic Neo-Latin Literature*, ed. by Lars Boje Mortesen and others <http://www. uib.no/neolatin/> [accessed 28 June 2014].

Translating Europe in Medieval Wales

HELEN FULTON

ONE OF THE MOST SIGNIFICANT aspects of Welsh as a vernacular is its long continuity as a prestige language in Wales. While Middle English endured an extended and often painful struggle with Norman French before emerging triumphant as a relatively high-status language towards the end of the fourteenth century, Welsh never ceded its position as the prestige vernacular of the elite. Consequently, medieval literature in Welsh has an antiquity, a variety of registers and functions, and an awareness of its own long literary history that are unusual among the vernacular literatures of Europe.

This is not to say, however, that medieval Welsh literature was parochial or insular. The early conversion of Wales to Christianity in the fifth century nurtured a strong cultural tradition of Latin writing, mainly of a religious nature but also in the form of annals, chronicles, and philosophical works.[1] From the twelfth century, the rapid foundation of a chain of priories and abbeys around Wales, particularly those of the Benedictines and Cistercians, enabled the keeping of substantial libraries which were shared among the various foundations and borrowed by noble families. Like England, Wales was subjected to conquest and colonisation by the Normans after 1066, with the crucial difference that Welsh literature retained its pre-eminence as a literary language alongside French. This was due in part to the politics and topography of Norman settlement in Wales, which divided the land into Marcher lordships held by the Normans (mainly in the east and south of the country) and independent patrimonial territories held by Welsh princes where the Welsh language retained institutional power.

In 1282, Llywelyn ap Gruffudd, prince of Gwynedd in north Wales, fell at the hands of the English army of Edward I and his entire territory, along with others ruled by Welsh princes, was annexed to the Crown.

---

[1] For a survey of Latin writing in medieval Wales, see Ceri Davies, *Welsh Literature and the Classical Tradition* (Cardiff: University of Wales Press, 1995), pp. 12–13. See also Patrick Sims-Williams, 'The Use of Writing in Early Medieval Wales', in *Literacy in Medieval Celtic Societies*, ed. by Huw Pryce (Cambridge: Cambridge University Press, 1998), pp. 15–38.

From 1284, Wales was divided into two different kinds of political unit, the Marcher lordships which operated separately from the king, and the Crown lordships, former Welsh princedoms, which were governed by a combination of English and Welsh administrators. The old Welsh aristocracy was brutally disposed of, by murder, imprisonment, or claustration, and the gentry class immediately below it in the hierarchy, the *uchelwyr* (literally 'high men'), found itself called upon to serve the English monarchy. Buttressed by imposing castles and new towns garrisoned by English immigrants, political power in Wales now depended on the co-operation of the upper echelons of the Welsh gentry.[2]

These families of landed freemen, many of them well-to-do and well connected with both Welsh and English powerbrokers, assumed the role of patrons of Welsh literature, a role they inherited – willingly or not – from the vanished aristocracy. Welsh poets, cast adrift by the events of 1282, now depended on this new group of patrons and adapted their literary styles accordingly, making their poetry less formal and adulatory, more flexible and contemporary. This stylistic adaptation to new times and new audiences included the widespread popularity of a reinvigorated metre, the *cywydd*, and a relaxation of traditional poetics to allow for a greater influence from another prestige literature, that of French. In both poetry and prose, the combined forces of Latin scholasticism and French courtly literature exerted a pressure on Welsh literature which turned it into a distinctively European cultural form.

We can say, then, that Europe was 'translated' into Welsh using two related processes: firstly in the form of literary and linguistic influence, and secondly in the form of translations, or rather adaptations, of European works into Welsh. It is the second of these which is the focus of this article, in particular the boom in literary translations evident in Wales in the fourteenth and fifteenth centuries which continued a tradition of translating that can be traced back to the mid thirteenth century and is likely to have been older still. While court poets after 1282 continued to practise a centuries-old tradition of Welsh praise-poetry to support their new patrons, leading gentry families also began to commission copies of key texts, translated into Welsh, which delivered the cultural capital

---

[2] For a detailed study of this period of Welsh history, see R. R. Davies, *The Age of Conquest: Wales 1063–1415* (Oxford: Oxford University Press, 2000). For the period before 1284, see also Max Lieberman, *The Medieval March of Wales: The Creation and Perception of a Frontier, 1066–1283* (Cambridge: Cambridge University Press, 2010).

required by a new class to establish itself in a multicultural environment.[3] As the emergent gentry class expanded to fill the place left at the top of the Welsh hierarchy by the disappearance of the princely class, their participation in a courtly culture shared by their Marcher and English overlords worked to institutionalise their own status position.

The influence and adaptation of European literary forms after 1282 seems to have been particularly vigorous in one area of Wales: the southeast of the country in the borderlands of the March. In the Anglo-Norman lordships of Glamorgan and Powys some of the key texts of French romance – the Charlemagne legends, some of the Arthurian prose tales from the Vulgate Cycle, and the romance of Bevis of Hampton – were translated into Welsh for Marcher noblemen. The monastic foundations of Wales, mainly Cistercian in the Marcher regions, provided sites of manuscript production and collections of manuscripts copied or borrowed from continental houses, including texts in Latin and French.[4] Translations from texts in French can be traced to a combination of lay patrons and their scribes, both monastic and lay, who commissioned and collected literary works in Welsh for themselves and their circles of readers in the multilingual spaces of south Wales. The business of translation, which accounts for a considerable proportion of surviving Middle Welsh prose, can be seen as a response by Welsh writers to their position on the border. In contact with other European languages and cultures, Marcher writers and their patrons participated in institutionally powerful ideologies, especially those of classicism and chivalry, which produced a distinctive cultural tradition operating on both sides of the border.

The 'matter of the March', taking shape in the thirteenth century and flourishing in the fourteenth and fifteenth centuries, is quintessentially European: it comprises works in English, Welsh and French, from *Fouke le Fitz Waryn* and the Harley Lyrics to *Sir Gawain and the Green Knight* and Welsh court poetry. From the Welsh side, the contribution to this Marcher literary culture is distinguished by an antiquarian preservation

---

[3] There is some evidence that the practice of commissioning translations from Latin began before 1282, supported by the native princes and their families. See Stephen J. Williams, 'Rhai Cyfieithiadau', in *Y Traddodiad Rhyddiaith yn yr Oesau Canol*, ed. by Geraint Bowen (Llandysul: Gwasg Gomer, 1974), pp. 303–11.

[4] On the spread of monastic orders in Wales, see F. G. Cowley, *The Monastic Order in South Wales* (Cardiff: University of Wales Press, 1977); Janet E. Burton, *Monastic and Religious Orders in Britain 1000–1300* (Cambridge: Cambridge University Press, 1994); *Monastic Wales: New Approaches*, ed. by Janet E. Burton and Karen Stöber (Cardiff: University of Wales Press, 2013).

of Welsh literary works from before 1282, a vigorous contemporary court poetry addressed to the new nobility after 1282, a resurgent practice of political prophecy, and a strong growth in translations from popular French texts into Welsh. As a coherent corpus, this material is united not by genre or content but by its location in the March, its assumption of multilingualism, and its production under the auspices of a particular social class, the *uchelwyr*, many of whom lived as social equals among the English and French-speaking elites of the Marcher lordships.

Welsh translation and classical reception

Translations from Latin into Welsh began before 1282, with the translation of monastic annals and native laws into the vernacular, though these Latin texts originated in Wales and not in Europe.[5] The majority of Latin texts adapted into Welsh from the thirteenth to the fifteenth century were religious, representing a continental tradition of religious learning and scholasticism that flourished at the monastic foundations in Wales, including 'Hystoria Lucidar', based on the *Elucidarium* (a popular dialogue on biblical doctrine, dating from the late eleventh century), 'Y mod yd aeth Meir y nef' ('How Mary went to heaven'), based on the apocryphal *Transitus Mariae*, and 'Credo Seint Athanasius', a translation of the Athanasian Creed. Lives of saints, including David, Catherine and Margaret, were translated into Welsh from the fourteenth century, together with various popular biblical and apocryphal narratives such as the gospel of Nicodemus ('Efengyl Nicodemus'), the story of Adam and Eve ('Ystorya Adaf ac Eua y Wreic'), and the vision of St Paul ('Breudwyt

---

5   On the Welsh historical chronicles and their basis in Latin annals, as well as Geoffrey of Monmouth's *Historia Regum Britanniae*, see J. Beverley Smith, 'Historical Writing in Medieval Wales: The Composition of *Brenhinedd y Saesson*', *Studia Celtica*, 42 (2008), 55–86; Brynley F. Roberts, 'Geoffrey of Monmouth, *Historia Regum Britanniae*, and *Brut y Brenhinedd*', in *The Arthur of the Welsh: The Arthurian Legend in Medieval Welsh Literature*, ed. by Rachel Bromwich and others (Cardiff: University of Wales Press, 1991), pp. 97–116. The earliest copies of the Welsh laws in Welsh survive from the mid thirteenth century, alongside contemporary Latin versions. See Thomas Charles-Edwards, *The Welsh Laws* (Cardiff: University of Wales Press, 1989). There is a very useful website of information on the Welsh laws by Sara Elin Roberts, *Cyfraith Hywel* <http://cyfraith-hywel.cymru.ac.uk> [accessed 5 August 2014].

Pawl').[6] Evidence of the influence of Latin school texts circulating in Wales include thirteenth-century Welsh adaptations of the twelfth-century Latin *Dialogus inter Corpus et Animam* ('Dialogue between Body and Soul') and Welsh examples, dating mainly from the fifteenth century, of the classical Latin genre of the *encomium urbis*, a praise-poem or epideixis to a town or city, which enjoyed a considerable vogue in late-antique and medieval Europe.[7]

A further example of translation from a Latin text is the Welsh prose narrative, *Ystorya Dared*, an account of the Trojan wars based on the sixth-century pseudo-history of Dares Phrygius, *De excidio Troiae historia*. The story of Troy became one of the major origin legends for a number of peoples who emerged as territorial nations after the fall of the Roman empire. Franks, Normans, English, Welsh and Irish all traced their origins to the Trojans and their descendants, with Geoffrey of Monmouth's *Historia regum Britanniae* providing an authoritative account of the foundations of Britain and the British people (direct ancestors of the Welsh) from the early settlement of Brutus, the surviving descendant of the group of exiles, led by Aeneas, who fled from the ruins of Troy.[8] *Ystorya Dared*, written in the early fourteenth century, follows its Latin source fairly closely; what is more remarkable is its inclusion in manuscripts alongside the Welsh chronicles, *Brut y Brenhinedd* ('Chronicle of the Kings'), based on Geoffrey's *Historia*, and *Brut y Tywysogyon* ('Chronicle of the Princes'), a continuation of the *Historia* up to the crucial date of 1282. By positioning *Ystorya Dared* at the beginning of this sequence, Welsh scribes redefined it

---

[6] For a list of religious works in Welsh based on Latin originals, see D. Simon Evans, *A Grammar of Middle Welsh* (Dublin: Dublin Institute for Advanced Studies, 1964), pp. xxxvi–xl. Jane Cartwright has published extensively on female saints' lives in Welsh, including *Celtic Hagiography and Saints' Cults* (Cardiff: University of Wales Press, 2003); *Feminine Sanctity and Spirituality in Medieval Wales* (Cardiff: University of Wales Press, 2008).

[7] For further examples of the *encomium urbis* in Wales, see Helen Fulton, 'The Encomium Urbis in Medieval Welsh Poetry', *Proceedings of the Harvard Celtic Colloquium*, 26 (2006), 54–72; Helen Fulton, 'Trading Places: Representations of Urban Culture in Medieval Welsh Poetry', *Studia Celtica*, 31 (1997), 219–30. The training received by professional poets in Wales was based on the classical grammars of Priscian and Donatus, whose name in Welsh, *dwned*, became a generic term for grammar or, to use the modern term, poetics. See Davies, *Welsh Literature and the Classical Tradition*, pp. 40–41.

[8] The significance of Troy for Geoffrey's account of early British history has been discussed by Frances Ingledew, 'The Book of Troy and the Genealogical Construction of History: The Case of Geoffrey of Monmouth's *Historia Regum Britanniae*', *Speculum*, 69 (1994), 665–704.

as the origin legend of the British people, the prequel to Brutus' arrival in Britain and the confirmation of Welsh rights to sovereignty that had been usurped by the Saxons.[9] The Welsh version of the Troy story indicates very strongly that a manuscript containing Dares' Latin text must have been available in Wales; the production of *Ystorya Dared* is associated with the Cistercian abbey of Valle Crucis, near Llangollen, known as a centre of manuscript production and probably the place where *Brut y Brenhinedd*, the adaptation of Geoffrey's *Historia*, was also made. There is a record of a manuscript of Dares Phrygius being held at the Cistercian abbey of Whit-land near Carmarthen and Latin manuscripts such as this were regularly lent to other houses for copying or translation.[10]

The fact that the Welsh version of the Troy story is based on Dares rather than on a later text such as Guido delle Colonne's *Historia destruc-tionis Troiae* of 1287 suggests that Dares was more readily available to Welsh clerics as part of a culture of classicism in the monasteries. The Trojan legends, known from Dares and perhaps other Latin sources, supplied a roll-call of heroes who could be invoked to confirm the great-ness of the lost Welsh princes. In *Brut y Tywysogyon*, a fourteenth-century Welsh chonicler composed a heartfelt eulogy to the Lord Rhys ap Gruf-fudd, prince of Deheubarth who died in 1197, comparing him to the great heroes of Greek legend:

Eil Achelarwy o nerth cledyr y dwyuron, Nestor o hynawster, Tideus o lewder, Samson o gedernit, Ector o prudder, Erckwlf o wychder, Paris o pryt, Vlixes o lauar, Celyf o doethineb, Aiax o vedwl, a grwnwal yr holl gampeu.

[A second Achilles for the might of his breast-bone, a Nestor for gentle-ness, a Tydeus for doughtiness, a Samson for strength, a Hector for prudence, a Hercules for excellence, a Paris for beauty, a Ulysses for

---

[9] The link between *Ystorya Dared* and the Welsh chronicles was noted in an early article by Brynley F. Roberts, 'Historical Writing', in *A Guide to Welsh Literature, vol. 1*, ed. by A. O. H. Jarman and Gwilym Rees Hughes (Swansea: Christopher Davies, 1976), pp. 244–47. For further discussion of the significance of *Ystorya Dared* in Wales, see Helen Fulton, 'Troy Story: The Medieval Welsh *Ystorya Dared* and the *Brut* Tradition of British History', *Medieval Chronicle*, 7 (2011), 137–150; Helen Fulton, 'A Medieval Welsh Version of the Troy Story: Editing *Ystorya Dared*', in *Probable Truth: Editing Medieval Texts from Britain in the Twenty-First Century*, ed. by Vincent Gillespie and Anne Hudson (Turnhout: Brepols, 2013), pp. 214–25.

[10] The manuscript is Exeter, Exeter Cathedral Library, MS 3514. See Smith, 'Historical Writing in Medieval Wales', pp. 84–85.

speech, a Solomon for wisdom, an Ajax for mind, and the foundation of all accomplishments.][11]

Translating chivalry and romance

In the early prose tradition of Wales, we can compare the 'native' tales, particularly those known as the Four Branches of the *Mabinogi*, with other tales found among the larger *Mabinogion* which show quite distinctive influences from French literature.[12] While the Four Branches, whose earliest redaction may be dated to the late eleventh century, evoke a legendary pre-Norman past, their occasional use of French loanwords and customs of *courtoisie* indicate the bilingual and bicultural circumstances in which the tales took literary form.[13]

[11] The text and translation are from *Brut y Tywysogyon or The Chronicle of the Princes, Red Book of Hergest Version*, ed. by Thomas Jones (Cardiff: University of Wales Press, 1955), pp. 178–79. See also Marged Haycock, 'Some Talk of Alexander and Some of Hercules: Three Early Medieval Poems from the Book of Taliesin', *Cambridge Medieval Celtic Studies*, 13 (1987), 7–38.

[12] The term *Mabinogion* is normally used to signify the collection of eleven prose tales in Middle Welsh found together in two fourteenth-century manuscript anthologies (the Red Book of Hergest and the White Book of Rhydderch) and composed at various times between the eleventh and thirteenth centuries. They are translated by Sioned Davies, *The Mabinogion* (Oxford and New York: Oxford University Press, 2007). The Four Branches of the *Mabinogi*, four linked tales identified in the manuscripts as a group, have been dated to *c*. 1050–*c*. 1120 though the texts as we have them are likely to be based on earlier versions including oral tales. See Sioned Davies, *The Four Branches of the Mabinogi* (Llandysul: Gomer, 1993). Using contextual evidence relating to the second Branch, *Branwen Uerch Lyr*, Patrick Sims-Williams argues that the assumed dates of composition are not stable and that the Four Branches may belong to a later period. See *Irish Influence on Medieval Welsh Literature* (Oxford: Oxford University Press, 2011), pp. 190, 214, 29.

[13] The linguistic context of medieval Wales, including evidence that many Welsh people used French as a spoken and written language, has been discussed by Llinos Beverley Smith, 'The Welsh Language before 1536', in *The Welsh Language before the Industrial Revolution*, ed. by Geraint H. Jenkins (Cardiff: University of Wales Press, 1997), pp. 15–44. See also Marie Surridge, 'Romance Linguistic Influence on Middle Welsh: A Review of Some Problems', *Studia Celtica*, 1 (1966), 63–92. For examples of the kinds of loanwords that came into Welsh from French (some of them via Middle English), see Surridge, 'Words of Romance Origin in the Four Branches of the Mabinogi and Native Welsh Tales', *Études Celtiques*, 21 (1984), 239–55.

The three tales composed before 1282 that present the strongest evidence of French influence and adaptation are the so-called Arthurian 'romances' of *Owein, neu Chwedl Iarlles y Ffynnawn* ('Owain, or the Lady of the Fountain'), *Gereint uab Erbin* ('Geraint son of Erbin'), and *Peredur uab Efrawg* ('Peredur son of Efrog'). These three prose narratives, probably composed in the late twelfth or early thirteenth century, have close affinities with three long narrative poems by Chrétien de Troyes, *Yvain, Erec et Enide*, and *Perceval* (*Conte del Graal*), poems which themselves preserved traces of early Arthurian legends from Wales.[14] Few scholars would now argue for direct influence from Chrétien's works to the Welsh stories; it seems more likely, based on the evidence of style and content, that the Welsh versions took shape in Normanised areas of Wales, probably in the south-east, and drew, if not on Chrétien's work itself, then on intermediary versions of it brought to Wales, in combination with older Welsh legends which Chrétien had also used to structure his own poems.[15] While the Welsh tales have adapted the French courtly diegesis to suit Welsh

[14] Chrétien de Troyes, writing towards the end of the twelfth century, is associated with the court of Marie of Champagne. The poems are translated into English prose by W. W. Comfort, *Arthurian Romances, Chrétien de Troyes* (Penguin: Harmondsworth, 1991). The three Welsh Arthurian tales appear in English translation in *The Mabinogion*, trans. by Davies, and are discussed individually in *The Arthur of the Welsh*, ed. by Bromwich and others. Ceridwen Lloyd-Morgan argues that 'in all three tales the narrative techniques, in fact the whole mode of telling the story, are essentially Welsh'. See 'French Texts, Welsh Translators', in *The Medieval Translator II*, ed. by Roger Ellis (London: Centre for Medieval Studies, Queen Mary and Westfield College, University of London, 1991), pp. 45–63 (p. 49).

[15] Proinsias Mac Cana supports the view that the three Welsh Arthurian tales 'were composed in the area comprising south-east Wales and the land around Archenfield in Herefordshire'. See *The Mabinogi* (Cardiff: University of Wales Press, 1977), p. 15. Arthur's court is located at Caerlleon, in the medieval region of Gwent, and Roger Middleton points out that the author of *Gereint uab Erbin* knew the local geography of the south-east, with events taking place in the Forest of Dean and Cardiff, and near the rivers Usk and Severn. See '*Chwedl Geraint ab Erbin*', in *The Arthur of the Welsh*, ed. by Rachel Bromwich and others, pp. 147–57 (p. 150). For the view that *Peredur* may have been composed in north Wales, see P. W. Thomas, 'Cydberthynas y Pedair Fersiwn Ganoloesol', in *Canhwyll Marchogyon: Cyd-destunoli* Peredur, ed. by Sioned Davies and P. W. Thomas (Cardiff: Gwasg Prifysgol Cymru, 2000), pp. 10–49. The process by which Welsh material may have reached Chrétien de Troyes is described by Constance Bullock-Davies, *Professional Interpreters and the Matter of Britain* (Cardiff: University of Wales Press, 1966). See also the review of this book by Rachel Bromwich, *Llên Cymru*, 9 (1967), 249–51, which comments on the importance of the south-east in the transmission of European material.

audiences – the tales are in prose, rather than poetry like the French texts, and the Welsh Arthur is less like a French king and more like a Welsh chieftain – there are evident traces of French chivalric themes centred on the figure of the knight as the main protagonist, including the knightly quest, single combat, marriage to an heiress, the hero's love-sickness, the conflict between marriage and martial prowess, exotic locations, and the knight's ambition for independent lordship. In following the basic plot outline of Chrétien's three poems, the Welsh adapters inevitably reproduce many of the French themes while translating them into a worldview that their audiences of Welsh nobility would recognise.[16]

After the watershed conquest and settlement of 1284, the proximity of French-language culture in Wales coupled with a flourishing of the Welsh language in the south-east generated a demand for French chivalric narratives translated into Welsh. These translations were commissioned by wealthy families in the March and supplied by clerics and lay scribes who shared the work of translating and copying. Evidence for the rise in translations during the fourteenth and fifteenth centuries comes partly from the production, movement, and ownership of manuscripts, and partly from references in Welsh court poetry that give some indication of the extent to which characters from French romance were known well enough by Welsh audiences to be integrated into the poetry on the assumption that everyone knew who they were. Describing his grief at the death of his friend, Rhydderch ab Ieuan Llwyd, Dafydd ap Gwilym, the pioneering court poet writing in the middle decades of the fourteenth century, refers to 'Amlyn' and 'Emig', the friends from the twelfth-century Latin *Vita Amici et Amelii*, a popular medieval tale which was translated into Welsh from the Latin text early in the fourteenth century.[17] In other poems he

---

[16] Erich Poppe discusses the concept of 'relative distance' between Welsh adaptations and their French sources, suggesting that the Welsh *Owein* is relatively far from the French *Yvain* compared with other adaptations from French to Welsh since *Owein* is 'neither predominantly chivalric in outlook, nor a romance in the narrow sense'. See Poppe, '*Owein, Ystorya Bown*, and the Problem of "Relative Distance": Some Methodological Considerations and Speculations', in *Arthurian Literature XXI: Celtic Arthurian Material*, ed. by Ceridwen Lloyd-Morgan (Cambridge: D. S. Brewer, 2004), pp. 73–94 (pp. 90–91).

[17] The Welsh text is called *Cydymdeithas Amlyn ac Amig* ('The Friendship of Amlyn and Amig'). Patricia Williams suggests an early fourteenth-century date for its composition, based on language and orthography. See *Kedymdeithyas Amlyn ac Amic*, ed. by P. Williams (Cardiff: Gwasg Prifysgol Cymru, 1982). For the reference in Dafydd ap Gwilym, see *Cerddi Dafydd ap Gwilym*, ed. by Dafydd Johnston and others (Cardiff: Gwasg Prifysgol Cymru, 2010), no. 10, ll. 16–17.

draws on the names of heroes from the Trojan legend (CDG 130), the character of Tyrel from the Charlemagne legends (CDG 83), Cyrseus, the sword belonging to Otuel (CDG 71), and 'Ffwg', or Fouke le Fitz Waryn, the eponymous hero of the Anglo-Norman romance composed on the March of Wales in the late thirteenth century (CDG 12).[18] These and similar poetic references, attested from the mid fourteenth century onwards, indicate the wide circulation of popular European texts translated into the style and cultural positioning of locally-composed Welsh literature.

By the middle of the fifteenth century, multilingual manuscripts containing texts in various combinations of Welsh, French, English and Latin were beginning to appear as anthologies or commissioned works, such as Aberystwyth, National Library of Wales, MS Peniarth 50 (c. 1445), a mixture of prophecy, religious works and historical pieces, and Aberystwyth, National Library of Wales, MS Peniarth 26 (c. 1456), containing prophecies and annals.[19] Though there are currently no manuscripts in French that can be identified as having been copied in Wales, there is some historical evidence that books containing French texts were circulating in Wales: when Llywelyn Bren, an anti-English rebel, was executed in 1317 an inventory of his books included a copy of *Roman de la Rose* along with three books in Welsh and two other unspecified volumes.[20]

---

[18] Poem numbers refer to *Cerddi Dafydd ap Gwilym*. *Fouke le Fitz Waryn* survives only in Anglo-Norman, though there was a Middle English version now lost. For other references to French and English literary influences in Welsh court poetry, see Rachel Bromwich, 'Allusions to Tales and Romances', in *Aspects of the Poetry of Dafydd ap Gwilym* (Cardiff: University of Wales Press, 1986), pp. 132–51; Helen Fulton, *Dafydd ap Gwilym and the European Context* (Cardiff: University of Wales Press, 1986); Huw M. Edwards, *Dafydd ap Gwilym: Influences and Analogues* (Oxford: Oxford University Press, 1996). Edwards argues that what appear to be influences from French in Dafydd ap Gwilym's poetry are more likely to be analogues from a shared tradition of vernacular popular poetry (see p. 129, for example).

[19] These manuscripts are described by J. Gwenogvryn Evans in the standard handlist of Welsh manuscripts, *Report on Manuscripts in the Welsh Language*, 3 vols (London: Eyre and Spottiswoode, 1898–1910), I, pt 2 (1898). See also Daniel Huws, *Medieval Welsh Manuscripts* (Cardiff: University of Wales Press, 2000). Some of the English material in MS Peniarth 50 and other Welsh manuscripts has been edited by William Marx, *IMEP XIV: Manuscripts in the National Library of Wales* (Cambridge: D. S. Brewer, 1999).

[20] *Cardiff Records*, ed. by J. H. Matthews, 6 vols (Cardiff: Records Committee of the City Council, 1898–1911), IV, p. 58. For a useful account of French manuscripts associated with Wales, see Ceridwen Lloyd-Morgan, 'Medieval Manuscripts at the

The man who best epitomises the 'matter of the March' in Wales is the manuscript collector from Glamorgan, Hopcyn ap Tomas ab Einion, who commissioned the manuscript known as the Red Book of Hergest (c. 1400).[21] This anthology, an enormous work which contains virtually the entire canon of medieval Welsh literature, including translations from Latin and French (but excluding most of the court poetry in the *cywydd* metre) was very likely designed by Hopcyn as a record of the literary heritage of Wales. We know that Hopcyn had a substantial library which included, according to the poet Dafydd y Coed, a copy of the Grail legends, almost certainly in Welsh but translated from the French Vulgate cycle:

> Mynawg Hopgyn, lyn loywglos,
> Mur heilddwbl cetgwbl catgis,
> Mwnai law, mae yn ei lys,
> Eurddar, y Lusidarius,
> A'r Greal a'r Yniales,
> A grym pob cyfraith a'i gras.

> [Noble Hopcyn, wine in his bright court,
> Walled with double provisions, complete bounty, battle strike,
> Hand full of money, he has in his court,
> golden leader, the *Elucidarium*
> and the Grail [stories] and the Annals,
> and the power of every law and its gift.] [22]

This list of books owned by Hopcyn indicates the importance of European material in the canon of medieval Welsh writing. The *Elucidarium* has been mentioned already, as a Latin religious text which became a popular Welsh version. The 'Annals' could refer to a set of Latin chronicles

National Library of Wales', in *Sources, Exemplars, and Copy-Texts: Influence and Transmission*, ed. by William Marx (= *Trivium*, 31 (1999)), pp. 1–12.

[21] Hopcyn ap Tomas of Ynysforgan, near Swansea, was active c. 1337–1408, though not a great deal is known about his life. On his role as a manuscript collector and commissioner of the Red Book of Hergest (Oxford, Jesus College, MS 111), see Christine James, 'Hopcyn ap Tomas a "Llyfrgell Genedlaethol" Ynysforgan', *Transactions of the Honourable Society of Cymmrodorion*, n.s. 13 (2007), 31–57; Prys Morgan, 'Glamorgan and the Red Book', *Morgannwg: Transactions of the Glamorgan Local History Society*, 22 (1978), 42–60.

[22] *Gwaith Dafydd y Coed a Beirdd Eraill o Lyfr Coch Hergest*, ed. by R. Iestyn Daniel (Aberystwyth: Canolfan Uwchefrydiau Cymreig a Cheltaidd Prifysgol Cymru, 2002), no. 3, ll. 91–96, my translation. Little is known of Dafydd y Coed who was active in the second half of the fourteenth century.

(*yniales* is an unusual form, borrowed from the Latin *annales*), but might just as likely signify one or more of the Welsh chronicles, perhaps *Brut y Tywysogyon*, which are based on earlier Latin annals. The reference to *pob cyfraith*, 'every law', suggests that one or more copies of the Welsh law codes were in Hopcyn's library. Finally there is *Greal*, the legends of the Holy Grail, whose transmission in Wales, through the medium of Welsh, is closely connected to Hopcyn and his manuscript collection.

The Welsh text known as *Y Seint Greal* (though this exact title is not given in the manuscripts) comprises abridged versions of two French romances, *La Queste del Saint Graal* and *Perlesvaus*, both of which recount the quest for the Holy Grail. The two French romances were composed in the first quarter of the thirteenth century, the *Queste* as part of the linked series of prose texts known as the Vulgate Cycle and *Perlesvaus* probably as an independent story in which Perceval, rather than Galahad, is the Grail hero.[23] The text of *Y Seint Greal* is found in five manuscripts held in the National Library of Wales, the earliest dating from the end of the fourteenth century (Aberystwyth, National Library of Wales, MS Peniarth 11) and a further two from the fifteenth century (Aberystwyth, National Library of Wales, MS 3063E and Aberystwyth, National Library of Wales, MS Peniarth 15), though the versions of the text found in these and the later manuscripts are all based on the one contained in MS Peniarth 11.[24]

---

[23] There are two manuscripts from France, dating from the fourteenth and fifteenth centuries respectively, in which the French *Perlesvaus* is juxtaposed to the *Queste*, as in the Welsh redaction, but it does not seem to have been a common practice and in fact caused considerable problems of cohesion. The manuscript evidence is discussed by Ceridwen Lloyd-Morgan, 'A Study of *Y Seint Greal* in Relation to *La Queste del Saint Graal* and *Perlesvaus*' (unpublished doctoral thesis, University of Oxford, 1978), pp. 4–7. Lloyd-Morgan states that the Welsh text is not directly based on any of the extant manuscripts of either the *Queste* or *Perlesvaus* (p. 11).

[24] The other manuscripts are Aberystwyth, National Library of Wales, MS Peniarth 118 (sixteenth century) and Aberystwyth, National Library of Wales, MS Peniarth 254 (seventeenth century). Only MS Peniarth 11 and MS 3063E contain complete copies, and the latter is copied from the former; the remaining manuscripts contain only fragments. For a more detailed description of the manuscripts, and an edition of the Welsh text of the first section of *Y Seint Greal* (that is, the *Queste*), see *Ystoryaeu Seint Greal, Rhan I: Y Keis*, ed. by Thomas Jones (Cardiff: Gwasg Prifysgol Cymru, 1992), pp. xi–xxi. For the possibility that MS Peniarth 15 represents a retelling, from memory, of the Welsh story as it appeared in MS Peniarth 11, indicating a continuing interest in the Arthurian legends in late-medieval Wales, see Ceridwen Lloyd-Morgan, 'The Peniarth 15 Fragment of *Y Seint Greal*: Arthurian Tradition in the Late Fifteenth Century', *Bulletin of the Board of Celtic Studies*, 28 (1978–80), 73–82.

This particular manuscript, like the Red Book of Hergest, was written by a scribe called Hywel Fychan and was almost certainly owned and commissioned by Hopcyn ap Tomas.[25] Hopcyn was clearly committed to making French texts available in Welsh; the reference to a copy of the *greal*, 'grail', among Hopcyn's books, made by the poet Dafydd y Coed and cited above, is the oldest recorded reference to the word – as a text or book – in Welsh, and it is possible that MS Peniarth 11 was the earliest translation of the romance to be made.[26] Another poet who composed a praise-song to Hopcyn, Meurig ab Iorwerth (*fl. c.* 1380), compared Hopcyn's court to that of Arthur in Celliwig (the native Welsh location for Arthur, in contrast to Geoffrey of Monmouth's Caerlleon) and referred to his patron's interest in French literary culture, perhaps as a translator as well as a reader, calling him 'koeth awdur messur moesseu ffrenghic' ('refined author of the style of French customs').[27] In the fifteenth century, copies of the *Greal*, of which there would have been very few, were eagerly sought after as gifts or loans. Guto'r Glyn, writing to Trahaearn ap Ieuan ap Meurig of Penrhos on the south-eastern March, asks for Trahaearn's copy of the book to be sent to David, abbot (*c.* 1480–1503) of the Cistercian foundation of Valle Crucis, near Llangollen on the eastern March:

> Am un llyfr y mae'n llefain
> A gâr mwy nog aur a main.
> Echwynfawr oedd iwch anfon
> Y Greal teg i'r wlad hon:
> Llyfr y gwaed, llafuriau gur,
> A syrthiodd yn llys Arthur;
> Llyfr enwog o farchogion,
> Llyfr at grefft yr holl Fort Gron.

[25] Daniel Huws groups MS Peniarth 11 together with other manuscripts written by Hopcyn ap Tomas's scribe, Hywel Fychan (*Medieval Welsh Manuscripts*, p. 60).

[26] This is suggested by Jones (ed.), *Ystoryaeu Seint Greal*, p. xxi. The Welsh dictionary, *Geiriadur Prifysgol Cymru*, gives Dafydd y Coed's poem as the earliest known reference to the word *greal*.

[27] *Poetry from the Red Book of Hergest*, ed. by J. Gwenogvryn Evans (Llanbedrog: [Privately printed], 1911), col. 1374 (my translation). Hopcyn ap Tomas was also interested in translations from Latin into Welsh. The two historical chronicles based on Latin sources, *Brut y Brenhinedd* (from Geoffrey's *Historia*) and *Brut y Tywysogyon*, are both contained in Hopcyn's Red Book anthology, along with *Ystorya Dared*. Copies of *Ystorya Dared* and *Brut y Brenhinedd* are found in another manuscript, Philadelphia, Library Company of Philadelphia, MS 8680, also commissioned by Hopcyn and copied by the same scribe who wrote parts of the Red Book, Hywel Fychan. See Huws, *Medieval Welsh Manuscripts*, p. 80.

Llyfr eto yn llaw Frytwn,
Llin Hors ni ŵyr darllain hwn.

[For one book he is calling out, which he loves more than gold and precious stones. A great loan it would be for you to send the fair Grail to this land: a book about the blood, pain of hard labours, which fell in Arthur's court; a famous book of knights, a book recounting the skill of the whole Round Table. A book also in the hand of the Briton – the line of Horsa is unable to read this one.][28]

This request indicates the close relationship between the Welsh nobility as patrons of literature and the monastic houses as sites of scribal copying and manuscript production. The reference to the English, the 'line of Horsa', unable to read the story of the Grail, confirms that Trahaearn's copy was in Welsh rather than English, but it also implies that the Welsh were ahead of the English in having a copy of the Grail legends in their own vernacular (and indeed the earliest surviving version of the Grail story in English, based on the *Queste*, is that of Thomas Malory in his *Morte Darthur* of the late fifteenth century).

It was not only the Arthurian legends that interested Hopcyn ap Tomas but also the other great story cycle from medieval France, the legends of Charlemagne. Welsh texts of *Cân Rolant* (*Chanson de Roland*), *Cronicl Turpin* (the Latin *Pseudo-Turpin Chronicle* attributed to Archbishop Turpin), *Rhamant Otuel* (from the Old French *Otuel* or *Otinel*), and *Pererindod Siarlymaen* (*Le Pèlerinage de Charlemagne*) are found together in about ten manuscripts from the fourteenth and fifteenth centuries, including Hopcyn ap Tomas's great anthology, the Red Book of Hergest.[29]

---

[28] The text is taken from the online edition of the poetry of Guto'r Glyn <http://www.gutorglyn.net> [accessed 5 August 2014], no. 114, ll. 43–52, with my translation. Ceridwen Lloyd-Morgan suggests that a complete copy of the Vulgate Cycle was available to Welsh writers at least by the fifteenth century and probably earlier than this: see 'Crossing the Borders: Literary Borrowing in Medieval Wales and England', in *Authority and Subjugation in Writing of Medieval Wales*, ed. by Ruth Kennedy and Simon Meecham-Jones (New York: Palgrave Macmillan, 2008), pp. 159–73 (p. 164 and n. 22). The transfer of books from one collector to another, whether lay persons or clerics, indicates the scarcity value of many of these texts. For a fuller discussion of the manuscript transmission of the Grail text, see Lloyd-Morgan, 'A Study', pp. 47–50.

[29] For the list of manuscripts and a full discussion of the manuscript history of the Charlemagne texts, see Annalee Rejhon, *Cân Rolant: The Medieval Welsh Version of the Song of Roland* (Berkeley and Los Angeles: University of California Press, 1984). Rejhon suggests that the translation of *Cân Rolant* was made in the first half of the thirteenth century and was based on a late-twelfth or early-thirteenth-

Another prose translation in the Red Book, *Ystorya Bown de Hamtwn*, is a thirteenth-century translation of the Anglo-Norman romance, *Boeve de Haumtone*, composed earlier in the same century.[30] The French genre of the *chanson de geste* clearly resonated with a Welsh nobility proud of their military service and seeking to strengthen their ties, already established through marriage, with the French-speaking Marcher lords.

There is one further link to be made between Hopcyn as a patron of literary translations and the appeal of French writing in the March of Wales. The French *Bestiaire d'Amour*, written by a northern French cleric, Richard de Fornival, in the thirteenth century, was translated into Welsh some time in the fourteenth century and a copy is included in a manuscript written partly by one of the three scribes who made the Red Book of Hergest.[31] Two other manuscripts containing the Welsh bestiary, dating from the sixteenth century, are also Marcher texts from Glamorgan and also contain other works translated from Latin and French, confirming the popularity of European material in that border region.[32] The bestiary uses

century Anglo-Norman manuscript of the *Chanson de Roland* (p. 89). For Welsh texts of all the Charlemagne stories, see *Ystorya de Carolo Magno o Lyfr Coch Hergest*, ed. by Stephen J. Williams, 2nd edn (Cardiff: Gwasg Prifysgol Cymru, 1968). Williams also notes that the translation of *Cronicl Turpin* from Latin to Welsh was commissioned by Gruffudd ap Maredudd, a lord of Ceredigion, some time between 1265 and 1282 ('Rhai Cyfieithiadau', pp. 303–05).

[30] The Welsh text is *Ystorya Bown de Hamtwn*, ed. by Morgan Watkin (Caerdydd: Gwasg Prifysgol Cymru, 1958). The Middle English version of the romance, *Sir Beues of Hamtoun*, was composed in the early fourteenth century and is therefore unlikely to be the source of the Welsh version. See Erich Poppe and Regine Reck, 'Rewriting Bevis in Wales and Ireland', in *Sir Bevis of Hampton in Literary Tradition*, ed. by Jennifer Fellows and I. Djordjevic (Cambridge: Boydell and Brewer, 2008), pp. 37–50. Poppe and Reck have published two articles which compare the French and Welsh versions of *Bevis* and other translations: see 'A French Romance in Wales: *Ystorya Bown o Hamtwn*: Processes of Medieval Translations. Part 1', *Zeitschrift für Celtische Philologie*, 55 (2006), 122–80; 'Part 2', *Zeitschrift für Celtische Philologie*, 56 (2008), 129–64.

[31] This is Aberystwyth, National Library of Wales, MS Llanstephan 4, dated to about 1400 and written partly in the hand known as 'Llyfr Teg'. Graham Thomas suggests that the manuscript 'was also one of Hopcyn ap Tomas's manuscripts, and that the Welsh translation of the *Bestiaire d'amour*, if not translated for him, was copied for him.' See *A Welsh Bestiary of Love, being a Translation into Welsh of Richard de Fornival's Bestiaire d'Amour*, ed. by Graham C. G. Thomas (Dublin: Dublin Institute for Advanced Studies, 1988), p. xviii.

[32] These manuscripts are Aberystwyth, National Library of Wales, MS 13075B (in the hand of a Glamorgan copyist, Llywelyn Siôn, *c.* 1540–1615) and London, British Library, MS Additional 15038, both described by Thomas (ed.), *A Welsh*

the conventional format of short sections describing individual animals, whose characteristics are applied, mostly negatively, to the complex negotiations of courtly love: 'Ag velly idd wyd ti y'm lladd j ag y'm dallv val i dalla'r helwr kywraint yr ap' ('And so you kill me and trick me like the skilful hunter tricks the ape').[33] Retaining the French epistolary form of a first-person address to the beloved, the Welsh adaptation remediates the courtly and learned traditions of northern France into the stylistic patterns and distinctive lexis of medieval Welsh prose, implicitly including Welsh audiences in the prestige game of courtly love.

The evidence of manuscript transmission, literary influences and the vigorous tradition of translations from French and Latin into Welsh, especially after 1282, all work to construct Wales as a region with close links with Europe, both cultural and political. When the translations are compared with their originals, we find a process of interpretation and adaptation that is just as creative as that used to turn Chrétien's Arthurian poems into Welsh prose tales: these are not word-for-word literal translations but creative remediations which transform Latin history and French courtly romance into the language and style of Welsh storytelling. These remediations are not simply linguistic; they construct the ideological positioning of the Welsh *uchelwyr* on the March, a relatively new nobility living in close proximity to an older and more powerful aristocracy whose prestige literature drew largely on classicism – the 'matter of Greece and Rome' – and chivalry, the 'matter of France'. Enriched by the multilingual context of south and east Wales, book collectors such as Hopcyn ap Tomas encouraged Welsh translations from this prestige material and in doing so helped to fashion the 'matter of the March', a literary culture on the border which looked to European trends as much as to the literary heritage of Wales.

Bestiary of Love, pp. xix–xxi. Thomas stresses that all four surviving Welsh versions of the text are copies of a previous Welsh translation now lost, and that the copyists were not working directly from a French text (p. xxx).

[33] *A Welsh Bestiary of Love*, p. 16, ll. 104–05, my translation.

Charms among the Chants: Verbal Magic in Medieval Bulgarian Manuscripts

SVETLANA TSONKOVA

THIS ARTICLE IS ABOUT medieval Bulgarian verbal charms preserved in manuscripts.[1] Here, the focus is on the medieval written contexts. After the functional typology of the medieval manuscripts, specific aspects of their contexts, content and usage are presented. The требници ('books of occasional prayers'), which are the most numerous type of manuscripts containing verbal magic, are discussed in particular. The written tradition is analysed in terms of interaction between canonical and non-canonical texts, and in relation to the daily life applications of verbal magic. In general, the year 1450 is kept as the chronological border. There are, however, important examples and parallels from later periods, which are included in order to demonstrate transmission and continuation.

The purpose of this article is to present a specific aspect of medieval Bulgarian written verbal charms, and to propose a hypothesis about the behaviour of Christian priests as practitioners of verbal magic. My aim is also to urge a more general scholarly discussion on the topic. This is very much needed, as the medieval and early modern Bulgarian verbal charms are rarely discussed in English language publications.

Functional typology of the source material

Significant numbers of medieval and early modern Bulgarian verbal charms are preserved in manuscripts. These books are written in Old Church Slavonic, and are dated between the thirteenth and nineteenth centuries. In my PhD thesis I analyse sixty-nine manuscripts, which contain

---

[1] This article arises from my doctoral studies on medieval and early modern Bulgarian verbal magic, conducted at the Department of Medieval Studies, at the Central European University-Budapest. See also, Szvetlana Conkova, '*Megégni tűz nélkül*. Betegségdémonok a késő középkori bolgár mágikus szövegekben' (Burnt without Fire: The Illness Demon in Late Medieval Bulgarian Magical Texts), in *Mágikus és szakrális Medicina*, ed. by Éva Pócs (Budapest: Balassi Kiadó, 2010), pp. 101–18.

173 charms, together with seven amulets containing seven charms. All these charms have been published by previous collectors and researchers of verbal magic.[2] Some of the published editions of charms do not provide exact and accurate dating. Thus, the numbers of manuscripts and their dating are approximate.

There are fifteen medieval Bulgarian manuscripts containing verbal charms that date from before 1450: thirteen manuscripts from the fourteenth century, one from the thirteenth century, and one from the first half of the fifteenth century. The manuscripts which contain charms are of the following types: *требник* (*trebnik*, meaning 'book of occasional prayers', plural *требници, trebnitsi*), *сборник* (*sbornik*, meaning 'miscellany', plural *сборници, sbornitsi*), *псалтир* (*psaltir*, meaning 'psalter', plural *псалтири, psaltiri*) and *часослов* (*chasoslov*, meaning 'book of hours', plural *часослови, chasolsovi*). The *требник*, the *псалтир* and the *часослов* are Eastern Orthodox Christian religious books. The manuscripts of the *сборник* type have mixed content, which may include religious texts. Most of the manuscripts containing verbal charms belong to the *требник* type.

In terms of content, my attention is focused on the genre of verbal charms. They, however, are always examined in relation to the other texts surrounding them. The rest of the manuscripts' canonical and non-canonical content (and especially the prayers) have close and intricate connections with the charms, especially as it is actually very difficult to make a clear-cut distinction between a verbal charm and a canonical Christian prayer.

---

[2] For example, the library catalogues by [B. Tsonev] Б. Цонев, *Опис на славянските ръкописи в софийската народна библиотека* (Catalogue of the Slavic manuscripts in the National Library in Sofia) (Sofia: National Library, 1910), I; [B. Tsonev] Б. Цонев, *Опис на славянските ръкописи в софийската нродна библиотека* (Catalogue of the Slavic manuscripts in the National Library in Sofia) (Sofia: National Library, 1923), II and [B. Hristova] Б. Христова, Д. Караджова и Н. Вутова, *Опис на славянските ръкописи в софийската нродна библиотека* (Catalogue of the Slavic manuscripts in the National Library in Sofia) (Sofia: National Library, 1996), V. Also the studies by [A. I. Almazov] А. И. Алмазов, *Апокрифические молитвы, заклинания и заговоры* (Apocryphal Prayers, Incantations and Spells) (Odessa: Летопис Новоросс. университета, 1901), 221–340; [A. I. Yatsimirskii] А. И. Яцимирски, 'К истории ложных молитв в южнославянской письмености.' *Изв. ОРЯС* 18, 3 (1913), 1–102 and *Изв. ОРЯС* 18, 4 (1913), 16–126 and [Donka Petkanova] Донка Петканова, *Стара българска литература в седем тома т. I. Апокрифи* (Old Bulgarian Literature in Seven Volumes. Vol. 1 Apocrypha) (Sofia: *Български писател*, 1982).

Specifics and contexts

The medieval Bulgarian manuscripts were part of various processes: translation, composition, transmission, adaptation and usage, to mention a few. Additionally, the manuscripts speak of divine and demonic supernatural powers, which in turn intervene within quotidian human experiences and needs. And finally, the books resulted from and existed in the overlapping spheres of written and oral texts. Therefore, we should speak not of one, but of many, multiple and various contexts, surrounding and influencing the manuscripts. Lotte Tarkka aptly points out that:

> The main problem with the notion of context is that context is in itself not a homogenic and unproblematic background, a given reality: it too consists of different cultural processes, different discourses, a multitude of things happening simultaneously or sequentially. Furthermore, the textualization of the culture as a whole into ethnographic accounts and descriptions of multiple contexts blurs the boundary between text, context and what could be called a meta-text: the presentation of the whole in manuscripts and secondary literature.[3]

This is very much true for medieval Bulgarian manuscripts containing verbal magic. Their milieux are not only extremely complex, but can also be very elusive.

The manuscripts of the требник, the *псалтир* and the *часослов* type belong to Christian liturgical literature. After the conversion to Christianity in the ninth century, these types of books were introduced in medieval Bulgaria: first as Byzantine originals, then as Old Church Slavonic translations.

Each type of manuscript has a typical traditional content, usually determined by the Church canon. The *псалтир* contains the psalms, which are part of every church service. The *часослов* contains the prayers, the psalms, the hymns and other liturgical texts, which are included in the twenty-four hour liturgical cycle. The manuscripts of the *сборник* type represent a more heterogenous group, not so connected with the Church canon. As the name suggests, they have mixed content, including a large variety of material. In some cases, a *сборник* is a miscellany, containing

---

3   Lotte Tarkka, 'Intertextuality, Rhetorics and the Interpretation of Oral Poetry: The Case of Archived Orality', in *Nordic Frontiers: Recent Issues in the Study of Modern Traditional Culture in the Nordic Countries*, ed. by Pertti J. Anttonen and Reimund Kvideland (Turku: Nordic Institute of Folklore, 1993), pp. 165–93 (p. 178).

all kinds of texts and images, religious or not. Culinary or curative recipes, verbal charms, divinatory texts, pieces of historical chronicles, lists of names, household calculations, personal notes and drawings of King Solomon's seal can be gathered together and mingled with canonical prayers, psalms, saints' lives, parts of theological treatises and drawings of the Virgin Mary and the Holy Cross. In other cases, a *сборник* is a miscellany with emphatically religious content. It may include canonical prayers, parts of the service, hymns, saints' lives and sermons.

In terms of content, function and application, the most important and most interesting for me are the manuscripts of the *требник* type. According to the Christian canon and traditions, the *требник* contains the rules and the texts for Christian services and rituals performed by the priest in special, private, peculiar and extraordinary occasions, outside of the Holy Liturgy. For example, the texts from the *требник* can be read for the purpose of blessing a new building or a new-born child, relieving a sick person's suffering or purifying wine, water or food, or at the occasions of baptism, marriage, death, war or travel. The *требник* was used at the begining of an activity or an enterprise, but also in the event of misfortune, bad luck or disaster.

The earliest known *требник* in Old Church Slavonic language is the *Euchologion Synaiticum* from the tenth century. Among other things, this manuscript is remarkable for its content of prayers for various occasions.[4] The texts in the *Euchologion Synaiticum* are exclusively practical, many of them with apotropaic functions. Here already we can see the beginning of a tendency: the *требник* is a practical book, used in the case of need. In later examples, its application grows broader and broader, beyond the cases determined by the religious canon. The way is open for practical non-canonical texts to find their place in the *требник*.

The *требници*, the *псалтири* and the *часослови* are part of the specialised literature of the clergy. Their content is topically organised and grouped, oriented towards specific occasions and extraordinary events. These manuscripts can be regarded as a peculiar type of *Fachliteratur* – manuals, providing both the texts and the practical instructions for Christian services performed in a variety of cases.

The term *Fachliteratur* is very much applicable to the *требник* in particular. This is the most practical Eastern Orthodox Christian religious book. Its content is explicitly arranged to be applied and read by the priest

---

[4] For more details about the manuscript, see Rajko Nachtigal, *Euchologium Sinaiticum. Starocerkvenoslovenski glagolski spomenik. I. Fotografski posnetek. II. Tekst s komentarijem* (Ljubljana, 1941–1942).

in peculiar, extraordinary and urgent cases. The *требник* is a book meant to be used in case of need. This is reflected in its Bulgarian name, literally meaning '(texts) that are needed'.[5] Often, the cases of need are actually cases of crisis: illness, injury and other health problems, natural disaster, famine, fire, pestilence and maleficent supernatural attack. The Christian service and the Christian texts from the *требник* are supposed to provide divine help, cures and protection, and to expel evil.

Due to this practical content and purpose, there is a large number of *требници* in Bulgarian medieval literature. Clearly, they were created, copied and transmitted in clerical and monastic milieux, and were meant to be used by the clergy. Equipped with the practical content of the *требник*, the parish or village priest was called upon to cope with critical situations and provide solutions for urgent problems in daily life.[6] The texts of the *требник* are divine words of power, helping with quotidian difficulties and protecting against supernatural menaces. Thus, the *требник* is not only a manual for the priest, but also a manual for successful crisis management through Christian prayers and rituals.

Content

The important practical role of the *требник* mentioned above determined and influenced the content of the book. Most probably, this is the reason for an interesting phenomenon: a large number of medieval Bulgarian *требници* contain non-canonical texts, such as divinatory texts, amuletic inscriptions, non-canonical lists of divine names and, most of all, verbal charms. This phenomenon continues and becomes more prominent in Bulgaria in the late Middle Ages and in the Early Modern period, especially in the sixteenth and seventeenth centuries.

The existence of a significant number of early modern Bulgarian *требници*, which have non-canonical content, has a complex explanation. Kazimir Popkonstantinov connects the introduction of the charms in Christian religious books with the quotidian needs and practices of the

---

5   According to the Church canons, the texts in the *требник* are called '*треби*', meaning 'needed things/texts/rituals'.

6   [Maria Shnitter] Мария Шнитер, *Молитва и магия* (Prayer and Magic) (Sofia: *Университетско издателство* 'Св. Климент Охридски', 2001), pp. 50–69.

local priests.[7] Maria Shnitter shares a similar opinion.[8] I agree with the general frame of their arguments. On one hand, the verbal charms are texts, practically oriented towards urgent quotidian issues and often apotropaic. Often, such texts have little to do with the Christian traditions, but have the formal and stylistic features of a Christian prayer. Alternatively, the charms include a mixture of Christian and non-Christian motifs and characters engaged in a narrative which imitates Bible stories and plots. Such formal similarities between the charms and the canonical prayers probably deceived the clergy (especially priests with low levels of education) into believing that these non-canonical texts are really pious Christian prayers which will help in a difficult and critical situation.[9] On the other hand, after the Ottoman invasion (at the end of fourteenth century), there were no official Bulgarian Church authorities to control and regulate the practices of the priests and the content of their books. Possibly due to these factors, the early modern Bulgarian *требници* are full of verbal charms.

This explanation is very probably valid for the early modern Bulgarian *требници*. In the medieval period, the situation may seem somehow different. The ecclesiastical authorities were present and active and their control was more effective, while the clergy of all ranks had certain levels of education, competence and attitudes towards non-canonical texts and practices. However, the practical apotropaic character of the charms is a fact. The difficult and demanding living environment was very much present too. Therefore, the increasingly frequent appearance of charms is probably due to their role as part of the coping mechanisms and problem solving methods needed for everyday life. In the form and style of Christian prayers, with pre-Christian elements well masked and difficult to recognise, the non-canonical magical texts took their place in the medieval Bulgarian *требници*. In support of this explanation, it should be mentioned that the charms are not written in the margins of the manu-

---

7 [Kazimir Popkonstantinov] Казимир Попконстантинов, 'Новооткрити епиграфски паметници от X–XI в. (апокрифни молитви върху олово)' (Recently Found Epigraphic Monuments from Tenth–Eleventh Century: Apocryphal Prayers on Lead), in *Трудове на II конгрес по старобългаристика* (Sofia: Balgarska Akademiia na Naukite 1996), pp. 16–18.
8 [Shnitter], especially pp. 40–50.
9 It can be debated whether the early modern Bulgarian monks and priests who copied and used the charms were really incapable of distinguishing between canonical and non-canonical texts. Possibly the village priests simply wanted to rely on all sources (canonical or not) which were available for coping with a difficult and demanding environment. See [Shnitter], pp. 59–60.

scripts. They are organically incorporated in the content, among the canonical texts.

Let us look at a good example from the source material. This is the *Зайковски требник* (*Zaykovski trebnik*), dated to the fourteenth century.[10] The manuscript is definitely written in a monastic milieu. Originally, it was thought that this was a monastery on Mount Athos, then later the manuscript was attributed to a scribal centre in western Bulgaria.[11] Regardless of the argument on the exact place of orgin, it is clear that the book is the product of a literate and sophisticated church environment, made by and for educated and well-informed members of the clergy.

The *Зайковски требник* contains the canonical prayers to be read at the occasions of baptism, marriage and confession. These are followed by prayer-type texts for various occasions: blessing of wine, slaughter of animals, protection against thunder, blessing of salt, blessing of polluted vessels, blessing of the willow branches for Palm Sunday, blessing of a new house, blessing of the Easter lamb, blessing of the grapes, protection against the bite of a rabid dog or wolf, blessing of meat, cheese and butter, and treating water retention in humans or horses. Finally, the manuscript ends with the canonical funeral prayers. The contents of the *Зайковски требник* represent an organic whole; the texts follow one another and there are no marginalia. The non-canonical parts (the verbal charms) are fully and organically incorporated into the canonical texture of the book.[12]

The *Зайковски требник* contains two verbal charms: a charm against the bite of a rabid dog or rabid wolf (fols 45v–46r) and a charm against water retention in humans or horses (fols 47v–48r). The first one is a typical narrative charm:

> When someone gets bitten, do this. Take wine, sour bread and your knife. Put the wine on the ground, take the bread in your hands and the knife in your right hand and say the following prayer to the Holy Mother of God: O, Lord! St John was walking through the holy moun-tain carrying a holy axe, to cut a holy tree. Mad dogs met him, rabid wolves met him, and he heard a voice from the Father, the Son and

---

[10] Kept in the National Library in Sofia as *Зайковски требник* MS 960. See [Stefan Mladenov] Стефан Младенов, *Зайковски светогорски требник* (Sofia, 1910), and the most recent study of the manuscript in [Tsibranska-Kostova] Цибранска- Марияна Костова и Елка Мирчева. *Зайковски требник от XIV век. Изследване и текст* (*Zaykovski trebnik* from the Fourteenth Century. Analysis and Text.) (Sofia: *Валентин Траянов*, 2012).

[11] [Mladenov], p. 200.

[12] [Mladenov], p. 156–59.

the Holy Ghost: John, John, turn back! Do not be scared, but give to
that man the Lord's flesh and the Lord's blood, to get healed and to
be smeared with it. Read this prayer nine times in the name of the
Father, the Son and the Holy Ghost, make the sign of the cross with
the knife. If the bitten person is near, give him wine and bread. If he
is far away, quickly pour out the wine, and at midnight put the knife
under a big stone and say the following prayer twice: In the name of
the Father, the Son and the Holy Ghost! St John was on the road and
saw iron soldiers and rabid wolves. He got scared, started trembling
and screaming. And God told him: John, do not be scared! Take the
Lord's flesh and the Lord's blood and give it to the man to eat and to
be healed from the east to the west in the name of the Father, the Son
and the Holy Ghost, today and forever. Amen.[13]

The text has the typical elements of a verbal charm: historiola, instructions on the performance of the ritual and the paraphernalia, and finalising
formula. The historiola is the micro-narrative, which places the event of
healing in a mythical chronotopos, and thus ratifies the curative power of
the charm. In summary, here we have a text which has features typical of
verbal magic, and little in common with the canonical Christian prayers.[14]
    The second charm is as follows:

In the name of the Father, the Son and the Holy Ghost. Three angels
were standing on the banks of the river Jordan, holding intestines of
copper. One was tying, the other one was untying, and the third one
was praying, saying: Holy, Holy, Holy Lord Sabbaoth! Fill the Heaven
and the earth with your glory! In the name of the Father, the Son and
the Holy Ghost. I went out in a fiery field and I found a burning lake.
Three sisters were sitting in it and holding three vessels full of crayfish
intestines. The oldest one was tying, the middle one was untying, the
youngest one was praying to God: O, Lord, please let the water pass
through this man (the person's name) in the name of the Father. In
the name of the Father, the Son and the Holy Ghost. Write on the

---

[13] My translation from the Old Church Slavonic original, published by
[Mladenov], p. 203.
[14] For example, the supernatural figures, the sign of the cross, and the trinitarian
formula are Christian. It is typical for a narrative of a verbal charm to travel
among traditions with its protagonists changed accordingly, while the core of the
historiola stays the same. The parallels and the later versions of the famous Second
Merseburg charm is a typical example of this process: the healing formula (*Bone
to bone, blood to blood*) stays essentially the same for many centuries, while the
superntural healer can be a Hindu deity, Odin or Jesus Christ.

front right leg Tigris, on the left rear leg Phison, on the front left leg Euphrates, on the left rear [sic!] leg Gyon. Let it travel around the world. In the Name of the Father and the Son. Read each one nine times.[15]

The human and equine urine is expected to flow as freely as the mythical rivers from the Bible.[16] The numbers three and nine are present too, which is another very common feature of verbal magic. A non-canonical narrative and pre-Christian elements are combined with the canonical Christian angels, biblical rivers and trinitarian formula.

It should be clearly emphasised here that I do not aim to present or discuss a binary opposition of the type 'pre-Christian–Christian'. Simply, I want to point out that an Eastern Orthodox Christian liturgical book from fourteenth-century Bulgaria contains two completely non-canonical verbal charms, organically incorporated in the body of the manucript. Two texts of verbal magic crept into a *требник* from the fourteenth century, and this can be seen as the initial stages of a process which developed to a much larger scale in the sixteenth and seventeenth centuries. The *Зайковски требник* is important evidence for the beginnings of the phenomenon of placing charms among liturgical material.

The verbal charms, as presented in the medieval Bulgarian manuscripts, are important instruments for coping with crisis situations. Taking a charm for curing a cow as an example, Ulrika Wolf-Knuts points out: 'the content of the charm was constructed in order to correspond to the needs of a certain situation in human life and the components were taken from several spheres, culturally inherited as well as self-experienced. We must assume that charms were used in critical existentially important situations where the person who utilised the text referred to his or her own environment.'[17] A crisis could put at great risk the economic wellbeing and the physical existence of a rural household. Therefore, the inhabitants have two choices: to give in, or to counteract the difficult situation. The

---

[15] My translation from the Old Church Slavonic original, published by [Mladenov], p. 203.

[16] This charm belongs to the *Flum Jordan* charm-type. Although not completely elaborated, this is clearly a ratification formula is of the type 'as ... so ...'. The biblical rivers provide a good magical paradigm. This mythical model is conjured to influence positively the health of humans and horses in a critical real life situation.

[17] Ulrika Wolf-Knuts, 'Charms as Means of Coping', in *Charms, Charmers and Charming: International Research on Verbal Magic*, ed. by Jonathan Roper (New York, 2009), pp. 62–70.

use of charms serves 'to oppose the powers that cause the crisis and try to thwart them. Saying a charm would be one of several ways of coping with the dangerous situation.'[18] As 'coping is a cultural, socially anchored, repetitive activity that opens a person's eyes to new opportunities in time of distress',[19] books with charms are important instruments of this system of coping in the context of a written culture.

Writing, using, transmitting

The manuscripts and their contents are parts of the traditional communication with the supernatural, through the means of special words of power. This interaction with the other world had its human actors and practitioners. As Lauri Honko writes, 'tradition is seen in relation to its user, an individual and a group, and to its arena, the physical environment which moulds cultural and socioeconomic activities.'[20] Apart from the charms themselves, however, the contemporary sources for medieval Bulgarian verbal magic are rather limited and the picture remains sketchy.[21] There is not enough evidence for the behaviour and practices of the parish and village priests.[22] Moreover, the non-canonical usage of the *требници* is not well documented. Usually, on this topic, two medieval Russian chronicles are quoted. The first chronicle is from the twelfth century and is entitled *On the True Books and the False* (О книгах истинных и ложных). The chronicle says: 'And the priests have false writings in their *Euchologia*, like bad Penitentials (*Nomokanony*) and the false Prayers for the Fevers. Heretics had distorted the traditions of the Holy Apostles, writing false words to deceive the vulgar; but the Council

---

[18] Ulrika Wolf-Knuts, p. 64.

[19] Ulrika Wolf-Knuts, p. 64.

[20] Lauri Honko, 'Thick Corpus and Organic Variation: An Introduction', in *Thick Corpus, Organic Variation and Textuality in Oral Tradition*, ed. by Lauri Honko (Helsinki: Finnish Literature Society, 2000), pp. 3–28 (p. 17).

[21] [Adelina Angusheva] Аделина Ангушева и Маргарет Димитрова, 'Другите авторитети: слова против магьосници и баячки в дамаскинарската традиция' (The Other Authorities: Sermons against Magicians and Charmers in the Tradition of the Damaskins), *Годишник на Софийския Университет 'Св. Климент Охридски' – Център за славяно-византийски проучвания 'Иван Дуйчев'*, 92 (2002), 81–99.

[22] Adelina Angusheva and Margaret Dimitrova, 'Medieval Slavonic Childbirth Prayers: Sources, Context and Functonality', *Scripta & E-scripta* 2 (2004), 273–90.

investigated them and cleansed them and cursed them.'[23] The second chronicle is a longer redaction of the same text, and dates from the fourteenth or fifteenth century. This chronicle says:

> And in their *Euchologia*, among the Divine Writ, the stupid village priests have false writings – sown by heretics for the destruction of ignorant priests and deacons – thick village manuscripts and bad Penitentials (*Nomokanony*) and the false healing Prayers for the Fevers and for infections and for sickness. And they write fever letters on prosphorae and on apples, because of sickness. All this is done by the ignorant, and they have it from their fathers and forefathers, and they perish in this folly. Heretics had distorted the traditions of the Church and the Canons of the Holy Apostles, writing false words.[24]

Taken with caution, this Russian material has some relevance to the medieval Bulgarian situation. As William Francis Ryan points out, practices like amulets, divination and pagan and quasi-Christian charms (placed in Christian context) are late importations into Russia through Bulgaria and Serbia: 'And it seems clear that the importers were for the most part the minor clergy, who until quite recently could be practitioners in magic and divination among the East and South Slavs, both Orthodox and Catholic, as they could in the West.'[25] In Russia the Church 'despite its official attitudes, was certainly one route for the importation of particular kinds of charms: uncanonical prayers and practices in many cases from fairly early periods of Christianity in the late antique Mediterranean world, with apocryphal motifs and persons and intermixed with pagan elements.'[26] In the light of such a transmission process, the quotations from *On the True Books and the False* are relevant. They are relevant because it seems that such practices reached Russia via Bulgaria, thus practices of this sort in Russia are likely to have been similar to Bulgarian practices of this sort.

[23] Robert Mathiesen, 'Magic in Slavia Orthodoxa: The Written Tradition', in *Byzantine Magic*, ed. by Henry Maguire (Washington, DC: Dumbarton Oaks Papers, 1995), pp. 155–77 (p. 162).

[24] Mathiesen, pp. 162–63.

[25] William Francis Ryan, 'Eclecticism in the Russian Charm Tradition', in *Charms and Charming in Europe*, ed. by Jonathan Roper (London: Palgrave Macmillan, 2004), pp. 113–27 (p. 121).

[26] Ryan, p. 121. According to Ryan, the exorcistic charm of St Sisinnius against the twelve fevers, the charm of St Paul against snakebite and the charms against the *nezhit* (personified illness) are some examples of such transmission.

The role of the clergy appears to be central in the process of compilation of manuscripts containing charms. First of all, there are the surviving
требници, with their mixture of canonical and non-canonical content,
including curative charms. The verbal charms have a stable presence in
the *требници*, and were rather systematically preserved, transmitted
and used continuously through centuries. Furthermore the heretical and
apocryphal Christian ideas, motifs and practices had a strong presence
in medieval Bulgaria. These ideas influenced both the content of the
требници and the attitude of the clerical authorities against the 'thick
village manuscripts'. A number of verbal charms from the *требници* also
contain elements which are to be found in later folkloric sources. It is
debatable who influenced whom, but it is possible that people who copied
or modified the texts in the *требници* were directly influenced by oral
folkloric tradition. 'The stupid village priests' were much more exposed
to such influence, and probably much more prone or willing to accept it.

In summary, the medieval Bulgarian *требници* and the charms within
them were used, modified and transmitted by priests, probably from the
low ranks of the church hierarchy. The practical apotropaic function of the
charms emerges as a possible explanation for the preservation and transmission of such texts in a clerical milieu and within clerical manuscripts.
Even more, the verbal charms were supposed to be read or uttered, as
part of a ritual. Thus, the non-canonical texts went together with non-
canonical practices, performed and perpetuated by the priests. In this
respect, we may say that medieval Bulgarian Christian priests and their
требници with canonical and non-canonical texts represent a case of the
'clerical underground', as it is aptly defined by Richard Kieckhefer.[27] The
manuscripts with words of power 'exist in two interactive domains, that of
popular oral composition, in which a large number of stock elements can
be arranged in a variety of traditional structures at the choice of the appel-
lant or performer, and that of the written spell-book, in which the spell
assumes a fixed form and may be transmitted, or collected, in this form.'[28]

---

[27] Richard Kieckhefer, *Magic in the Middle Ages* (Cambridge: Cambridge
University Press, 2000), p. 2.
[28] Kieckhefer, p. 116.

Crisis writs and crisis rites

The *требници* employed words of power for practical purposes. This is rather clear for their canonical content, the normative Christian prayers and blessings. The non-canonical content also fits well for this aim. The charms can be divided into two thematic groups: health-related and protection-related. The first group deals with prevention, treatment and cure of various ailments. Health is the predominant theme in medieval and early modern Bulgarian verbal magic. The second group provides protection against evil supernatural powers and against forces of nature.[29]

All the charms have emphatically curative and apotropaic functions. Their aim is to provide protection and help through supernatural means and powers. In this respect, the charms have roles identical with the roles of the canonical Christian prayers. They are all words of power, and they share not only formal and stylistic features, but common curative and apotropaic functions. In terms of both form and content, the verbal charms are shaped to be magical (and often apotropaic) instruments. Thus, the organic incorporation of canonical prayers and non-canonical charms is not surprising. In the framework of the *требник* as a book of necessary prayers, the verbal charms are especially suitable and fitting.

The notion of natural selection in folkloric terms is a good summary for this stage of the discussion:

> [the] absence of performance arenas, invalidation of past mythologies, low memorability and other factors acting on a population of charms eliminates those examples less well adapted to their environment. The examples surviving to be passed on would tend to have characteristics with survival value to their offspring and in time the composition of the population would change in adaptation to a changing environment. The characteristics with survival value for verbal charms include memorability and perceived effectivity.[30]

The medieval and early modern Bulgarian manuscripts containing words of power represent a completed stage in this natural selection,

---

[29] In my doctoral research, I also identify and analyse charms for good luck and success. They come from manuscripts dating from the sixteenth, seventeenth and eighteenth centuries.

[30] This statement is applied by Jonathan Roper to Estonian and English verbal charms. See Jonathan Roper, 'Traditional Verbal Charms with Particular Reference to the Estonian and English Charm-traditions' (unpublished M.A. thesis, University of Sheffield, 1997), p. 41.

preserving prayers and verbal charms with high survival value, namely
high effectivity. Both the canonical and non-canonical texts were subject
to variation. The verbal charms are even more so, as they were (and are)
always between the oral tradition (which is more fluid) and the written
record (which is more fixed or at least not as fluid). However, the essence
and functions of the texts remained the same, and their themes and aims
unchanged. They all were written down, preserved and transmitted in
durable book form. Thus, the *требници* represent a complete written
cultural product with immense survival value in terms of verbal magic,
crisis management and cultural history.

At the same time, the notion of natural selection gives a different
perspective on the question of charms-users and charms-practitioners:
'charms can undergo transmissible changes in the period between initial
reception and eventual transmission onward. Such changes may just be
random mutation, but may also be deliberate on the part of the charmer,
and the next recipient of the charm could transmit this deliberately altered
form.'[31] In my mind, the Bulgarian *требници* and the charms inside
them are products of such deliberate modifications.[32] I think that the
continuous and stable presence of specific charms inside the *требници*
can be seen not as random inclusion, but as a deliberate action on the side
of the users. Thus, the clergy not only used the charms, but also modified,
changed and re-shaped the nature and the applications of these liturgical books. The priests transmitted the modified *требници* and the next
clerical recipient received an alloy of canonical and non-canonical words
of power that were proven to be effective. In my mind, 'the stupid village
priests' were among the main actors and factors of the medieval Bulgarian
verbal magic. They influenced the 'natural selection' of the verbal charms,
making it a complex cultural process. Through the *требници*, they also
influenced the whole written tradition of medieval Bulgarian liturgical
books.

Still, it is difficult to make any definite conclusions about the users of
the medieval Bulgarian manuscripts containing verbal charms. Clearly,
this field has several elements. There are the verbal charms, the manuscripts that contain them, and the clergy who wrote, copied, transmitted
and used these books and texts. All these elements are related to a difficult, demanding and even aggressive living environment, with a large
number of serious daily life issues, problems and challenges. According

---

[31] Roper, p. 42.
[32] Especially the late medieval and early modern *требници*.

to the Church canon, the *требници* have a legitimate central role in the management of the critical situations in this environment. The verbal charms are a non-canonical, but logical and natural, part of the same crisis management. The clergy employed both canonical and non-canonical words of power for the successful performance of crisis rites. Thus, 'the stupid village priests' shaped and developed a flexible and practical coping strategy and proved themeselves to be not so stupid at all.

Index